INSIDE
Family Law

CONVERSATIONS FROM THE COALFACE

Zoë Durand

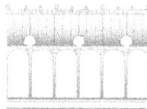

LONGUEVILLE
MEDIA

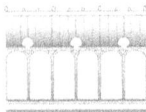

LONGUEVILLE
MEDIA

First published 2018 for Zoë Durand
by
Longueville Media Pty Ltd
PO Box 205 Haberfield NSW 2045
www.longmedia.com.au
info@longmedia.com.au
T. 0410 519 685

Print ISBN: 978-0-6483398-4-7
POD ISBN: 978-0-6483398-7-8
eBook ISBN: 978-0-6483398-5-4

NATIONAL
LIBRARY
OF AUSTRALIA
A catalogue record for this
book is available from the
National Library of Australia

This book is dedicated to my husband Francois for his support, and my one year old daughter Alice who let me know the draft manuscript was ready by (literally) eating it.

May this book be just the start of an ongoing public space for discussion, where individual's stories can be heard, because as Karen Blixon said:

*'All sorrows can be bourne if you can put them
into a story or tell a story about them.'*

Contents

Q&A Index

This Q&A Index provides 60 useful questions for those navigating the family law system.

GENERAL

1. When should I seek legal advice?
    ▸ Heng, Robyn Sexton, Huesch, Hutchings

2. What are the 4 essential questions I should ask my lawyer in the initial conference?
    ▸ The Hon. Justice Rose

3. What are the first things I should do if I am thinking of separating?
    ▸ Robyn Sexton

4. What should I be considering when choosing a lawyer?
    ▸ Robyn Sexton, Huesch, Barry, Heng, Jarman, Brown

5. What should I consider when choosing a barrister?
    ▸ Blackah, Nolan, Kenny

6. What are the kinds of pathways a matter might take from very start to the finish?
    ▸ Huesch

7. How can I best work with my lawyer?
    ▸ Edwards, Knight, Barry, Saab

8. How can I best prepare information for my lawyer?
    ▸ Edwards, Barry

9. What are some strategies for how I can best manage my legal fees?
    ▸ Hutchings

10. What steps should I take if I have limited funds to pay for a family lawyer?
    ▸ Jarman, The Hon. Justice Rose

11. What services and information are available if I have limited funds for legal fees, but am not eligible for legal aid?
    ▸ Edwards, Jarman

PARENTING

PROPERTY

Key practical points for lawyers

1. The 4 questions you should give your client an answer to
    ▸ The Hon. Justice Rose

2. How best to run family law matters, including focusing on the key issues
    ▸ The Hon. Justice Rose

3. What lawyers' general approach should be in family law
    ▸ Judge Harman

4. Analysing your client's case and providing realistic advice
    ▸ The Hon. Justice Rose

5. Working with your client: getting instructions, reality testing
    ▸ Stephen Scarlett

6. Qualities clients perceive as favourable in lawyers
    ▸ Jacqui

7. When and why clients become dissatisfied with lawyers
    ▸ Robert, Brooke, Ryan

8. Working with the other parties' solicitor
    ▸ Stephen Scarlett, Nolan, Heng

9. Judges' expectation of lawyer's level of preparation prior to a court appearance
    ▸ Judge Harman

10. Preparation of court documents
    ▸ Stephen Scarlett, Tockar

11. Preparing affidavit evidence
    ▸ Blackah, Kenny

12. Preparation of affidavits in family violence matters
    ▸ Robyn Sexton

13. Preparation of correspondence and letters
    ▸ Tockar

14. Requesting a preliminary hearing on family violence only
    ▸ Robyn Sexton

30. Process for preparing expert business valuations
   ▸ Pickup, Lipson

31. Summary of the main methodologies used in expert business valuations, and when each is appropriate
   ▸ Pickup, Lipson

32. General tips for lawyers from the perspective of a forensic accountant/ expert business valuer
   ▸ Pickup

33. When lawyers should jointly contact the expert business valuer orally rather than in writing
   ▸ Pickup

34. Options for your client if they have separated and there is a family business
   ▸ Pickup

35. Process for identifying hidden monies and assets
   ▸ Lipson

36. Updating business valuations (and why it is not just a matter of "putting in another financial year")
   ▸ Lipson

37. Challenging expert business valuations and cross examination
   ▸ Lipson

38. Instructions to expert property valuers
   ▸ Bird

39. Expert property valuations becoming outdated
   ▸ Bird

40. General tips for lawyers from the perspective of property expert valuers
   ▸ Bird

41. Challenging expert property valuations
   ▸ Bird

42. Practical financial implications of when parties divide assets, including considering the "mix" of assets
   ▸ Viola

43. Tax implications of division of assets
   ▸ Viola

44. Superannuation following separation
   ▸ Viola

45. Child support and your client's tax return
   ▸ Stephen Scarlett

Preface

Why Inside Family Law?

This book exists because of something that happened when I was starting my career in family law. I went looking for a book about the perceptions of people with first-hand experience of the family law system and could not find it. There was a gulf between the family law text books and the self-help divorce guides.

I have tried to do two things in these pages.

First, I have gathered the views of some of the leading experts in the field. I have interviewed Judges of the Federal Circuit Court and Family Court, family lawyers, barristers, family report writers, Court expert psychiatrists, Court expert real property valuers, forensic accountants and family therapists and many others that work in the family law area. This allows readers to pick the brains of the leading experts in the field. I have focussed on two key questions:

1. What are the key practical tips for both someone who is separating and for lawyers, from that professional's perspective?

2. Looking to the future, what should we be changing about the family law system?

Second, I have shared the experiences of those who have been through the system, including those who were children at the time. I think it is important to hear their stories.

Overall the aim of this book is to tell the *inside*, behind-the-scenes, story about family law, through dialogue with those at its coalface.

Empowering individuals

I have observed that many people entering the family law system after a relationship breakdown feel daunted by the complicated processes, jargon and paradigms in family law. One of my key motivations in this book is to demystify the family law system by offering readers the closest experience possible to having their own fireside chat with Judges, experts and professionals they may not otherwise have access to. I want to give everyone access to the local knowledge that professionals in the field gradually acquire over years.

The first way *Inside Family Law* empowers those in, or entering, the family law system is through interviewees sharing their key practical tips and strategies. The *Q&A Index* on page xii, provides a full list of the practical questions *Inside Family Law* provides answers to, but very briefly this book provides tips with regards to choosing, working with and what to ask lawyers, managing costs, pathways a matter can follow, being a self represented litigant, supporting children through separation, how expert reports are prepared and challenged, tracking hidden monies, mitigating the financial impact of separation and many more fundamental points. This *Q&A Index* allows readers to dip in and out of the book and find the key pointers that are applicable to their situation.

The second, more subtle, yet nonetheless powerful way *Inside Family Law* assists readers is that it unlocks the key concepts and jargon in this specialised field in a way that is accessible and conversational. Piece by piece, with each interview, readers will absorb the family law language and thinking.

Finally, *Inside Family Law* is also of value for lawyers, as I have asked Judges, barristers, experts and professionals their pointers for family lawyers (see the *Key practical points for lawyers* on page xvii). I also believe these conversations facilitate lawyers and other professionals to understand the perspectives of the other professionals they work with in family law. Most importantly firsthand narratives and children's stories remind lawyers of how their clients' experience the process.

Ideas for Reform

I have also asked interviewees about their ideas for the future of family law.

Delay and resourcing

Almost every interviewee emphasised the problem of delays. Interviewees in various states mentioned delays, however they are the worst in Sydney where it can take three to four years for a matter to be heard from start to finish.

To address delay, overwhelmingly interviewees said funding for more Judges, Contact Centres and family report writers is needed. Former Federal Circuit Court Judge Stephen Scarlett estimates 100 Judges, not the current 70 in Sydney are needed. The Honourable Justice Rose also expressed the view delays would continue 'unless there are governments that actually have the political will to do something and provide substantially more resources rather than just talking about it.'

Efficiency, merging and streamlining

Interviewees suggested novel ways to increase efficiency. For example short form judgements for interim hearings (Greg Kenny), standard set time limits and processes in interim hearings (Claire Nielsen) standardised financial agreements (Tash Nolan) and standardised wording for orders (David Barry). Real property valuer David Bird also suggested the valuation report process could be reduced to having experienced valuers provide an initial opinion from a desktop database.

Interviewees raised concerns regarding how families are moved between the Family, Federal Circuit and Children's Courts respectively. The Family Court is about to merge with the Federal Circuit Court, but should the Children's Court be next? Lawyer Joanna Knight also proposed 'a referral system for matters from the criminal courts, where an Apprehended Violence Order (AVO) has been granted.'

Overall many interviewees felt Courts that deal with families should either be merged or have better interface. On a global level barrister Sandrine Alexandre-Hughes recommends greater international consistency with improved recognition of overseas Orders and Financial Agreements in Australia, which currently is a potential loophole for international families.

If power is given to Judges to act more decisively and not jump through the hoops as much, this means the public must place more faith in the judiciary. The Honourable Justice Rose was concerned about 'the quality of resources' government provide, namely he thinks 'there have been some other Judicial appointments that can only be explained for reasons that have nothing to do with family law.' Barrister Trevor Tockar proposed Judges be 'chosen a different way' for example via a 'judicial services commission where candidates may be interviewed and chosen on a non-political basis.'

Uniqueness and specialisation

On the other hand, some argue that in our current family law system, unique aspects of families and individuals are not always appreciated. Dr Milch says 'Every family has their own culture' and later observes there is a risk of black and white thinking in law.

In my conversation with barrister Tom Hutchings we discussed how family structures common in, for example Chinese families, where grandparents can play an extremely important role in caring for children, do not seem to be fully understood in the current system, as there are hidden Anglo Australian norms embedded in the law.

Similarly Retired Federal Circuit Court Judge Robyn Sexton discusses how in her view there are still issues of feminisation of poverty, particularly for older women who have had limited time in the workforce. However one father expressed the view that the system has hidden biases against men as gendered beliefs limit what can be understood about family violence, namely he says, that men can be victims of (in particular psychological) violence.

One possible way to better respond to the unique aspects of each matter is to have more specialised courts or lists. Robyn Sexton spoke in detail about the specialised Indigenous list she was running in her later years on the Bench. Sherlene Heng proposes a specialised list for small property pools.

The adversarial system

Another question raised in *Inside Family Law* is, how radical should changes to the family law system be? Is adversarialism a poor fit for families? Does it contain an inevitable paradigm of competition, winners and losers, as 'parties are encouraged to put on affidavit material disparaging their former partner' (lawyer Tash Nolan), and 'takes a vulnerable family system and places it in an amplifying chamber of tit-for-tat legal responses' (psychiatrist Dr Milch). Conversations in this book also include alternatives to litigation such as arbitration or mediation. In particular interviewees also raised if we should consider compulsory mediation prior to filing in property (as occurs in relation to parenting cases).

Robyn Sexton supports a 'place for a more inquisitorial' approach, particularly in parenting cases, including for example Judicial Mediations, which she anticipates may be available from 2019. Family consultant Linda Campbell supports a 'collaborative, child-centred approach' where parents have 'access to professionals' to 'coach and educate them about how to best meet' their children's needs. However both Robyn Sexton and Linda Campbell acknowledge such an approach is problematic in matters with violence.

Tom Hutchings makes what I personally think is an accurate observation, that already 'the reality is many Judges at the coalface... operate in a quasi-inquisitorial fashion'. He ultimately concludes the 'checks and balances' built into an adversarial system are 'preferable on balance to an out and out inquisitorial system'.

Lastly this book has focused on the experiences, rights, and needs of children and if the law could be improved in this area, for example, in how children are represented in family law matters. Lawyer Stephen Page, in particular, discusses his concern about how the rights and identities of children are ignored under current surrogacy laws. I felt it was important to tell the stories of those who were children when they experienced the family law system. I think in general we need to make more space in public discussion for children's voices.

*

In our age of empowerment for everyone, empowerment is not just about people being *given* power, but *taking* it. It is for separating parents to 'be part of the culture change themselves for their family' (Judge Harman) and for all practitioners in the family law community to advocate for reform where they see it is required.

I hope the insights and stories in this book provide practical strategies to assist and empower individual parties, because everyone has a role to play. So in the words of Stephen Scarlett, 'come on, let's try a bit harder' – lawyers, politicians, Judges, parents and clients, law societies and bar associations, and professionals – everyone.

Judges of the Family Court & Federal Circuit Court

Former Federal Circuit Court Judge Stephen Scarlett OAM RFD

Come on, let's try a bit harder

Stephen Scarlett OAM RFD was a Judge of the Federal Circuit Court of Australia, federal magistrate of the Federal Magistrates Court of Australia and a Senior Children's Magistrate in the Children's Court of New South Wales. Prior to this he worked as a lawyer for several years.

In 2015 Stephen Scarlett was included in the Queen's Birthday Honours List and was awarded the Medal of the Order of Australia for service to the Judiciary, to the law and to professional organisations.

Since his recent retirement from the Bench, Scarlett works as a Senior Member of the New South Wales Civil and Administrative Tribunal, as a barrister and mediator. In this interview he looks back and provides a wide overview of the history of modern Family Law in Australia, from the inception of the 1975 *Family Law Act* and the very first days of the Federal Circuit Court (then Federal Magistrates Court).

⁙

Tell me a bit about your path to becoming a Judge of the Federal Circuit Court.

I was a solicitor originally, first in Sydney and then I started work in the country town of Parkes and I thought I was going to do conveyancing and probate, but my employer, the late Tony Matthews, on the first day I was there (which was the first day the District Court was sitting), said, 'Come on, let's have a little look at what the Court is doing'.

As we walked diagonally across the road to the court house, he said, 'You'd better get used to this walk because I'm not going to do it anymore. Litigation is all yours.' I thought, oh, ok, I'm doing litigation, am I?

And it started from there.

As an articled clerk I was involved in some matters under the old *Matrimonial Causes Act*. That Act was still in force when I went to Parkes.

Then, when the *Family Law Act* came in, I thought this was actually a really big deal. It was a huge step, a big change, that I had better learn this.

So, I got in on the ground floor with Family Law. I wasn't actually in Court on 5 January 1976 (when the Act first came into force), but I think I was pretty close to taking instructions from a client.

There was a huge flood of divorces. People who couldn't get divorced under the old Act were now relying on the irretrievable breakdown of the marriage evidenced by 12 months' separation being the only requirement. And out they all came. Of course, when they brought divorces, they brought other Family Law matters, such as maintenance or access to children. So, in Parkes, I was the main Family Lawyer.

I found that country people liked to have their own lawyer present. Even if they had to go to Bathurst or Dubbo or Parramatta, they liked to have a familiar face there. I got used to doing the long drive, and sometimes going down the night before. As happens, the more you do, the better you get, and the better you get, the more you do. I was doing a lot of Family Law as well as crime and personal injury work.

In 1988 there was a change of government and Mr Greiner became premier. He said the state court system was running too slowly and they were going to appoint seven extra crown prosecutors and seven extra magistrates. My then wife and I were thinking whether we were going to stay in Parkes or not. The local magistrate encouraged me to put up my hand to be a magistrate, so I went down for an interview. The interview was interesting. I got the feeling they had decided something, but I didn't know what. And then a month later I got the phone call: 'Do you want to be a magistrate?' I did. I moved down to Sydney and rented my sister's flat.

I did a lot of Children's Court work as a magistrate. In 1995 I became the Senior Children's Magistrate and was head of the Children's Court from then until 2000, when they were looking for federal magistrates for the Federal Magistrates Court. I went for a couple of interviews. The second-round interviews were conducted by Daryl Williams, who was Attorney General at the time. That was interesting. And, lo and behold, I was sitting at Bidura Children's Court and the magistrate who was next to me said, 'You'd better get off the Bench. I heard Daryl Williams leave a voice mail message for you.' I had been offered a job as a federal magistrate.

A few weeks later, there I was, at a training course at Wood End, near Mt Macedon, in Victoria, and in the middle of winter, which was like going to the Antarctic. I was there with the original appointees. They were all people who had been knocking around the Courts for 10, 15, 20 years and I thought this was a pretty good group. We spent some time working out the ethos of the Court. We heard lectures by all sorts of people, such as Supreme Court Judges and psychologists. On the Thursday they shipped us in to Melbourne and there was a mass swearing in, because at that stage the only federal magistrate was the Chief Federal Magistrate, Diana Bryant, so she swore the rest of us in.

I returned to Parramatta and went in to Court on the first day and it just took off from there. Of course, the work got busier and busier. In 2013 we became the Federal Circuit Court and we became Judges. We kept getting more and more work, and our jurisdiction kept expanding. From about 2009 I was doing almost exclusively Family Law and child support. Prior to that I also did some migration and bankruptcy matters.

Since retirement from being a Judge, you are working as a barrister and mediator. Can you tell me about mediation and how that works for people going through a separation?

I think it's pretty important. Firstly, to commence parenting proceedings, people are required to attempt mediation, often at a Family Relationship Centre, and if mediation doesn't occur, you are issued a Section 60I certificate.

What it meant for the Court was that once the Family Relationship Centres were set up, a lot of the easier cases were filtered out, and at the Court we just got the hard cases.

> I am more and more convinced that mediation is important. It's quicker and significantly less expensive.

Mostly, you can do it in a day, and if people approach mediation with a reasonable attitude and in good faith, it's amazing how much can be achieved. They can end up with a solution that usually doesn't have a winner or loser, but allows both parties to walk away with their dignity intact, an outcome they can live with and then get on with their lives.

The saving is considerable. People can spend hundreds of thousands of dollars on litigation. Recently, I had a mediation on various parenting matters before the matter was back in Court for contravention proceedings, and in a full day we resolved everything, with consent orders being prepared and the contravention proceedings being withdrawn, with a better set of parenting orders than the ones they had come in with, which really took into account the important things about them or their children.

Not all matters settle, but most of the matters I have done have resulted in a settlement.

> In a property matter I had, the parties said, 'We are $70,000 apart. This isn't going to resolve.' And I said, 'You'll spend that in the next 12 months and you still won't be at a final hearing. Come on, let's try a bit harder.' An hour or so later they reached an agreement where they were content with what was agreed.

You can have mediations where people have tried to resolve things before, but it has fallen over later. I say, 'Look, you have three options: you can agree here, you can go to court and fight it, or just spend all this money and walk away from it and do nothing. Don't try that third option. You already have tried that before and look where it has got you. So, it's either mediate and agree, or go to court.' In that case the parties and lawyers were keen. The husband and his lawyers came from Perth for the mediation and they found it worth the investment.

The other point is that the courts are full. There are now 70 Judges. When I left, there were about 65, but that is hardly enough to keep pace with the influx of work.

> To get ahead of the work, they would need 100 Judges and that just isn't going to happen. I hear horror stories of the delays in getting to a final hearing. I used to tell people it would be two years from filing to get a hearing. These days it is a good three years.

So, people are involved in litigation for years and years. It's costing them money, and the emotional toll is immense.

And not being able to move on too.

You can't move on, physically or emotionally, if you are involved in the here and now. I think it's like being a soldier in the middle of war. What you are involved in is the battle that's going on at the moment. you are not thinking about what you are going to do when it's peace time.

And of course you are spending big money, which goes to the lawyers. A lot of lawyers who arrange mediation are, to their credit, committed to mediation, because they can see that a speedy result for their client in property, parenting, or both is in their client's interests.

I don't find I get parties coming along to see me with their lawyers telling them not to do this. Usually, the lawyers are supporting the process and advising their client not to be obstinate and dig their heels in, to listen to what's said and come up with something constructive. I have only had one matter where the lawyer was being obstructive.

As a former Judge and mediator, I often tell people what they have already heard from their lawyers. So, I am validating the advice they already have got. I don't have people who are forced to attend mediation. The people have voluntarily agreed to be there.

You mentioned you have been on the ground since the very beginning of the *Family Law Act*. What changes have you noticed over the years?

Initially, in the first few years, we did heaps of divorces. All these people wanted a divorce (often so they could formalise their present union). They all came out of the woodwork.

It was not uncommon to go to Court and do about half a dozen divorces a day. These days they are done before registrars, but they used to be done by Family Court Judges.

Also, until the mid to late '80s, you were doing a lot of child maintenance matters, either under state legislation or the *Family Law Act*. That went once the various child support acts came in, noting that these came in in reverse order. The *Child Support Registration and Support Collection Act* came first, and it wasn't until a year later that the Child Support Assessment came in, which took child support as an administrative process out of the courts. For about a year you would still be doing child maintenance matters in front of a Judge or a magistrate, but you could then register those maintenance orders with the Child Support Agency, as it was then. They were collecting child maintenance orders. In fact, it was possible then, and still is possible now, to register spousal maintenance orders for collection by the Child Support Registrar. I don't know if many people do it, but it's there.

In 1989, child support came in and child maintenance stopped, and it was an administrative procedure. It was largely taken away from the Court, which caused a lot of confusion for lawyers, and they never really got the hang of it. I had to get the hang of it as a Judge, and in fact I did the child support list. That was a huge change.

With the Federal Magistrates Court, in 2000, when we started, we had limited jurisdiction in parenting and property. We could do interim parenting orders, but we could only do final orders by consent. If someone didn't consent, we had to send it off to the Family Court.

With property matters originally, we had a ceiling of only $300,000. Even then, that was below mean value of the average home in Sydney. It might have been alright in Launceston, but people would consent for you to have a higher jurisdiction.

A year or so passed and the jurisdiction of the Federal Magistrates Court increased, so we got more and more matters we could do as of right, rather than having to send them to the Family Court.

Then it was brought about that federal magistrates could do contraventions. So, we could deal with contraventions of Family Court orders as well as our own.

Initially when we first started the Federal Magistrates Court, we did a whole lot of divorces. The divorces went from the Family Court to the Federal Magistrates Court, and most of us were doing 100 to 120 divorces every week. It became very much a court for solicitors, as normally you didn't need a barrister to do a divorce. Solicitors found it was a fairly approachable court. If they'd done the divorce for a client in the Federal Magistrates Court, they often elected to stay there for the property or parenting case.

It got people in the doors. It got lawyers in the doors. A lot of lawyers appreciated the simple, robust approach we took to dealing with Family Law matters in those days. It was very much a 'get 'em in, get 'em on, get 'em out' approach.

Of course, more and more work came. It just got bigger and bigger and bigger. So, they were huge changes.

The other thing I noticed was there would be a different culture in various states and registries. The Family Court is a national court and could sit anywhere in Australia, other than Perth which has its own Family Court. But sitting in Sydney, compared to Melbourne or to Brisbane, became very different. Darwin was more like sitting in a country town, which surprised me for a national court.

Melbourne people were falling over themselves to settle. About a third of the lawyers in a list wanted time to talk about the matter. The Sydney registry was much more aggressive and combative. Parramatta, as a registry, never seemed to be as aggressive as Sydney.

Judges from other states that came to sit in Sydney used to comment that they 'needed to put on a helmet and a flak jacket just to go and sit in Court.'

Why is it like that in Sydney? I mean, what is in the water in Sydney? Is it because it's one of the larger cities?

Well Melbourne is big too, but I don't know why it is less aggressive. Is it because they have a more conservative culture? I don't know.

Did you see any changes with how technology is being used?

Very much so. The courts have embraced technology and there's electronic filing. That's really taken off in the last two to three years.

The downside is that Registry staff have been exercising less of a monitoring effect on what was being filed electronically; the stuff was just coming in. Fewer documents were being rejected by the filing clerks. People were more or less picking a list they would go into, and you'd have parenting or property matters coming up in your child support list, which wouldn't have happened if the documents were being filed over the counter.

But electronic filing is the way we are going and it will just continue to increase.

And what about social media?

That's had a huge effect on proceedings.

> A lot of litigants don't realise that what you SMS or
> put in an email is not ephemeral.

So often you see text messages annexed to affidavits, and people post things on Facebook commenting on their proceedings or partner, naively thinking this wouldn't rebound on them. Oh yes it will. Get off social media; shut up until your matter is over.

> So many times you go to court and there would be howls of outrage
> from one side because the other party made comments about them
> on Facebook. It was never conducive to settlement.

I had a case where the wife sought to remove the husband from living in a granny flat out the back of the house, claiming he intimidated her. But from about 11pm (when she probably had been drinking) she'd send [him] vitriolic and abusive texts, and any claim she had that she was intimidated was completely disproved by all these appalling messages. If anything, he was frightened by this dreadful stuff that was coming in.

> Social media has affected what has come into courts. My advice to litigants is: Don't post anything on Facebook that is relevant – resist the temptation. If your former partner has access to passwords for your email, (1) Tell them they no longer can use the password, but (2) Change it anyway. You do get people trying to hack each other's emails.

Everything is traceable.

Yes. I mean, you can delete something, but it's not permanently deleted; it's still recoverable. If you send something to the other side, they have it just as clearly as if you had put it in a letter and posted it to them. But people don't seem to realise it.

Any other tips for those going through the Family Law process?

> In parenting matters, don't think about winners and losers. Think: 'What effect will this have on my children?'

In most cases children love both parents, and bitter fights between parents can cause distress for the children. So often you see cases of parents abusing each other at changeover. That's terrible for children. If parties can't help but abuse each other when they see each other, they should make arrangements so they don't see each other, because the effect on children can be damaging and long term. If you are the parent of young children, you will be a parent for years, and will have to deal with them for years.

> If you adopt an aggressive abusive manner, that's the reply you will get. The likelihood that you can settle matters just reduces and reduces and reduces. Every abusive text, every abusive phone call, just pushes a proper settlement that much further away and will just run up more financial expense and more emotional expense.

> So often you see parents use their children as clubs to beat each other with. It's not good and it does nothing positive for the children. I am very strong on that, because I have seen it so often.

People need to think: I'm not going to be in this litigation forever. The best way to do it is with proper legal advice and working out reasonable negotiated settlements with the other side. Spend as little money on lawyers as possible, and as little time in court as possible; that's what you should be aiming to do.

Any words of wisdom for the lawyers?

Get good instructions early on. Apply a reality test to what your client tells you. You don't want to be in a position to find out something about your client in court as a surprise. Check what your clients tell you because they may give you a sanitised version.

Dealing in a courteous manner with other lawyers is very important. So often the Court sees reams and reams of abusive letters from lawyer to lawyer annexed to affidavits. All the Court sees is a slanging match between the lawyers. Lawyers need to realise they are hired guns, mercenary soldiers. They aren't their client's best friend. They are not to take on their client's case as a personal crusade, but to give objective advice. If they become too close to their client, they lose their ability to see things objectively. You don't do your client - or your professional reputation - any favours.

Prepare your documents properly and - an old bug bear of mine - turn up to Court on time. I would give the above advice to lawyers probably in any jurisdiction.

Family law litigation can be emotionally draining, physically tiring, and sometimes you need to download. Talking to friends in the profession is often a good way.

Don't make enemies in your profession; make friends with them. There are a lot of nice people in your profession. Try to offload it and then leave it behind when you go home and lead a normal life. Keep a work–life balance.

You have a lot of experience with child support matters and, as you say, a lot of Family Lawyers feel they are on shaky ground with child support. I know many lawyers also complain about the child support system.

I hear a lot of complaints about the Child Support Registrar. Lawyers and litigants say the Department of Human Services is very difficult to deal with and can be bureaucratic and unreasonable.

It's not entirely black and white, and one of the problems is that a lot of lawyers don't understand the system.

I was lucky, as I saw it all start up. I knew it was designed to be an administrative system and the idea was originally that the money would just be collected, just like pay-as-you-go tax, to take all the emotion and difficulty out of it. And, in fact, the original Child Support Registrar was the Deputy Commissioner of Taxation a long while ago.

A lot of lawyers don't understand child support. As a barrister I get several briefs asking me to advise on aspects of child support, and I am happy to do this, having done a lot of child support as a Judge, and I can at least give people an idea on the procedure and prospects of success if they are bringing litigation and drafting notices of objection to reviews.

I don't know how we could really reform child support offhand. I think people need to learn how the system works and accept the fact that it's very black-letter law and seek advice to that end.

The first thing you should always advise your client to do with regards to child support is to get their tax return in on time. If they don't, the Child Support Registrar has the power to deem their income, which is never in their favour.

Any other views on reform?

In interim proceedings, the Courts should be able to hand down short-form judgements. On a hotly contested interim matter, a Judge can't do an ex tempore (at the time) judgement. They then need to reserve and then turn around a written decision which is as lengthy and complicated as a decision on a final hearing.

My view is with many interim decisions courts should be able to come out with a judgement contained to one to two A4 pages setting out the essential matters. Certainly, without having to go through a tick-the-box arrangement, including so many things which aren't relevant but again they feel they have to do. I think that would improve things.

I think the Federal Circuit Court could make more use of registrars. The time has come for registrars to be dealing with first court date matters, rather than Judges, but that a Judge, into whose docket the matter is going to go, be available to have a matter sent to them on the day. I think the Court could use registrars for a lot of interim hearings, the way it seems to happen in the Family Court.

> The Federal Magistrates Court embraced the docket system in 2000 wholeheartedly, little realising that the workload was just going to expand exponentially. So, a lot of judicial time is not used effectively, instead dealing with administrative matters that a registrar could do.

I also think the courts should be strongly advising people to go to mediation, and unless a matter has been to mediation unsuccessfully, the Court should be asking why the matter should be given a final hearing date.

Do you think, in the way there are the Section 60I certificates, there should be a requirement for mediation in property matters before even entering the court system?

Whether you do the mediation just before filing or shortly after the first date I don't think matters.

I think conciliation conferences are a good idea, but I believe the rate of settlement is only one in three. The problem is that there's so much work, the registrars can't give enough time to a conciliation conference. When they are doing three a day, there isn't enough time to work towards a resolution of the matter.

Sometimes conciliation conferences, like mediation, need some further reality checking by the registrar, and we either have more registrars to do conciliation conference or more property matters sent out to mediation.

> I think [mediation] should be mandatory. There should be a really good reason why you would get a final financial hearing if you haven't been to mediation, and I think that would clear a lot of the matters.

I also think the profession should consider offering more mediations on a pro bono basis for those in difficult financial circumstances.

Given your experience in child protection, do you have thoughts about the intersection between Family Law and child protection?

I think a number of cases come before the Court that have serious child protection issues that should properly be brought to the attention of the Department of Family and Community Services.

Certainly, the Judges have the power to refer such matters, but I can't recall a case where the Department has picked up the ball and run with it. It seems to me - and I may be wrong - that these overworked departments in various states take the view that if the matter is before the Courts, it's being attended to anyway, whereas Judges are at times frustrated because there's a serious need to have the child protection issues dealt with for the benefit of the children.

I did a lot of care proceedings as Senior Children's Magistrate. There, you have a Court really focussing on what's in the best interests of the children. Care proceedings are, in my view, a good way of dealing with child protection issues. Children's Courts have a number of powers that Judges in the Family Law system don't have. I think child protection can sometimes suffer from the fact the Judges are overworked.

I know people say there are a lot of spurious child protection issues raised in Family Law proceedings. I have no doubt there are some, but I find in my experience that most child abuse matters raised in Family Law proceedings do have a strong legitimate basis. It is the exception where people have actually made these things up. It happens, but it is the exception.

Do you have any thoughts about Independent Children's Lawyers that have appeared before you over the years?

Yes, certainly. I think they can do a great deal to assist the Court and the parties. Good ones are worth every cent of their money. In particular, the in-house ICLs employed by Legal Aid New South Wales, and probably also the other legal aid agencies in other states, are above average in their ability. When they brief Counsel, they usually brief someone who is experienced in appearing for an ICL, so the Counsel will also add value.

The standard of ICLs in the private profession varies considerably. Some of them are extremely good; some of them are not quite so good. But on the whole, most Judges are delighted when they see a good ICL has been appointed, and Courts will rely heavily on them, and they really do try to work towards a resolution in a matter for the child.

Retired Federal Circuit Court Judge Robyn Sexton

Not a case of one size fits all

Recently retired Federal Circuit Court Judge Robyn Sexton practised as a family lawyer in her own practice for many years prior to being appointed a Judge of the Federal Circuit Court in 2004. She had been a member of the NSW Medical Tribunal and Social Security Appeals Tribunal, a member of the Family Law Issues Committee of the NSW Law Society and a Commissioner on the NSW Legal Aid Commission. Prior to studying law, Robyn was a public affairs researcher in ABC television, and worked on the Royal Commission on Human Relationships under the Chairmanship of the first Chief Justice of the Family Court, the Honourable Elizabeth Evatt.

In her later years as a Judge, Robyn Sexton has been increasingly involved in improving the access and experiences of Indigenous Australians in Family Law, and in this interview she speaks about the Indigenous list she established in the Sydney Registry of the Federal Circuit Court in 2016, and her hopes for how this may develop going forward.

Although, when I interviewed her, she was just weeks away from retiring from the Bench, I found Robyn Sexton to be visionary, forward thinking, and focussed on the future of Family Law, including new ideas for reform. I was given an overriding sense that she believes it is 'not a case of one size fits all' and we need to consider expanding the options and responses to Family Law disputes, including the specialised Indigenous lists in Family Law, judicial mediations, a more inquisitorial approach to matters, and changes to how parenting matters are dealt with. Robyn

Sexton also spoke about the vexed issue of family violence, and why the feminisation of poverty is still a real issue.

Just to start, how did you come to work as a Judge of the Federal Circuit Court?

I had been a solicitor in Family Law exclusively for probably about 10 years. I'd been a lawyer for about 20 years and I had been involved in other areas of law before I became involved in Family Law. I had done Tribunal work on the Social Security Appeals Tribunal and the Medical Tribunal. I realised I enjoyed hearing both sides of the story and coming up with a decision, and that judging was essentially problem solving, which I enjoyed. I had gained considerable experience over the years, so when I was asked if I was interested in becoming a Judge, I thought it would be a very satisfying way to practise law.

What would you say to someone who might be reading this book and has just separated?

It's obviously very hard to make general statements about what might work for one person or another. But my general perspective is that people shouldn't rush in to Court immediately after separation. Generally, it takes time for things to settle down and for people to adjust to their new circumstances, which can be stressful and frightening. Often, there might be a sense a of panic, a sense of overwhelming sadness, and when someone's emotions are running high like that, it's very hard for that person to think clearly about what might be the best way forward.

> I find parties who rush into court when emotions are still running high find it much harder to resolve their matters than those who have had time to give things a bit more thought.

So, as a general rule, where there's no major urgency, I would encourage people to wait awhile before they try to make final decisions.

Having said that, I think it's quite helpful for parties who are thinking of separating to get legal advice before they separate. And that doesn't mean it should be done with the knowledge of the other party. I think it's helpful for a party contemplating separation to go and see a lawyer, talk about the realities of what the likely outcomes will be, in relation to parenting, property, and maintenance, before taking that final step.

If it's clear the separation is going to happen, it is useful to think about what material you are going to need; what documents you are going to copy from the matrimonial home; what you might need to protect your position before taking the separation step.

Of course, human beings don't necessarily behave in that methodical way, and there are circumstances where there needs to be urgent action because there's violence, abuse, or financial intimidation, or because circumstances are such that you need urgent help.

> It's often hard for people to know when they should see a lawyer. I think as a general proposition it is best to get advice early even though no legal action may be taken for quite some time.

Of course, it's hoped that, ultimately, parties won't end up in a courtroom, and most parties don't. It's very helpful if parties have reached a stage where they are both accepting of the separation and are able to talk to each other about what might be the best way forward, particularly where children are involved. But when money is involved, as well.

In the courtroom we see the extreme cases. We see some terrible cases involving violence and abuse of all kinds. We see cases where people behave very badly and it is necessary to come to Court to get things sorted out. But as a general proposition, I would say the comments I've made would apply.

You mentioned the importance of legal advice early. What should people look for in a lawyer?

It's a very good idea to see a solicitor who has been recommended by someone you know, whom you trust and respect.

> I think it's generally better to see an accredited Family Lawyer,
> because they are going to have the necessary experience in Family
> Law, which is really important if you want to be well represented
> and advised.

Ideally, you'll see a lawyer who is not overly litigious, a lawyer who has
a reputation for being sensible about trying to resolve matters and knowing
when to make an application to the Court. You are looking for someone
who is experienced, smart, and sensible.

> The best Family Lawyers are not in Court a lot at all. They are doing
> most of their work in their offices, working with the solicitors for the
> other side and helping their clients achieve sensible resolutions.

**You mentioned that a lot of matters don't go to Court. What are the benefits
of resolving the matter before court?**

You'll save a huge amount of money. Most people cannot afford to come to
Court, so it's saving of money and it's also less stressful. Court can be very
inflammatory, given the adversarial nature of litigation.

Parties don't have the same direct control over their arrangements when
litigating as they do when they can work out arrangements themselves.
When represented, the lawyers take over, and although lawyers act on
instructions, it is not always easy to convey those instructions to the Judge,
particularly in a busy duty list. Some parties can be frustrated by the Court
process when they haven't had the chance to clearly express their point of
view.

Judges have very busy lists. Judges aren't going to give everyone the
amount of time they probably deserve and need and want because the Judge
doesn't have time for that. They'll be moving through the cases, asking the
lawyers to summarise what's going on and whether there are urgent issues
to be addressed. Often, there isn't time for the Judge to reflect on how

the litigant might be feeling about how the matter is being run. The Court process can make a party feel they have lost control.

If you settle a matter, there's not going to be a costs order against you, and you won't end up with an appeal against the orders. And when there are children involved, the less conflictual the parties, the more likely the parties will be able to keep working together into the future. Ending up with an inflammatory, hostile, and uncooperative relationship with a former partner is going to make life very hard for the children. That's why I say to wait for emotions to calm down if at all possible.

Often in a relationship breakdown, one party is way ahead emotionally compared with the other. For one party the marriage might have broken down some time ago, well before the separation. That party has long accepted that the marriage is not working for them and that, in time, they will separate. The other party may be unaware or unable to accept that the relationship is not working, and that separation is inevitable, so they will get a tremendous shock when the separation occurs; that party will be in a completely different emotional space from the person who has thought about separation much earlier. You need time for that party to catch up emotionally so that sensible settlement discussions can take place.

I understand you are quite involved in improving Family Law experiences for Indigenous Australians. What do you feel are the current challenges in Family Law for Indigenous Australians? Where can we go from here?

Indigenous Australians have a fundamental fear of courts. Their experience is almost exclusively criminal courts where their sons, sisters, brothers, and members of their community have been locked up. Or the Children's Court, where their children, or children in their families or community, have been placed in out-of-home care. In the Sydney Registry, we were seeing relatively few Indigenous Australians making applications to seek parenting or property orders when compared with their numbers in the community at large.

About five years ago, the Federal Circuit Court entered into a Reconciliation Action Plan with Reconciliation Australia. We were the first Court in the country, as far as I'm aware, to do so. And that plan was designed to help Indigenous Australians use the Family Law division of our Court more effectively, to help them and their families.

There were Judges from all around Australia appointed to the Court's Indigenous Access to Justice Committee, and I was a representative from the Sydney Registry. Another colleague on the Committee and myself spent time in the community talking to Indigenous people about what Family Law is all about, and what benefits there might be for their family members to use the Family Law process when children were seen to be at risk in their immediate family.

Over the last four years or so, we have arranged functions at the Court, in Reconciliation Week, in NAIDOC Week, and three years ago we introduced an annual evening gathering for Indigenous law students to come to to the court to meet our Judges and have the Federal Circuit Court's work explained to them. Those initiatives were successful, but a couple of years ago I decided that we needed to do something more and the Chief Judge gave his full support to my proposal.

We wanted to make the Court a more accessible environment, so I started a list called the Indigenous list. Once a month we would have a special list in the Court, where only matters in which one or both parties were Indigenous would be listed. I invited Indigenous support people from various agencies in the community to come to the Court on list days to create a safe environment for Indigenous litigants.

I only allowed one case in at a time because Indigenous Australians don't like their business being shared – not that anyone does, but they particularly don't. We put the Aboriginal and Torres Strait Islander flags behind me in the courtroom, and we added Aboriginal art to create a more culturally friendly environment. Instead of sitting at the Bench in my usual position, I sat at the Bar table with the parties directly opposite me at the same level, as well as the members of the family interested in the subject children, along with the lawyers and Independent children's lawyer. And, at this mention or interim stage, I conducted a 'yarning' session to help the parties and the family work out the best solution for the subject children. It's an inquisitorial rather than an adversarial process.

The aim of the Indigenous list is to encourage parties to come in early when a problem arises in the family so that the Court can stabilise the child's circumstances, ensure the child is safe, and then look to how it can assist the family. Maybe the parents are using alcohol or drugs, so we might be able to send them off to programmes, and we might place the children with granny or aunty in the meantime, to ensure the children are safe. If the children are safe, the Department will not need to take the matter to the Children's Court. Those Indigenous litigants who have used the Court in this way, as well as the support workers, have said that this is a much more accessible process for Indigenous people, and those who appear aren't frightened.

The word is going out in the community that it's worth coming to the Federal Circuit Court because you will be treated with respect, you'll have your say and you'll be listened to. It's a non-threatening process in which the Court is looking to how it can protect children from risk of harm and work out parenting arrangements which keep the children within their extended family and community.

The Indigenous list is at a pilot stage, and it's early days, but...

> I believe it is necessary to have specialist Indigenous lists if we are genuinely committed to improving Indigenous people's access to justice. I hope that eventually there'll be a specialist list or Court in all States in Family Law.

Do you see anything we can learn from the Indigenous list that shows us something about potentially how we could do Family Law differently, not just for Indigenous Australians but more generally?

I think so. I think we do learn from this process. I think there is a place for a more inquisitorial rather than adversarial approach, particularly in parenting matters.

There are cases where it wouldn't work, such as when high-level violence or when you need to make findings of abuse of any kind, really. But in many, many cases, my view is that an inquisitorial approach would work better and result in more child-focussed outcomes.

Well, funnily enough, actually I was about to ask you about the judicial mediations that I know you have been running too.

I have recently conducted numbers of judicial mediations to reduce the number of matters that I am transferring to other Judges on my retirement.

The judicial mediation process is inquisitorial and a more informal process, though I sit on the Bench. The process allows the parties to speak about what they see as the issues and why they see those issues as important. It involves having parties listen carefully to each other about their views, and why that party holds that view, in a more controlled and relaxed environment where each party and the Judge are trying to come up with solutions and orders that can work.

I believe there is a real place for this inquisitorial approach. Having had thirteen and a half years on the Bench making decisions after an adversarial hearing, I believe there are many cases, both parenting and financial, in which an inquisitorial approach which allowed the parties to be actively involved, would have been of greater benefit to the parties.

Since I have been saying to people, 'Look, I think you can probably resolve this; would you be prepared to come to a mediation with me in the Courtroom?', I've had only one party in a matter say they didn't want to. All the others have jumped at the chance, said yes, and so far, touch wood, all the matters have settled and therefore did not require hearing dates. It is very satisfying work.

Wow, all of them have settled? Well, that speaks for itself.

However, it's time intensive. You have to be very well prepared as the Judge and have parties there who want to resolve the matter. But I have found in the 15 or so that I have done, the lawyers have been extremely helpful and quite enjoyed the process, because they can see the outcome is likely to be more lasting, given the parties' direct input into the result.

So, where are we at with these judicial mediations? I must confess I was not aware you were doing these till we spoke today.

Well, it has only been happening in my docket because I am retiring; it is not yet happening elsewhere, but it will. I would anticipate that, in 2019, at least some of the Judges will start doing judicial mediations in selected cases, so it will hopefully be possible for parties to say, 'Your Honour, would you consider our case for a judicial mediation?' It will also hopefully be open to the Court to ask the parties if they would be willing to come to judicial mediation to try to resolve the matter without a full hearing.

Although the cases I have mediated have been well down the litigation track, I think there would be cases you could list for judicial mediation at the first return date.

There's an issue with resourcing though, as you say.

A big issue. I think what will happen – and, look, I may be completely wrong – is that there will be certain days allocated to slot these into, and so they will fill. And then, when they are full, they are full. There will be certain days allocated to hearings, certain days allocated to these judicial mediations, certain days allocated for duty lists, et cetera, and so there will be a limit to how many will be done. But I think, given the backlog of cases, we should consider all the options.

And are there any other reforms that you think could be considered?

The ALRC [Australian Law Reform Commission] is presently conducting an inquiry into Family Law generally. My understanding is that they will look at how Family Law is actually delivered to the public. There is criticism of the current system, as we know from lawyers, social scientists, litigants, and children. There is criticism from people who have been through the adversarial system.

This is a problem across the world – there are too many matters and not enough Judges. It is the age-old problem of too few resources, and we are dealing with human behaviour, which is hard to predict, and at times needs to be pulled into shape rapidly and firmly by judicial officers to protect the interests of others, most particularly children.

Not every Judge would be comfortable about doing judicial mediations. And not every Judge would be comfortable doing an Indigenous list, so it's best for those who do feel comfortable to do it, and for those who prefer to do trials to do trials.

It's not a case of one size fits all, necessarily.

It will be interesting to see what the ALRC recommends. I think they will also be looking at clarifying and simplifying Part VII of the Act, a complete rewrite.

> It is generally accepted that there are a multitude of problems with the presumption in favour of equal shared parental responsibility, and there's a lack of focus in the Act on the developmental needs of young children.

There are other parts of the Family Law Act where changes could help.

What do you think are the issues with the presumption of equal shared parental responsibility?

There's a fundamental misunderstanding in the community about what that presumption is. There's a sense that the presumption in favour of equal shared parental responsibility means there's a presumption in favour of equal shared care, and it doesn't say that; that's not the law.

> The law says that when parties are going to share parental responsibility equally, the Court must consider whether an equal time arrangement would be best for the child or whether a substantial and significant time arrangement would be the best outcome for the child.

But there are many, many cases I have determined where I have made a decision that there should be equal shared parental responsibility, but I have not found that there should be an equal time or even a substantial and significant time arrangement, because I did not consider either arrangement to be in the best interests of the child. The best interests of the child will always be the overriding principle. That's not always understood.

> I think the presumption [of equal shared parental responsibility] has created a lot of unnecessary litigation. I think it has focussed people on the wrong questions in parenting matters: 'How do I get

equal time?' 'I want equal time.' 'I'm entitled to equal time', is the
catch cry, not 'Is equal time the best outcome for my child?'

The question should be: 'What is in the best interests of my child?'

A rights entitlement kind of perspective, you mean.

Absolutely. 'I am entitled to equal time; I am just as a good a parent as she
is.' There's this view that fathers have missed out and fathers have been
excluded from the lives of their children that I don't think stands up anymore. I think, historically, that was a more valid position to put, but as
women take their place in the workforce increasingly and men take their
place in domestic life increasingly, if one examines determined cases, one
will find there are many hundreds of cases where children primarily live
with their fathers as opposed to their mothers.

When very little children are involved – and by 'little' I mean children
from birth to approximately four years.

We need to look at their developmental needs and what little
children can manage at their developmental stage. This often gets
lost in this whole equal-time argument ...

and it's been a real concern to me during my time as a Judge that orders
have been proposed that are not developmentally appropriate for a child
of that stage and age. I can't think of a case where it would be appropriate for a child under four years of age to be in an equal-time arrangement, because it would be likely to have such an adverse impact on their
developmental needs.

**You mentioned the changing gender roles and how this has filtered through
into Family Law. Are there still any gender issues in the Court or Family
Law process that persist?**

I still think – and, again, this is a generalisation – we are seeing a problem
with women's financial positions, in particular, older women. We are seeing

women with almost no superannuation who have either not worked at all in the marriage or worked in limited part-time employment, so they don't have financial security, and remain dependent on their former partners who do not want to pay them spouse maintenance, expect them to find a job, and want them to move on. It is difficult to find a job at aged 50-plus when you have qualifications well out of date, and little or no work experience.

It is difficult to achieve a just and equitable outcome in such cases. If you look 10 years ahead and ask, 'Where is this woman going to be (in a financial sense) in 10 years, versus where is this man going to be in 10 years?' it is likely that he will be a lot better off because he will have worked more, will have a higher-paid job, will have superannuation and he will take his income-earning capacity with him. The significance of an ongoing solid earning capacity is well recognised by the authorities.

That's certainly not always the case, and we are seeing cases where women earn more than men and are well off financially, with plenty of superannuation.

But we do see a lot of cases where older women, in particular, are going to be poverty stricken later in life, and it is sometimes very difficult to fix that. Often, there are insufficient assets to overcome the problem that has emerged from a partnership decision made 30 or 40 years ago.

You are referring, I think, to the idea of feminisation of poverty?

That feminisation of poverty is still real and we see it. It is not common to see final orders for long-term spouse maintenance. Orders for interim spouse maintenance and orders for limited spouse maintenance, while a party does a computer course or a child care diploma, for example, are made regularly. But an ongoing final spouse maintenance order is rare, unless there are significant health or disability issues.

If you think about it, a woman who needs ongoing spouse maintenance when there is limited property isn't going to be able to afford to fight that case, and thus she will settle. It is very hard to get a settlement on the basis that she gets 95% of the asset pool and he gets 5%, because he is walking away with a $250,000 income a year. But 95% of a couple of hundred thousand dollars is not very much when we consider property prices in Sydney.

So, women who are older, have had long marriages, and have not been anywhere near equal participants in terms of income earning capacity, in my view, are still worse off.

In a parenting situation, I think the perception of bias - actually, I don't think it is bias - arises in those very early years where if you have a competent, capable mother, she will generally have been the primary carer from birth, and through those early pre-school years. This will mean that the child's primary attachment is to the mother. Children have a hierarchy of attachments. They may have a strong attachment to the father, but it will be a secondary attachment. That's when you are going to want to protect the attachment with the primary carer to ensure a strong secure attachment foundation for that child so that, in the future, they can form other strong secure attachments. If you disturb the development of a secure primary attachment, the child will suffer.

So, that's where I think bias is perceived, but I think it's the right bias because it is a bias in favour of the child. If there is a true focus on the child's needs, and not 'I want...' and 'I should have...', that's the right answer.

Of course, there are cases where you have an incompetent mother who is perhaps alcoholic, drug addicted, seriously mentally ill or personality disordered; a mother who lacks the capacity to be the primary carer.

And cases where dad has been the primary carer too.

Absolutely. And the dad is sometimes the primary carer even with a baby, because in the circumstances of that case - for example, he may have always been the primary carer of that baby - that is the outcome which is in the child's best interests. I have made orders for a grandfather to be the primary carer of a very young child when circumstances dictated that outcome. So, there's no rule.

I suppose, going back to your first question, in terms of what do you say to parties when they are facing separation, you should tell them to think hard about their child and the likely impact of the separation on that child.

> If you are in a relationship which is tolerable, it might not be
> the happiest of marriages but it is a working relationship, the
> child is thriving, and you are both actively involved parents, then
> separating when the child is very young is not child-focussed. In my
> view it is adult focussed.

Even if you realise that ultimately you will separate, I would advise waiting until the child is at least a few years old.

If the child has a strong foundational relationship with both parents
before separation, there is a far greater prospect of that child moving into
a substantial and significant arrangement because the child has a strong
loving relationship with both parties and the child will be able to manage
such an arrangement.

But if you separate when the child is six months old, or 18 months old,
or even two years old, they are unlikely to be developmentally ready for that
substantial and significant time arrangement. You need to think long and
hard about when to separate when children are involved.

Of course you should separate if there's violence or abuse, because your
first priority is to protect your child from exposure to conflict and violence.

You mean people who are, say, feeling bored in their marriage?

Exactly, I am talking about situations where you are, say, bored in your
marriage, or you have met someone at work and they are a bit more attractive. Think about it, because the ones who separate when the mother is still
pregnant or the baby is three weeks old, or six months old – they are the
really problematic cases to sort out, because the non-primary carer is going
to have to be patient.

**You mentioned violence or abuse. I did want to ask one more question about
where are we at with the understanding of family violence. For example, there
were the amendments in 2012 to increase the scope of what family violence
was understood to be. Do you think there needs to be further reform? Or is
family violence misunderstood still?**

Well, the Court is often criticised, isn't it, for the way it manages family violence cases.

In my experience, in almost all parenting matters that run the full course to final hearing, there is family violence. It is not often that I see a matter in final hearing for parenting matters where there is absolutely no allegation of family violence. Those matters usually settle along the way, or before they get near a Court.

If every matter that involved some form of family violence meant that the perpetrator never saw the children, there would be an awful lot of children with no fathers. Generally speaking, the violence is coming from men, but that is not always the case. I made a decision recently where the mother would have been the more violent of the two, without a doubt. But putting it in a general context, one has to seriously examine what is going on in terms of the violence. Is this situational violence? Is this a reactive one-off violent exchange? Or is this coercive and controlling violence? There is a lot written about the different types of violence and its damaging impact on parties and children.

All serious conflict in front of children will be damaging to children. But some children are chronically exposed on a daily basis to some form of violence. Those matters are looked at very differently from a case where a child might have heard their parents shout at each other abusively on one occasion. What's important for lawyers and litigants is to really detail what violence and intimidation has occurred.

There are different forms of violence, including financial, verbal, physical, sexual and emotional. All forms can be extremely serious, and often we find more than one form of violence occurring in a household. For example, there might be the occasional physical outburst, but also isolation from friends and family, and financial controls. All those forms of intimidation need to be carefully detailed and dated. Any person reading this book who is a victim of this kind of behaviour needs to keep a careful diary of what has happened, because if there are proceedings down the track, those details will be imperative to ensure the Court is fully aware of the extent of the behaviours complained of.

In my experience, when an affidavit details carefully and comprehensively what has gone on, there's no way the Court cannot take careful note of it and be careful of the time arrangements put in place, if any time arrangements are determined to be in the child's best interests.

I have had cases where there has been violence resulting in no time at all, because it is simply too risky.

I have determined cases where there is forever supervision because it is too physically or psychologically risky to permit any other arrangement, or too risky emotionally, because the content of face-to-face communication is so destructive.

When it is properly pleaded in affidavits, I think our Courts deal with family violence effectively. I think the broadening of the definition of family violence has been helpful. We now have to deal with a child's safety as the priority factor when considering a child's best interests.

> The Court must consider as primary factors the benefit of a child having a meaningful relationship with both parents, and the need to protect a child from harm, but the latter is the factor to which we must give priority.

> So, if you write: 'He was always violent to me' in your affidavit, with no detail, it won't help the Court. But if you detail the incidents carefully, the allegations will be taken extremely seriously.

When there are family violence allegations and the other party says that none of it happened, which is frequent, it is open to the Court to list a preliminary hearing on just the question of whether the violence occurred. If the Court finds the allegations of violence were false, which, can I say, is unusual, but if that were the case, the matter would proceed without the complication of the violence factor.

If, on the other hand, findings were made in favour of, or partially in favour of, the victim, the matter would proceed on the basis that violence occurred. That may shorten the litigation process considerably, as the Court has dealt with the issue that is really causing the need for a final trial. There have been occasional cases where I have said, 'I want a preliminary hearing on family violence'. If you are dealing with a 15-year-old child who has a solid relationship with both parents, even if there has been violence, you are unlikely to order a no-time arrangement, because at that age the child will just vote with their feet anyway. But if you are talking about a child who is five months or five years old, you certainly would want to do something about it.

Returning to the issue of preliminary hearings on family violence, are you suggesting that we should think about, in Family Law, determining the issue of violence as a matter of priority?

As a lawyer or self-represented litigant, you can ask the Court to determine that issue as a preliminary matter, because one party is saying these things have happened and the other is saying none of this has happened.

But is it automatic? I mean for people who are reading this book, they may be wondering if there has been family violence. And bearing in mind that the meaning of family violence in the Family Law Act is perhaps more expansive than what the average person may think, is it automatic, if there has been family violence, that there will be either no time or supervised time forever?

No, definitely not. Every case will be different and the outcome will turn on the particular findings of fact in each case. Few cases overall result in a no-time or long-term final supervised contact order. If there's been serious coercive controlling violence that's been ongoing, chronic, and has clearly impacted the children, there may be a no-time order or long-term supervision order.

> The outcome will depend on the nature and severity of the conduct, on the nature of the relationships between the perpetrator, the victim, and the children, and the likely impact of ongoing contact on the victims of the violence.

In the majority of cases, even when serious violence is alleged, the victim is not asking the Court to make a no-time order. There are significant variations in outcomes in cases involving family violence. If there's been a pattern of violent behaviour over a long period and pre-school children are involved, absolutely there could be no-time or supervised time on a final basis. If the children are older and the perpetrator's behaviours are likely to continue, there may well be a no-time or supervised time on a final basis. But if the children have solid, loving relationships with the perpetrator, it may not be realistic to cut the children off from the perpetrator, and it may be preferable to order therapy for the perpetrator in the hope the violent behaviours can be stopped.

So if you are a litigant or lawyer and you ask for a preliminary hearing to determine if family violence has occurred, is that something Judges would be willing to do?

Well, each case would be considered on the merits of the argument.

Speaking only for myself, if you put it in a way to me that satisfies me that a preliminary hearing on the question of whether family violence occurred is likely to lead to the matter being resolved, I would give your request very careful consideration. Because even the person who is the perpetrator can say, 'Well, look, there are findings against me that I've behaved in this way, so I have to accept those findings. I have to go and do a 16 week anger management course, I have to see a psychologist for 12 months, and have supervised time while I get my act together, but I hope that means that supervision will end.' I have seen that happen.

The Honourable Justice Peter Rose AM QC

Former Justice of the Family Court, mediator and arbitrator

The less glamorous part of it

The Honourable Justice Peter Rose AM QC is a seasoned Family Court Judge having served for approximately 13 years before retiring from the Bench in 2011. Prior to this, he was a leading Queens Counsel, specialising in Family Law cases. He is an Adjunct Professor in the Faculty of Law at the University of Sydney and also lectures at other universities, including the University of New South Wales, the College of Law, China University of Political Science and Law, Renmin University of China, and Tsinghua University, Beijing.

Justice Peter Rose has served as the Chair of the Advisory Committee on Advanced Legal Education for the College of Law, and as an honorary consultant to the Australian and NSW Law Reform Commissions. He has been a member of the Family Law Council and an executive member of the Family Law Section of the Law Council of Australia. Justice Peter Rose continues to bring his extensive experience in Family Law to his work as an arbitrator and mediator.

In this interview, the overriding message I took away from Justice Peter Rose was we need to focus more on 'the less glamorous part of it', on being genuine, on reality over appearance - for parents to provide practical financial support (rather than just talk about how much they love their child), for lawyers to give 'professional advice with integrity', and for politicians to 'provide substantially more resources rather than just talking about it' to the Family Law Courts.

⸭

May I start by asking you how you became Justice of the Family Court?

Well, I was a leading specialist in Family Law and a QC for 10 years. I was fortunate to be briefed in high-profile cases and also engaged in legal politics with Law Council Australia, so I had developed a profile. The Attorney General of the day, who had lost in a case in which I had appeared, decided he should get rid of me from practice and offer me a job.

I worked for approximately 13 years as a Family Court Justice. Because it is a national court, I sometimes heard cases interstate, and from time to time I sat on the Full Court which heard appeals interstate.

What drew you to Family Law?

I preferred dealing with people rather than documents. When I was a solicitor I did a fair amount of Family Law. When I went to the Bar I was doing personal injury work, and other work as well, suddenly three leading barristers were all appointed as Judges around the same time, and so the younger barristers were given cases they otherwise might not have had for some years. Fortunately, that worked out ok for me and it developed a steamroller effect.

What changes did you notice in terms of the way Family Law was being practiced, or the kinds of cases that were being run, or the way they were being run?

In terms of the way it has been practiced, I think there have always been no more than a handful of solicitors who were sophisticated and well prepared, but as time has passed, there are more of those who lack necessary knowledge and were poorly prepared. There have been some barristers who fall into the same genre.

On the other hand, Family Law has become more complex, with changes relating to superannuation, third-party rights, and big changes in relation to children and parenting proceedings, compared to what the law was before.

Could you please elaborate further with regards to children and the changes that have occurred here?

With children, the current state of the law in parenting matters is, in my opinion, far too complex and much more than is necessary, and that was because of a parliamentary enquiry in 2005. It was a classic example of why you shouldn't leave changes to the law to politicians, because their agenda and what they want to achieve is not always what the average citizen wants to achieve.

So, it became very prescriptive, and it required a whole host of factors to be taken into account, with all sorts of presumptions that must be dealt with, and the consequence of that was that it made the best interests of the child far more complex to deal with and created a lot of false expectations – for example, equal time.

> There wasn't, and never was, a provision that a parent must have equal time. There's a provision for equal parental responsibility, but equal time is just a factor to take into account. This was misconstrued by politicians and others, and gave people an incentive to litigate, instead of an incentive to try and reach agreement.

You would have come across litigants who wanted equal time and saw it as their right to have equal time, as opposed to thinking about the rights of children.

Yes, it provided incentive for people who weren't getting proper legal advice and who only followed what they read in the media to think that they were entitled to equal time. The only immovable feature of the law is that it is about the rights of children, not about the rights of parents. That doesn't mean parents' rights are irrelevant, but they don't occupy the top of the flag pole compared to children's rights.

You mentioned that you felt the law became unduly complicated with regards to parenting.

I would repeal the whole of the *Family Law Act* that deals with children, with the exception of the sections that deal with the best interests of the child as the paramount consideration. I would leave in the section that lists the factors you have to take into account. And I would leave in the provisions about parental responsibility, but remove everything else.

If I could ask further with regards to children, do you think the way children are represented by the Independent Children's Lawyer could be different?

I think the Independent Children's Lawyer generally does a good job. It is a very difficult role to fulfil at times because often the child is too young to have an intelligent, mature discussion. Sometimes, the child has been heavily influenced by a parent and pressurised to tell the Independent Children's Lawyer what the parent wants told. But, overall, I think there are a number of experienced ICLs who do an excellent job.

Do you have any views about children's involvement in Family Law proceedings and striking the balance between participation and protection?

Firstly, this is a big myth and misconception that children's voices aren't heard. It's absolutely rubbish. Children's voices have been heard since 1976, when they started to have reports by Court counsellors and children's experts following interviews with children, so, to that extent, children's voices have been heard for a long time.

Secondly, a child can always be interviewed by a Judge, but in my experience that has happened rarely, because unless the child is of a certain maturity, it places the child in an invidious position. The parents will want to prime the child as to what they should say and will want to know afterwards what the child did say.

There's the question of how it will be handled, because the Judge can't become a witness in the case. The usual procedure was, and still is, as far as I know, that when on the rare occasion you interview a child who is at an appropriate stage of life and maturity, it is only done by consent, and no detailed notes are taken. The notes won't be subpoenaed. The Court Counsellor has to be present, as a witness, and a memorandum is prepared which provides a summary of what the child or children said, and that, in turn, can't be challenged. If parents, through their lawyers, agree to those restrictions and there is no better way of hearing what the child's views are, then that can work quite well. But, given we have child experts to interview children who can then be cross-examined, it is a rare situation when a Judge will need to interview a child.

There's been a lot of focus on family violence recently. Do you think we could be doing things differently in terms of any reforms to legislation with regards to family violence?

Look, I think that the legislation that we have that deals with family violence in Family Law cases is fine. It doesn't need any changes, because legislation doesn't change someone's behaviour. They don't walk around with a copy of the *Family Law Act* in their pocket. And concerning people who have psychiatric disturbances or mental health issues, or alcohol or drug issues, which are often the main causes of domestic violence, that is not going to change because legislation changes.

Somehow or other, we need to be able to educate children at high school and university level about what is expected of their behaviour. Part of that problem is made more complicated because sometimes, in their own home, that's all they have seen, so they think this is the norm.

It is highly complicated and I think what you are referring to is the sometimes intergenerational nature of violence.

Well, it is about how you deal with people who are affected by substance abuse or poor temperament or mental health issues. No amount of legislation is ever going to change that.

For example, a few years ago, there was a big announcement by the state government that there was going to be a portfolio given to a minister in prevention of domestic violence. Has anyone ever heard of anything that has been achieved in that Department? I'd be very surprised. Might have given a lot of lectures, but has it translated to reducing domestic violence? All the information to date indicates the reverse.

On a related issue, what do you think about where we are now with the intersection between Family Law Courts and Children's Court?

There definitely needs to be federal and state legislation in harmony to enable better legislative and court-related responses to often dealing with one or more of the same people and children. Currently, because of the division between child welfare laws, which is a state province, and Family Law, which is a federal province, there is a limit as to how much can be done. But if there exists the political will to do it, then I am sure ways can be found to overcome it.

In some overseas countries the Court dealing with Family Law also deals with criminal law. For example, in China, the Court has a power to deal with, for example, domestic violence as a criminal act as well as dealing with the civil side and Family Law. I am not saying that is necessarily the way we should go, but it is an example of how, in other jurisdictions, the Courts try to deal with everything instead of sending people from one court to another.

Do you think it would, or would not, be helpful if, for example, Judges in the Family Law Courts had the same powers that those in the Children's Court have?

I think in theory it would be good. The problem is the current state of affairs which has existed for a long time, that the Family Court and the Federal Circuit Court are under-resourced, which has contributed to long delays.

If they had to deal with more matters, though, there would be even more delays, unless there are governments that actually have the political will to do something and provide substantially more resources rather than just talking about it.

Did you see, when you were a Justice of the Family Court, the change in Court delays and this under-resourcing getting worse and worse?

Yes. There were two Judges and I who, for a period of time, would each have two trials listed for the same period of time and we would send out people in one trial to have discussions while we heard the other case, and if that didn't reach a settlement, then somehow or other we would juggle both cases.

That was unsatisfactory in the end to everyone because it made people feel frustrated that their cases weren't being dealt with as efficiently as they should have been, and it pushed up legal costs. Delays have certainly gotten worse.

I don't think it is just a question of more resources. It is also a question of what the quality of resources are. For example, it's been noteworthy that the best Judges are those who have been highly experienced, knowledgeable family lawyers in all aspects of Family Law, not just children's matters.

There have been some other Judicial appointments that can only be explained for reasons that have nothing to do with Family Law. So, unless there's a bigger commitment by governments to improve the quality of the resources they provide, nothing much is going to change.

When you were first appointed as a Justice of the Family Court, what was the rough time limit for how long it would take to hear a matter from start to finish?

Well, Sydney has always been one of the busiest registries, so, using Sydney as the example, at that time, assuming that both lawyers were efficient and could get instructions in a timely way, the delay was something like 14 to 15 months. Now it is something like at least two years, if not longer.

Yes, two to three years, I think. So, moving onto property issues, following on from the *Thorne v. Kennedy* case, do you think, as the media say, prenups (or binding financial agreements) are 'dead in the water'?

I don't think they're dead in the water, but there are an increasing number of lawyers who won't prepare prenuptial agreements even before that High Court decision because they are too susceptible for challenge.

Secondly, from the lawyer's point of view, their Lawcover insurance is capped, and if it involves one or more wealthy people, and the junior lawyer makes a mistake, then the damages that might have to be paid might exceed the insurance cap. So, I think lawyers are realising, particularly after the High Court decision of *Thorne v. Kennedy*, and where there's an imbalance of power monetarily and emotionally between a couple that propose to get married, that this is ripe for litigation. I think there are going to be specialist lawyers who are going to be more and more reluctant, in a lot of situations, to have a prenuptial binding financial agreement.

Do you have any thoughts about how property is determined?

I think that that's one of the few good things. There are many years of jurisprudence, with principles that have been laid out. The manner in which discretion should be exercised has been traversed in numerous appeal judgements and overall property cases decided without much controversy.

Tell me about the work you are doing in arbitration.

Firstly, arbitration can only be held by consent, and only in relation to property matters. If the lawyers on all sides are efficient and knowledgeable, you should be able to have an arbitration fixed for hearing in six weeks from the time that you agree to have arbitration.

If the arbitrator is sufficiently knowledgeable and experienced, and the best ones in terms of decision making being former Judges or leading barristers, they should be able to hear and determine the case on the real issues without necessary delay. The expectation is that the award with reasons, which is similar to writing a Judgement, should be able to be delivered within 14 days after the arbitration hearing has been completed, and that has been my experience. That leaves it well ahead of what can be achieved in Court. Again, that has been my real experience; I'm not just talking in theory here.

> Arbitration also has the advantage for the litigants in that they can choose their own decision maker.

That's a big plus. While the initial costs are higher than if they were waiting for a court hearing, it is a drop in the ocean compared to the preparation and running of a trial that might last for a few days, not to mention the prospect of an appeal as well.

And just the shelf life of having a matter in court as well, for two to three years, that also incurs legal fees. I mean there is a cost to just keeping a matter running through the court system.

No comparison. And provided the arbitration award is registered in court, which is just a formal process, it has the force and effect of an order, so it can be enforced.

And what about the mediation work you are doing? For those separating and reading this book, is that something that is suitable in most cases?

I think that, in most cases where there are many substantial facts in dispute, the answer is yes. Because it has the big advantage of helping people reach their own decision rather than having the decision forced upon them, so they own the result, and if it's a case involving children, the children will know that it is their parents who have reached that decision, rather than a stranger in the Court forcing it on them.

Do you think there is another way we could deal with cultural issues correctly?

Well, I can't speak for everyone in the Court, but I know that, for many years, cross-cultural issues have been very prominent in seminars and legal conferences. There are, in children's cases, experts who are highly experienced in that area, and I think they are being appreciated in a far more knowledgeable and sophisticated way than 20 years ago.

But it is a big issue, and most people can't get away from their cultural upbringing, so that, in turn, raises expectations that can't always be met. But the important thing is that Courts should be sensitive and alive to these issues, and have some appreciation that what might be attractive to a couple with an Anglo-Saxon background isn't necessarily going to be the right approach for people with an Asian or Indian background.

When I speak with men and women who have been through the system, some women feel it is still quite patriarchal, and men feel that it is biased against men. Do you think we have the right balance with issues that may be particular to either gender?

I do. You have to be careful to draw a distinction between the Federal Circuit Court, which is set up to deal with a high volume of cases, and the Family Court, which isn't. In the latter, in the pressure to finish cases quickly, it can seem they aren't as sensitive to gender issues as the other. I think the question of male and female bias is a myth that's been promulgated by special interest groups to suit their own agendas. A lot of people need an excuse for a result that was unavoidable, and this is a convenient excuse. In my experience, both in practice and in the Court, I don't think you could say with any real substance that there's gender bias. But for people who are determined to find there is gender bias, nothing will persuade them otherwise.

You mentioned before about solicitors being properly prepared. Are there any other key tips for lawyers in Family Law?

I think it's important to try and analyse, and be focussed on what the real issues are, not what peripheral issues are, not to chase every rabbit down every hole.

So, what are the real issues? And am I preparing material, such as affidavits, that are admissible? Those are the things I would concentrate on.

The other is that you should always remember there is at least one other party involved in your client's matter. You can't become the worst litigator, someone who only sees their client's side of the case and who's not capable and has no desire to stand back and provide a professional view of the case with integrity. That means analysing not only the strengths but the weaknesses in your client's case and determining how you would challenge those issues if you represented the other party. Good litigators in any jurisdiction do that.

But there are plenty of bad litigators, or people who are very enthusiastic, or fall in love with their client's case, who seem to be incapable of doing that. The result often is that the client is done a huge disservice and gets a result they were given no previous advice on as to its possibility. Inevitably, they say to the lawyer, 'Why didn't you tell me this might happen?' That lawyer might end up being sued for negligence.

> Just remember that, as a lawyer in litigation, you're not a politician. You're not there to win popularity. You're there to give professional advice with integrity. And if you can't do that, or you're not willing to do that, or you haven't got the time to do it, then you shouldn't handle their case.

Good, sage words of advice. And for the litigants – the mums and dads, the husbands and wives who are going to Court, which is hugely a new forum – do you have any key tips?

Yes. They should ask their lawyer what the procedure will be.

They should go down and sit at the back of the courtroom and experience the atmosphere and see what goes on, and they'll realise that it is not an episode of Law and Order or LA Law, and it's not such a frightening experience as they might otherwise have thought.

Otherwise, they should insist on their lawyer giving them advice as to the range of possibilities.

Ask, 'What is the worst possible result? What is the best possible result? And what is all this going to cost me?' And then, finally, 'What steps can we take in the meantime for mediation?'

Any thoughts about how social media is being used in Family Law proceedings?

Yes. It is often an advantage to one person and a big disadvantage to someone else, because the thought processes that end up finding their way into social media can then become admissible in a case.

The only advantage in social media that I can think of is as an avenue to try and find a missing child.

Otherwise, it should be avoided at all costs. Also, be aware that text messages are capable of being reproduced in court.

Text messages should be limited to arrangements and constructive or positive comments. Anything else should remain in the mind.

Some litigants feel they can't afford solicitors, yet they are not eligible for legal aid. Do you think it is possible for someone to run their own case without a lawyer?

Generally, no. Even for those who have education and the sophistication to do it, it's an emotionally taxing experience dealing with your own children's issues or hard-earned assets. And as a non-lawyer grappling with the emotional pressures, the idea that you will be able to conduct your case properly is ridiculous.

The person in the situation that you mentioned should be trying to get enough money together to get a solicitor to organise a mediation, if possible, or to use the Court's early processes for meeting with a family consultant; or otherwise a conciliation conference at Court which registrars run should be approached in a constructive and positive way to try to reach agreement.

All very sound advice. If I can ask you a final question about child support: What are your thoughts on the current system?

The system we currently have is excessively bureaucratic and slow, and works on a formula such as the last income tax return that may no longer be current. As a consequence, people ask for an appeal or a review, which all takes lots of time, and in the meantime the one who suffers is the child, because they aren't getting enough support.

My own view is that if you love your child – and most parents say they do – and if you are dedicated to the child's financial support and upbringing, why do you need to get a bureaucratic child support assessment? You should be providing suitable financial support without someone in a government office telling you based on some complicated formula how much you should provide.

Unfortunately, if we went back to the old system, where that bureaucratic system didn't exist, courts would become clogged with child support cases, and the delays for other cases dealing with children's care and financial property settlements would be even greater than they are now.

So my message would be that if you and your former partner have had differences, it is not the child's fault. They are an innocent party in all of this.

> Your child needs not only your emotional support, and statements about how much you love them; they also need the less glamorous part of it: providing suitable financial support, not at the lowest possible level.

If you claim to really love and be dedicated to your child, you can do that without needing a child support assessment.

Judge.Joe Harman[1]

Judge of the Federal Circuit Court

Not the dollar, not the corporation,
but the family

Judge Joe Harman was appointed to the Federal Circuit Court (then known as the Federal Magistrates Court) in 2010, after 25 years of practice as a family lawyer and Family Dispute Resolution Practitioner. In both his legal and mediation careers, Judge Harman has been involved in researching and advocating with respect to issues of domestic violence, mental health, and culture within the context of Family Law disputes. Judge Harman has written and presented on Family Law issues at domestic and international conferences and as a lecturer at the University of Western Sydney and Sydney University.

Since appointment to the Federal Circuit Court, Judge Harman has developed practices within his docket focussed on achieving better parenting outcomes, and engaging community-based services within the Court process, and in working with parents. He is currently working on making mediation services more accessible to litigants.

This broad experience was very clear in his interview, as Judge Harman weaves in law, academia, and popular culture references, and provides intellectual insights infused with a wry sense of humour. He shares his

[1] The views expressed in this interview are Judge Harman's own views; they do not represent the views of the Federal Circuit Court of Australia or other judges. These views do not indicate how Judge Harman would decide a case after having the benefit of evidence and argument.

views on mediation and its role in Family Law, family violence, on how we represent children, and why the adversarial system could work in Family Law if lawyers focused on resolution of disputes and multi-disciplinary practice to assist parents heal and change. Overall, Judge Harman believes we could be doing better by families as a society and that they are the priority: 'Not the dollar, not the corporation, but the family'.

I'd like to speak with about your mediation project. Before we get to it though, could you tell me just a bit of background? What was the path that you took and how did you come to Family Law?

A lot of chance. I'm one of Gough's children. I went to university because Gough Whitlam had made education free, so my generation of my family, my eldest sister and I, are the first people in my family for 300 years who have been to uni.

I did law because my father suggested I should, as I had a job cadetship as an engineer and it fell through – the company went bust – so I went and did that. I had no idea what I was doing or why I was doing it. I got to the end and by then I thought, I've got a law degree, I've got to get a job. So I got a job. It just so happened the first job I had was predominantly Family Law.

You obviously had an interest in it or you wouldn't have stuck with it, I'm guessing?

I certainly have an interest in it. I probably now have more of a passion for it; I really like what I do. I spent the first seven or eight years just being a lawyer, then trained as a mediator in the early '90s and by the time I got appointed as a Judge in 2010, I was doing about 50% mediations and about 50% being a lawyer, predominantly representing kids.

I'm aware that you're working on a mediation project at the moment. What exactly is that?

I've got a lot of projects about mediation. I am keen on the idea that mediation, or alternate dispute resolution in general, are how we should be dealing with families. So, for the reader, there are facilitative ways of resolving disputes through negotiation, mediation, or counselling, and there are determinative models, like arbitration and the court. I've done a lot of research through my job in the Court in this area.

Over the last few months I've been trying to put together lists of FDRPs [Family Dispute Resolution Practitioners] with help from the Attorney General's department so that I can have lists to give to all my fellow Judges and to my Head of Jurisdiction of the accredited FDRPs and what they charge, where they work, and what their qualifications are, because it's just impossible to find a list of FDRPs that lets you make an informed choice about who you might actually use for mediation.

I'm hoping that we're at a point in history where maybe we start to think seriously about what we're doing, and I think we are. There's the Law Reform Commission Review of Family Law, in general. The Senate Committee's report last year suggested we really need to be looking at structural and systemic change for our system.

> Mediation [in parenting matters] has been, theoretically, a compulsory requirement for 12 years now, but in reality, I would observe that many people do not go to mediation before they come to court in parenting cases.

In property cases, no-one has to go to mediation before they come to court. And they generally don't. So, I'm really hoping that all of this drive and this momentum we have might move us towards recognising that relational disputes in Family Law have better ways of being dealt with than people coming to Court and beating each other up in an adversarial system.

What do you see is the benefits of mediation as opposed to a Court adversarial system, in the context of Family Law?

I suppose, to start with, not every matter is suitable for mediation. There are disputes that need Courts. People who have horrific histories of violence and fear of their partner probably need to come straight to court.

Most parents, even if they have concerns and issues in their relationship with each other, are not of the magnitude where they're ever talking about their children spending no-time with a parent.

> The problem with an adversarial system is it can set you up as competitors in the system, where you're fighting each other.

You adopt a position, you defend it for your life, and the process in an adversarial system then becomes about persuading everyone how you're right and everyone else is wrong.

> Mediation is self-empowering and self-determinative. People get to focus on their needs and interests rather than their positions.

It gives them an opportunity to preserve relationships. They can develop, or at least not damage their co-parenting relationship further – and hopefully even improve – how they communicate with each other. Because, if anything, a Court order is dependent upon how people can communicate and their capacity to implement it and work together. It's almost like the medical Hippocratic Oath: If you do so much damage in the process to get to an end result, there's just no point at all in having gone through that process.

Recent cases have highlighted horribly aggressive lawyering. Not adversarial lawyering, because people conflate the idea of an adversarial system with an aggressive system. I think adversarial lawyering is just really about getting to the truth, and people who are aggressive, who obfuscate, who don't provide disclosure, who engage in silly fights about meaningless issues just don't seem to understand what their role is in the system.

Are you hoping that there would be, for example, more of an uptake of mediation because of this project you're working on? Is that the goal?

I think my goal has been essentially two things. Firstly, to ensure that there was good available information to let people make informed choices about accredited mediators – nationally accredited mediators and FDRPs – rather than just going back to some idea that mediation is just something people do. We have accreditation systems. I think it's important that they're honoured and validated, and that we use accredited mediators.

But secondly, I'm just very conscious that while it's great to talk about how people should go to mediation, the practicalities on how you actually find a mediator and choose one are very hard. Most of the sites you can go to just bombard you with names, and you've then got to phone 50 people to find out what their qualifications are, what they do, what they charge.

There should be a more user-friendly interface with that sector so you can look at a list of 'here are the people in my area; this is what they charge; here's their qualifications and experience; let's pick one'. Because otherwise you're just shopping on price, or you're shopping blindly, and have no idea what you're getting.

Something somewhat related: I've come across, through interviewing people who've been through the system, is this sense that they're getting on and off bus stops. Like, their lawyer is just shuffling them from place to place. They don't really feel empowered, and they feel that they've lost control of the matter, wondering what's going on.

Yeah, I think that's very valid.

It's particularly relevant I think to family violence cases that the definition of family violence is focussed around coercion, control, and fear. The Court is coercive, controlling, and can even generate fear in people, especially as, for most people, a family law dispute is an awful time in their life and their kids are really important to them. Courts can determine where people's children are going to live, when they see them – or if they see them – whether their house is going to be sold ... Court is just a disproportionate reaction for most people's disputes.

Our common law system is designed so that everyone who has understanding of the law, which predominantly is intended to come through getting competent legal advice, is going to know pretty much what a Court's going to do for them anyway.

One of the things that is often left out of that advice is how long it's going to take, what it's going to cost financially, what it's going to cost them in terms of their relationship, their stress, their time off work.

I think one of the problems is that there's been a falling down of the legal process in terms of how lawyers have come to be viewed and how some lawyers see themselves. Some have become aggressive mouthpieces, champions of people rather than zealous advisors who tell people what's actually going to happen. You tell them, 'The reason you don't want to go to Court is because ...', or 'If you take this to court, you're going to lose', or, as Abraham Lincoln said, 'Even if you win, you'll still lose'. Because of what it's going to cost you in terms of time, money, broken relationships, it's just not going to achieve what you want.

Plus, if you were to ask most parents what they want for their children, they'd all have the same answer: 'I want my children to be happy. I want them to have the best life they can have. I want them to be well educated.'

Going to Court and creating fights between parents that they don't need to have is just counterintuitive. It destroys any prospect of achieving what those parents actually want to achieve.

One thing also I'd like to ask you about is whether you think that there should be, say, mandatory mediation in property matters, not just parenting matters?

Yeah, I do. I think it's important though that we don't start to see mediation as a cure-all, or it will just become a failure as well.

Mediation needs to be prepared for, just like a court case needs to be prepared for. You need to be able to create a balance sheet that's pretty well agreed with what you own, what you owe, what all the figures are. And a lot of people approach mediation either flippantly, as though it's just a waste of time, or as though it is this cure-all, that the mediator will fix it all, but the mediator can't determine what a house is worth. So, the parties have to do that work to get there.

But I think ...

the vast majority of parents, particularly in financial cases, given the time, given the option, and given the opportunity to just sit down with competent advice, and having done the work they need to do to understand what their dispute is actually about, can sort it out very quickly and easily without coming to Court and fighting.

You mentioned family violence before. Obviously, there's been a lot in the media in recent times on family violence. Just anecdotally, is it at a crisis point? I mean, that's what's talked about in the media.

Well, I can talk about it more specifically than anecdotally, because the research I do around mediation is particularly focussed on what the cases that come to a court or go into mediation look like in terms of their characteristics, how often they involve family violence. About 80% of the cases that come through the Federal Circuit Court at Paramatta involve allegations of family violence. Now, they're not all the same allegations, although I'm very conscious that ...

family violence is very personal to individuals and it's very experiential. It's silly to try and arbitrarily decide what is serious family violence and what is not; it depends upon the individual.

The reality is that the vast majority of cases involve allegations of family violence. There's a lot of controversy and a lot of academic debate around the appropriateness of mediation when there are allegations of family violence. But there's some excellent work being done by people like Rachael Field around lawyer-assisted processes which acknowledge that well.

A process where a person is actually well supported and well protected through a system of mediation is much better for them and much better procedural justice than coming to Court, where they have no control whatsoever over the outcome.

Is it an epidemic? I try and avoid the epidemiological discussion of it because it suggests that all of a sudden people started being violent, and I think we've had family violence as long as we've had relationships, and as long as we've had families. It's just that we've learnt to name it, to identify it and to recognise it, and to respond to it in a way that perhaps 10, 15, 20 years ago we didn't.

It's a complex issue but our legal process has a very clear definition of what family violence is, and we have a very clear definition and understanding, from social science and neuroscience, of the impact of family violence. It's really about focussing on what this means for kids and what it means for people who experience it and have lived with it. I think we still have a long way to go with family violence, but I don't think it's an epidemic. I think it is a continuum of behaviour that we've just gotten much better at recognising and understanding, and we still have some way to go with it.

This week I've been hearing cases where arguments have been put to people who've experienced family violence that 'it can't have been that bad or you would've gone to the police, or you would have left the relationship', which I thought we might've left behind in the '70s, but it still arises. There's certainly a lot of academic discussion again about how well Judges and lawyers are trained to understand and respond to family violence. I think Judges of both courts understand family violence well and the National Judicial Council is working hard to deliver training to ensure that the issue is clear and to the forefront.

The Victorian Royal Commission, the Batty Inquiry – all had a lot to say about those things and very valid and appropriate comments about it. But we do need to get better; we need to get far more coordinated with information sharing. One of the real barriers we have to that is just the system we have in this country, where we have two different systems of courts, state and federal. The Department of Family and Community Services and police, as the investigative bodies, are state-based, and the Federal Circuit Court and Family Court don't have the ready access to their information we'd always like. Those agencies don't always have the ready information to us and the information that we would like. But a lot is happening to change that.

What could we change there? (NB: This interview was conducted prior to the announcement that the Family Court would merge with the Federal Circuit Court.)

Ideally, and it's my view, we would have one system that deals with every family. Constitutionally, that's not easy to do as things presently stand, but we could, like we have with corporations law, etc., have a uniform code that applies in every state, dual commissions so that federal judges could exercise state powers. Or, alternatively, the states just refer their powers over care and protection, for example, to the federal system, so that children are all dealt with in one system.

There's not a clear delineation between the population of children who come before Courts. About a third of the cases in the Federal Circuit Court have had significant involvement with the Department of Family and Community Services and potentially end up in the Children's Court. Parties might spend two years going through a federal system, and then something happens and they end up in the state system and start all over again.

Domestic violence issues are dealt with in the state system. Then in a parenting case the federal court finds out about it, deals with all that information, but it has to be gone over twice. The duplication of resources, which again, the Victorian Royal Commission has focussed on, and the Australian Law Reform Commission led by Helen Rhodes will look into and comment upon as well, are real problems; they really mess people about.

Politically, there are solutions by referral of power or devolution back to state jurisdiction. They are ultimately matters for government. But we really do need to find solutions to those problems, because we've known about them now for a very long time and they need to be fixed. For a family to go to a federal court for their property and parenting dispute, the Children's Court for a care and protection matter with the same facts, a Magistrates Court for their protection order on the same facts, a Tribunal for mental health issues based on the same facts, must be confusing and exhausting.

So, what do you think? It just needs the political will there?

I think it needs political will; I think it needs leadership and advocacy by law societies and Bar associations. But I think we owe families a better outcome than they get at the moment.

They might be going to a state system for domestic violence issue, a criminal issue, a mental health issue, a child protection issue, so they're going through potentially three or four courts or tribunals at a state level. It would be great if we could have a unified court system that can deal with all of the issues that families face.

Of course, this would probably take funding. There's a huge issue with funding.

There is a huge issue with funding and that's a matter for government. I appreciate there are competing priorities for every dollar of taxpayer money and where it goes. Since 1948, Australia has been a signatory to the Universal Declaration of Human Rights, which Australia and especially Dr Evatt had a very proud and prominent role in drafting and implementing, and that recognises that ...

> the family is the fundamental unit of society – not the dollar,
> not the corporation, but the family.

And if families are the fundamental unit of society, every law we pass should be protective of and recognise the importance of families. There is a very good American academic, Clare Huntington, who talks about structural Family Law. In terms of structural laws, every law should have some consideration for how this is going to impact children and families; for example, when you cut penalty rates, and parents suddenly are working all weekend, having to pay for child minding or finding some level of care, but not getting paid any extra money to fund that let alone casualisation of workforces and zero hours contracts. Being required to work four days on, four days off, when their child has a seven-day-a-week calendar, and how that's going to work for families that are together, let alone separated. So there's a lot of shifting of focus I believe we need to, and could be doing, around the idea that if families are really important, how are we reflecting that in our laws?

Something else that has come up through some of the other interviews is whether we should move towards a more inquisitorial system in the courts. Do you have any views about that?

I do. Again, my very personal view is that I think the adversarial system, when all of its components work well, is a wonderful system, because an adversarial system is not intended to be a knock 'em down, drag 'em out fight. Our system has evolved on the basis that everyone is represented. But it's a reality that not everyone is. Part of that problem is just that lawyers, in some respects, price themselves out of the market, but they are expensive and they have big overheads, and some people can't afford them.

There are certainly changes we could make to an adversarial system to make it far more user friendly, but the system itself, I don't think, is the problem; it's the failure of individual components within the system that is the problem.

One of the reasons Courts have not been functioning particularly well is resources. Courts have not had what they need in order to do what is expected of them. Not just Judges, but family consultants. But there are other problems. This is very much my personal view, but there has been a decline in some quarters of the legal profession as Justice Benjamin spoke of recently. Some lawyers have stopped understanding what they do. Their job is to be problem solvers, to help people find resolution of conflict, rather than to generate conflict, to fuel it, to create it where it didn't previously exist. It's a bit like what Woody Guthrie said, that if there was no profit to be made from war, we would have no war. In a lot of parenting disputes before Courts, if there was no profit to be made, there would be no dispute, and the parties don't profit from it.

Lawyers should be courteous to each other, focussed on identifying what's in dispute and what the issues are between parents and finding solutions to those issues whether in law or by engaging parents with counsellors, psychologists and similar folk to help and support parents. Separation is both a legal and health issue. Some lawyers, not all, seem to adopt the attitude that it's just not their job to give people bad news, like telling them that their case won't succeed. Well, they'll run it whether it's going to win, lose, or not.

I think a return to basics in lawyering and a stiffening up of the legal profession and their ethical obligations is called for.

I'm not trying to hold myself out as having been a better lawyer than anyone else - I wasn't, and I don't hold myself out for one moment as being a great lawyer. But lawyers have one basic role and that is to assist parties to resolve their disputes. You can't help to fix a problem if the problem is not clearly identified and the focus of all that is done. And if children's best interests are the paramount consideration for the court, then they should be the paramount consideration for everyone. If we could fix that, the adversarial system would work as intended.

There are some elements of inquisitorial-ism that I think would work very well.

So, again, my personal view is that our system of independent representation of children could be better. I think that, rather than lawyers representing the interests of children, family consultants or similar people should represent children, and they retain a lawyer who represents them in the court process, very much the English model, or that a lawyer and a social scientist together represent the child, to some extent the Ontario model in Canada. We would then have a hybrid between a family report writer and the person who is actually representing and advocating for a child, and them being represented in court, as opposed to being thrown to the wolves, as family report writers presently are, where if you agree with them that's great, and if you don't, you attack them vociferously.

I think there are changes we can make within our structure which are far from dramatic and which would provide better due process. I'm conscious that lots of changes we contem plate and consider about addressing failings of individual components of our system, whereas the system itself isn't the problem, it's just individual parts of it aren't working well. Because there aren't resources, or people aren't focused on their purpose, or people aren't using FDR and accordingly the system starts to fall apart, and we look for a new system rather than saying, 'What's wrong with the system? Why isn't it working?' I think Helen Rhodes will look at that brilliantly. She's a wonderful academic; she'll have a lot of intelligent things to say about that, which I hope gets a lot of attention.

Another thing I did also want to speak to you about is when you talked about family violence before. I still think, as a practitioner (and this is just

me speaking, anecdotally) the understanding in the public is that family violence is just the physical. There isn't that awareness still, I don't think, even though the definition changed in 2012. Would you elaborate for readers what your understanding of family violence is?

Certainly. It's fundamentally found in our definition in Section 4AB. It is behaviour that causes coercion, control, or fear. We still have such a struggle around family violence. Firstly, I think that by putting the word 'family' in front of the word 'violence', it sometimes, for some people, creates a different category of behaviour that, in their mind, excuses the fact that it is violence. Violence is violence, whether it's between strangers or between people who have been in an intimate relationship.

We don't seem to have any difficulty in coming to terms with physical violence, where somebody strikes another person; for example, our fairly unanimous and appropriate support for a strong reaction to one-punch assault, when a complete stranger comes and thumps someone in the street. That should have a really harsh reaction. I cannot comprehend, for the life of me, why anyone would ever (and I don't suggest anyone necessarily does) think it is any different - in fact, I would've thought it significantly worse - if you experienced violence with someone with whom you were in an intimate relationship, where part of that relationship involves trust and mutual support, whether it is physical or otherwise, that it could possibly be anything other than violence. In fact, it's much worse violence. I don't condone strangers hitting each other, but nor do I think that there's anything excusable about people with a degree of intimacy hitting each other.

And, again, it's a very old wisdom, in that Oliver Wendell Holmes, US Supreme Court Judge from the 1800s and 1900s, said, that it was clear that the closer the proximity of people, the greater their abandon in treating each other with disdain and disrespect. And it shouldn't be. If you're in a relationship - and I don't want to be old-fashioned about it - but if you feel that you can control, or be violent to your spouse, you really need to be looking at yourself, about what's wrong with you, not your partner.

And I appreciate that violence can also be perpetrated by women, but it's perpetrated by women significantly less often than it is by men. However, violence is perpetrated by women against women, and women against men, and by men against men, and men against women, and predominantly by men. Data consistently suggests that about 95% of the time the primary perpetrator of violence is a man against a woman.

The second problem, I think, with violence is that in criminal law we have always understood that an assault doesn't necessarily require physicality. An assault is behaviour that generates fear. All you have to do is make someone fear for their safety and that's assault. We've understood that since the 1700s, and yet when the definition was changed in Family Law in 2012 to make it the same test as the criminal law, everyone reacted as though it was some fundamental attack on men. It was just bringing Family Law into line with the criminal law, and saying that if you behave in a way that makes someone fearful, that is violence.

I think violence is an incredibly complex issue. Recently, Mark MacDiarmid, wrote a piece in *The Guardian* about the culture of how we raise men, that violence is acceptable. You know, men play contact sports in which violence is an inherent part of what they do, albeit a very controlled and regulated type of violence. But without always quoting song lyrics, there's a wonderful song by an American artist Gil Scott-Heron that says that peace is not just the absence of war; it's the absence of the rules of war, the absence of the acceptance of war.

I think the problem we have in our society is that violence is such an inherent part of many things that we do. It is such a fundamental part of the establishment of the nation. Violence does not require an element of physicality at all. It just requires making people scared and con trolled. We do that in many aspects of what we do in society, including, as I've said, through our legal system. Linda Steele refers to this as acceptable state sanctioned violence. But we also do it through our whole structure of how we approach prison penal ties, punishment, etc.

Violence has just been acceptable for so long in Anglo-normative society. The very fact that for hundreds of years, women have been subjugated and treated as less in relationships, still paid less on average than men, etc., is just unacceptable.

If we accept one element of that perpetration of discrimination [against women], it leaves open the door to accept all of them, and we shouldn't. It should just be that violence is intolerable.

We know from neuroscience that, particularly for small children, exposure to violence affects brain development, their entire development as an adult. It almost begs the question of, well, is what we're seeing now in terms of violence in society perhaps a reflection of how poorly we dealt with violence in the 1940s, '50s, and '60s?

One thing that has been raised in other interviews is matters of international law and Family Law. I know of cases, for example, where there is a prenuptial binding financial agreement type document made in France, and while it's given some weight in Court in Australia, it's not regarded with the same weight as a document drafted in Australia would be.

I think, again, that's largely an aspect that's absent the Federal Circuit Court's jurisdiction. A first instance Trial Court tends not to deal with those issues. I think when it arises, it's a conflict-of-law issue between different systems, how they oper ate. I don't think our system at all, and particularly not Judges in the Family Court, is in any way disrespectful of overseas jurisdictions.

It's just an issue of an agreement made in one country. Purporting to bind how a Court in another country will work, or how property in another county will be divided, I think, is not quite something the world has got its head around. For example, it was probably never contemplated when the Hague Convention was being drafted so many years ago now, that we would become quite such a global community, I think we've still got some work to do in that field.

I think it becomes a very dangerous thing, in terms of world order, let alone the rule of law, if we start being less than entirely respectful of over seas jurisdictions.

The other thing that has come up when I interviewed other people is – and I want to put this respectfully – there is a concern that the Court is not

predictable. There are very different outcomes. But I think you have to have some discretion, because of how the Court has to make the best decision in different situations, so I'm thinking, as I review my other interviews: How do you get that balance between having that adaptability and being nimble and able to respond to each unique situation, but then creating what people perceive as consistency and thus fairness? It's a difficult issue.

I would challenge the basic premise on this basis:

> The common law system is intended that the Court, as a tribunal of fact, will determine what the facts are (one would hope predominantly by the parties having engaged in disclosure and discussion and having agreed on most of them), and then apply settled legal principle to those facts.

I think there is a popular public conception that the range of outcomes in property matters is more unpredictable than perhaps it is. The legal principles, I think, are quite settled.

There are certainly reasonable differences of opinion amongst appellate judges, so that a not dissimilar case in front of a differently constituted full bench might have a slightly different outcome. But the differences are slight. I think we have a very strong appellate system, not just in the Family Law jurisdiction but in all our jurisdictions in Australia - criminal sentencing, etc. - where the principles are, in fact, incredibly clear.

There is some room for difference in their application. I think one of the things that's often misunderstood (I'm not trying to be pejorative of the argument) is that there is an exercise of discretion in how one applies principle to fact. It can be seen as a problem with the Court. Personally, I see it as a great benefit. It does mean, certainly, that you can run the same case on the same facts in front of two different Judges and get two slightly different outcomes. I would challenge the suggestion that they're dramatically different, but they are different, because there is, as we recognise in law, the potential for reasonable difference in reasonable argument. One argument on one day might be a 5% difference in a property adjustment as opposed to the same argument on another day in front of another person.

But the principles that are applied consistently are a strength of our system, and having discretion so that there is the potential to produce a different outcome in a different and individual circumstance is an enormous strength of our system. If you look at two examples, criminal sentencing and child support. The Child Support Agency is probably the most dreaded agency in our country (and unfairly, as regards to their employees). Everyone criticises the arbitrary outcome that the formula is sometimes suggested to produce. But if we went back to a system with discretion, people would be equally dissatisfied. By having a formula where you punch the numbers in and it tells you an answer, it produces a lot of very happy customers as well as some unhappy customers. There is discretion but not at first instance.

It's similar with criminal sentencing, where there are now many constraints, guidelines, and mandatory considerations in sentencing. There is so much criticism now, that wasn't there 10 years ago, about criminal sentencing. So, the more you constrain discretion to some extent, I think, the more you produce the absolute opposite of what those who criticise discretion want.

It's a controversial example in terms of present terms, but if you look at a criticism of ball tampering in international cricket, some might say 'Why is the person who tampered with the ball getting a lesser sentence than the people who actually didn't touch the ball?' It's because it takes into account, as an exercise of discretion (with all due respect to the Australian Cricket Board), the leadership role they had, their position of responsibility. It would be the same as if somebody, who should know remarkably better (so, for example, to go back to reported cases), there's the case of being sentenced to imprisonment for being untruthful about who was driving a car for a speeding fine. If that was a tradesman who knew he was on his last point, who depends on his licence for his occupation, who lied, it's reprehensible, it's wrong and inappropriate, but the penalty should be different to a someone with responsibility for sentencing people for those offences. If you remove discretion, they all get the same. And that would mean it's going to produce injustice in a variety of ways.

I don't think the range of outcome is actually that broad; if people studied cases, it'd probably be maybe 5-10% from the best to the worst that you might expect in most circumstances, and I think that's something actually to be cherished. You don't want to walk into court (or perhaps some people do) knowing that the outcome is going to be 53.2% no matter what. But the downside of that is your great argument about the fact you've introduced the property is going to be a problem.

Take, for example, 'communal-property' jurisdictions, where once you've been together for a certain length of time, everything's 50/50 – there would be a lot of people in this country who'd be very dissatisfied with that system, and it would tend to be the people who introduced a lot more property or have real financial disadvantage from the care of children. Whereas the people who came in with nothing but debt might have no financial disadvantage and be very happy with that outcome.

I guess we can't please everyone; that's the thing.

No, and I think that ties in with... I know there's a lot of dissatisfaction about the perceived attitude of courts towards binding financial agreements and how easily they're interfered with, but I think part of the problem with that is the agreement itself.

If two parties enter into an agreement that says that, whatever they do, it's going to be 50/50, but at the end of a 20-year relationship, a wife, for example, is left with three children in her care. She's been out of the workforce for 20 years looking after the children, has no superannuation, her employment skills are now out of date, and she's effectively unemployable. Her husband meanwhile has continued on: continuous employment skills, superannuation, earning a very good income. That woman would be very aggrieved at the idea of saying your BFA says 50/50, no matter what, and it's going to be enforced.

Now, you mentioned before the role of the Independent Children's Lawyer and some of your personal views about potential reform. Do you have any other views about children's voices or perspectives, and how these are heard in Court?

Within our present system, again, one issue is that it's all very dependent on the quality of the representation. When you're representing the interests of a child, it is a special responsibility.

Children have a legal disability:

... they don't have the capacity to provide instruction; they're in a unique position in that their interests are the subject matter of the proceedings, even though they don' t have direct representation in the proceedings; and the parties who are involved as the parties to the proceedings are people who have very different views about what might be best for the children often intermeshed with their needs and their grief and pain.

So, I think quality representation is important. One thing I'd love to see is, as they have in Ontario – an office of children's representation, where we have people whose speciality is representing kids, and that's what they do.

I think, secondly, we do have issues about hearing the voice of children in proceedings, because we have a deficit of resources in terms of family consultants, so we probably don't get reports as much as might be ideal.

There's a big debate in Australia about Judges meeting children; in other jurisdictions it's not as big a debate. If you spoke to a Judge from Israel, Germany, or most states in the US, meeting children is what they're man dated to do. But there is a very valid argument against meeting them as well, because then you're making a decision potentially based on your emotional response to your meeting with the child, rather than purely the objective evidence in the case, which is very important.

So, I think there are mechanisms we could use through better representation, better facilitation, of children's involvement in proceedings. One of the ironies we have is that we start talking about system abuse if children are becoming involved. It's not necessarily an abuse of a child to give them a voice in proceedings. In fact, I would argue it's an abuse of a child to deprive them of that voice. If they've seen a lot of people, you have to be careful around how many more people they see, and how much more they become involved.

I met with a child in Court this week, with an Independent children's lawyer present. The child had expressed, at age 12, a very strong desire to meet the Judge who was going to make the decision about her case. I fundamentally accept that ...

> I'm in the minority of Judges
> who have probably ever met children.

I have only done it a few times and would never do it without a lot of thought, a purpose and a plan. But I think it's just respectful that, if I'm going to make a decision that is going to impact on your life, not to meet you for the purpose of interviewing you, or find out what you want (because we have ICIs and family reports for that) but to at least be able to say, 'I'm the guy who's going to make the decision', to be able to eyeball them, let them see the courtroom, to let them see what it's about. That is all this child wanted.

That was very prominent, for example, in New Zealand until only a few years ago. But in this country we've, perhaps explicably, struggled conceptually and philosophically with the idea of ever having children involved in proceedings by meeting a Judge or by having any active participation in the case. I think if we want to give any meaning to the international convention that says a child has a right to participate, they should have some say as to how they participate.

As the disability sector says, 'There's no decision about me without me'. They should have some say.

Something I wanted to ask as well: I know every situation's different, but do you have any words of wisdom for someone who's going through separation?

I do not have wisdom. But I would say:

> Parents have a choice of whether they want to focus
> on the past and on problems, or whether they want to find solutions.

Do they want to be part of the culture change themselves for their family, or do they just want to be mired in arguing about what did or didn't happen in the past?

The past is important, but ultimately what they have to live in is the present and the future, so that's what they should be focussed on. And they should be helped by lawyers, and everyone else they work with, to do that.

Secondly, I would say to any parent: You need to understand that you were, before you separated and you still are, a family. You're a different-looking family. You're a separated family, you have two different houses, and possibly lots of other people involved now, with new partners, etc., but you're still a family.

You need to be focussed on what's actually important for your kids. Engage in the very important exercise, which is horribly difficult for adults, of self-reflection, owning problems. What have I done to contribute to how broken this is, and what do I need to do to fix it?

The worst cases are parents who, when they're provided with all that information, say, 'Thank you for all of that. That's helpful for me to understand the damage the other parent is doing to our children', whereas they assume they're doing nothing at all. They probably need to be very focussed on the fact that their dispute is not a real thing. It's not tangible. It's dysfunction between two people, and they can choose to change it, or they can choose to live with it. As Felstiner, Abel and Sarat opined *'Disputes are not things: They are social constructs'*. And if they choose to live with dysfunction, just like the James Stewart film *Harvey*, it will become real, their pooka; it will follow them around. They need to set a place for their dispute at the table so it can become part of their daily life.

I think the other thing that I would tell any parent to do is get legal advice, to make sure it's good, and that a good lawyer is one who is not going to gee them up, who's just going to tell them the truth and tell them all of their options, legally and socially. They'll talk to them about mediation, arbitration, and everything else that is a means to sorting stuff out, but to just stay focussed. That's really what it's about. You love your kids so stop stressing about things that don't matter.

Do you have any other thoughts about reform? Obviously, I accept it's not the view of the Court, that it's just your personal view.

I don't have any insight into what Professor Rhodes will recommend, other than it will be incredibly sensible and well thought through. I think our system has the potential to work well. It's not just about resources though.

I think its important to read and understand Rule 21 of the Uniform Solicitor's Conduct Rules, about not invoking the Court's jurisdiction other than as a last resort, and using it responsibly. Lawyers need to become dispute resolvers who understand what disputes are about, who understand their dynamics, who understand their impact on people. Lawyers need to think about (and I'm really not trying to berate them or lecture them) the fact that they are a profession that engages in the conduct of law, and that all of the discussion of legal principles and ethics from the 17th century onwards is real. I think too many people have forgotten it.

I understand those pressures. Legal practice is really hard in this day and age. The overheads are huge and the pressures are enormous, but the role of lawyers is fundamental to society. Hence, Shakespeare said, often misquoted, "The first thing we do, let's kill all the lawyers". His idea was that if you want to produce chaos and oppression, you must first get rid of the people who are responsible for ensuring society functions properly. And that's what lawyers are intended to do, but they don't do that when they think of what they do as a business.

Russel Norman, a restaurant critic, says that to open a restaurant to make money is wrong, but your restaurant has to make money. (Quite apt, as we're sitting here in a restaurant!) If the purpose of opening is just to charge people money, you're probably not going to make very good food and you probably won't make much money. Whereas ethical lawyers – and by 'ethical' I don't mean that lawyers are unethical – but focussing on their ethics, their duty to the rule of law and society and it's functioning, is fundamentally important to a society. I genuinely believe that, and hold it very close to my heart. And I get very disappointed when, for example, a lawyer comes into Court and I ask them 'What orders does your client want?' and they can't tell me. Or I ask them, 'What authority are you relying upon to persuade me to make these orders?' 'Oh, I haven't turned my mind to that,' they say.

That just tells me people aren't doing their job. So, the system isn't failing; the individuals who are part of it are failing. I think self-serving as it may be, the Judges of the Federal Circuit, every Judge of every Court in this country, is hard-working. Judges have a desire to see the people who come into our Courts not be there, because we know they can produce an outcome for themselves if someone just helped them to do it.

There are exceptions. If you've experienced significant family violence – a person who just can't and shouldn't be expected to deal with their partner – they're the cases the Court should be hearing, and, sadly, they get delayed while we deal with people's resolvable property cases, where they're both asking for something that common-law precedents says they cannot achieve.

Lawyers need to focus on being dispute resolvers who bring peace, calm, and resolution to families. If we rip a family apart, as the Productivity Commission has pointed out, it costs an enormous amount of money. But leave the money aside, because that's not actually that important. What's important is that it produces children who are unhappy.

As any parent who comes into Court knows, children should be happy. Not in an idealised sense; it's only 140 years since we sent nine-year-olds to work in coal mines and factories. We're a rich, privileged country. Children should be well parented, and if they're not well parented there should be state intervention, but parenting should be judged by what the parents can provide. We shouldn't be arbitrary about it. Parents are what they are. Every parent is flawed, but parents shouldn't be having fights about things that just don't matter, and too often they do.

Mediation is a much better way to focus on that because they're looking at their needs and interests, and someone will ask them fundamental questions like, 'What do you want for your child?' as opposed to 'What order do you want made?' Because a court order can't change people. I can mandate a therapeutic intervention, but I can't mandate a therapeutic outcome. If people want to change, they'll change. A good joke a social worker once told me: 'It only takes one social worker to change a light bulb, but the light bulb has to want to change'.

It's too easy in our current system for parents to just fall into this conflictual arrangement, and adversarial is not conflictual, it's not aggressive. Adversarial is about comparing fact with fact to

produce truth, and if we focussed on that as a system, we would get
to an outcome.

I think it's too important what we do with our children today to produce a
society in 20 years' time, in this current world we live in of four-year election
cycles and 24-hour news cycles, not to be worried about investing properly in
their future. Not only Family Court processes, but all of the structural Family Law that I started with, of making sure parents don't have to leave their
kids in day-care seven days a week while they go to work trying to survive in
Sydney, where it's just so expensive to live. Maybe we don't need to adopt
the Tongan measure of gross domestic happiness, (though there would be
nothing wrong in doing so), but at least looking at how every law we pass
will impact children and their families, because I think if we had applied that
criteria to a great many laws, we may not have passed them in the first place.

Parenting Matters

Court experts and other professionals

Dr Antony Milch

Expert psychiatrist & expert report writer

To forgive each other

Dr Antony Milch has established a career as one of Sydney's leading child, adolescent and family psychiatrists and is well known as a respected expert in family law matters. Over the past 25 years he has worked extensively with children, adolescents and their families in both private and public settings on the Lower North Shore and Northern Beaches. Dr Milch has contributed to programs for adolescent mental health at The Black Dog Institute. His private practice is based in Mosman at Family in Mind.

Dr Milch is available for clinical assessments, therapeutic intervention has a particular interest in medico-legal assessments as a court expert in the Family Court of Australia and other jurisdictions relating to child and family mental health.

Dr Milch regularly lectures and presents at conferences. He is a contributing author to the *Practitioner's Guide to Psychoactive Drugs for Children and Adolescents*. He is the former chair of the NSW Department of Health stimulants subcommittee and the Northside Cremorne Clinic medical advisory committee.

In this interview Dr Milch discusses, amongst other things, parental alienation, the damaging effect of delays on children in our Court system, and also makes an important point about the uniqueness of each family and each child and how we need to be careful to avoid 'cookbook' approaches to psychology in Family Law when the legal system often demands black-and-white divisions. He also speaks at length about the kind of behaviours that damage children and makes the point that 'we are thinking about the next generation'.

I often find in Family Law litigation there exists a kind of inertia towards a hardening of positions by parties (and/or their lawyers) and a tendency to polarise into binary thinking: good/bad, win/lose, wrong/right, villain/victim. By contrast, Antony's interview emphasises an opening and softening. He speaks about things on a spectrum that is not necessarily black or white, and about there being different ways of parenting ('many paths') and how each family has its 'own way'. He observes that 'no-one is perfect, especially when it comes to parenting', and to reach for flexibility when possible and 'try to forgive each other'.

⸬

For our readers, what is your role in the Family Law system?

I am a child and family psychiatrist who assists the Court in the capacity of court expert. My role is to conduct assessments to assist in the understanding of family dynamics, mental health issues, and special needs of children and their parents. Family reports and court expert reports under chapter 15, part 5, of the *Family Law Act* are requested to assist the Court in determining what's in the best interests of the children. Assessments are conducted as a single expert before the Family Court and Federal Circuit Court, with the involvement of all relevant parties and review of all relevant information.

Although there may be concurrent property matters, my assessment is focussed on issues that impact parenting capacity.

There are specific areas in which a psychiatrist with experience in working with children, adolescents, adults, and families can assist the Court.

These specific areas include child and adult mental health, personality vulnerabilities, and complex relationship dynamics.

If children have developmental issues, such as autism spectrum disorder, attention deficit/hyperactivity disorder, anxiety, or depressive disorders, they may have special needs which should be considered. If there have been allegations of exposure to family violence, parental mental illness, abuse, or neglect this may warrant a risk assessment.

The parties are interviewed separately and together with the children. Ideally, all family members residing with the children and involved in their day-to-day care are interviewed. A developmental perspective is crucial in assessing the children.

Some of my clients have been nervous before meeting with an expert who is doing this kind of report. Would you just break down the basics of what would actually happen in a day when you meet the parties?

Each expert conducts assessments differently. Psychologists may utilize standardized rating scales and psychometric instruments.

My approach is to interview the family over two days, typically for a total of eight hours of interviews. Assessments may also be conducted on a single day. Each parent is initially seen for two hours after having read the relevant documentation. That said, documentation produced under subpoena and updating affidavits may be subsequently perused.

Initially, I introduce myself and explain my role: necessarily that there is no confidentiality as a report will be prepared for the Court, and typically all parties involved in the proceedings will have access to this information. Although the report will hopefully be of assistance, it is not designed to be a therapeutic intervention but, rather, a forensic inquiry.

I clarify each parent's experience and provide an opportunity for them to air their concerns, allegations, and responses. A child and family psychiatric assessment is conducted. This involves understanding their developmental history, personality development, relationship history, mental health, and substance use. Their perception of their children's experience and needs, and their awareness and response to their child's developmental needs, speak to the key issue of parenting capacity.

On the second day, the residential parent attends with the children. I observe their interactions. When the children are comfortable, I interview them on their own. The children are then seen with their non-residential parent and members of the extended family. The parents, their partners, and other relevant family members are also interviewed.

I am particularly interested in observing the interactions of the children with family members with whom they have day-to-day contact. I find it useful to use a video link to observe interactions when not in the room. This is not, however, standard practice and is only undertaken with the consent of all parties.

I am trying to put this respectfully, but I must raise it on behalf of my clients over the years and some of the other litigants I have interviewed in preparing this book. Some people have questioned how it is that an expert can, say, diagnose someone with a personality disorder, for example, in meeting them for a day or two? This is a question I have consistently been asked. Do you have a view about that?

Many parents raise such concerns. They question if it's possible for a one-off assessment to adequately assess parenting capacity and address core issues of diagnosis, special needs, and risk. I am respectful of such concerns.

The assessment relates to their presentation on the day, including a mental state examination and observation of family interactions, within the context of the family narrative.

The review of relevant documentation is thus of importance. This will depend on the legal representatives and the Court providing the expert with the relevant source material.

After all, any assessment is as good as the information it is based on.

Source material will include the parties' affidavits, supporting documentation, and relevant documentation produced under subpoena. The observations of therapists, psychiatrists, and teachers are particularly relevant. With the consent of the parties, they are contacted and their reports perused.

If further material is presented, this will be addressed. If a parent is uncharacteristically anxious or angry, this will be taken into account.

If this is a longstanding and pervasive pattern of behaviour, this speaks to a person's personality.

The assessment conducted can be tested during cross-examination in Court. If additional information is put to the expert which is inconsistent with the view formed, this may alter the opinion and recommendations.

Often, matters are heard in Court sometime later. Subsequent events will also be considered. Competing allegations are a core aspect of adversarial proceedings. It is a matter for the Court to determine matters of fact. The competing narratives will typically result in different opinions and recommendations.

In addition to ensuring the relevant information gets to the expert, do you have any other tips for litigants?

A lot of damage is done within the Family Court process. It is important to hold in mind that at the end of the day you will both remain parents of the children.

It is in the children's best interests to maintain a good relationship with both parents, except in cases of abuse or neglect damaging to the child's developmental experience.

Exposing children to conflict is stressful and damaging. In our society there is a lack of recognition of the impact of traumatic events such as domestic violence on younger children, as they don't have a memory of this.

A traumatised child under the age of two will not have a narrative memory, so they are unable to tell the story of what happened. Nonetheless, their procedural memory will affect them developmentally and impact the security of their core attachment relationship. The resultant insecurity, emotional dysregulation, hypervigilance and behavioural problems can be harder to manage, as they can't work through the experience.

It is critical to adopt a developmental perspective. Thus, a one-year-old requires a secure base and should not be placed in equal shared care. The challenge is to think about arrangements from the children's point of view, rather than focusing on parental rights.

Protecting the children from information that is not developmentally appropriate will help. The 'parent as teacher' model is thus useful. Think about 'What am I teaching them by such an approach?' Core values of trust, respect, and goodwill are lost in adversarial interactions. Co-parenting requires a model of collaboration.

> Do not use the children as go-betweens or confidantes.
> Do not use the children to justify your views.

Parental alienation is not a syndrome but, rather, a developmental pathway for children unable to maintain a loving connection with two warring parents. A successful future will be grounded in a good relationship with both parents, both extended families, and in respect for their cultural background.

> I endeavour to use a trans-cultural approach.
> Every family has their own culture.

The children will benefit from an integrated response to their developmental experience, whether this relates to culture, religion, education or activities.

My primary criticism of the Court process is that it is an adversarial system. It takes a vulnerable family system and places it in an amplifying chamber of tit-for-tat legal responses. This is counter-therapeutic and promotes a conflictual approach to family life. It helps to return to the adage 'What about the children? What am I teaching them?' Adversarial legal processes fuel conflict, whilst conciliatory processes contain it.

Sometimes, I witness parents justify unconscionable actions on the basis of their legal advice. Such behaviour can undermine their children's core relationships and stability. I would caution litigants, because at the end of the day they remain the parents. They are responsible for their child's experience.

Thinking about the developmental stages of children, what about cultural issues? For example – and this is speaking anecdotally – in Chinese families the baby is with one parent, then sent to China to be cared for by the grandparent for some time, then back again to a parent in Australia. I mean, I have to be careful because I don't want to generalise, but do you see patterns of such things across different cultures or ethnicities? Is this a cultural issue, or is it just that attachment theory applies and therefore there is an issue there?

This can be tricky. Attachment theory is a useful guide in considering children's developmental experience.

It is inappropriate to approach family life from a one-size-fits-all point of view. One of the problems with cookbook approaches to child and family psychiatry is that each case is unique, each child is unique, each family is unique. A resilient child will cope better than a child with a difficult temperament and disrupted attachment.

Thus, if a child has an autistic spectrum disorder, their needs will be different from other children, even in the same family. The meaning of particular developmental experiences will be different within different societies, such as in this example of a Chinese family. After all, it is both the experience and how it is interpreted which will influence the outcome.

If parents are not coping and the child is exposed to an environment which is out of control, characterised by neglect and abuse, being placed elsewhere – with extended family or in childcare – can be protective, as it serves to provide the child with a stabilising influence. Thus, it is not as simple as saying the child should always be placed with the primary caregiver.

Unfortunately, many fathers complain that the Court is gender-biased. They are often focussed on their rights as a father and struggle to truly think about the child's experience. The Court process is not about parental rights; it's about thinking about the child's best interests.

Tragically, all too often the best interests of the child are long gone. We are thus searching for the least detrimental alternative. It really is about thinking about the child's needs and assisting parents to meet them.

That doesn't mean wrapping the child up in cotton wool, or protecting them from adversity at school, in social relationships, or within the family, but rather to help them to incorporate and manage those challenges in their lives. It can be problematic if parents are excessively protective. Just as it can be inappropriate to push too hard, it is also inappropriate to not push hard enough.

One of the aspects of parenting capacity that I always look for is balance: a balance between care and control, a balance between love and discipline.

One of the challenges for all parents is to find balance. For a particular child, in considering their capacity and needs, how do we facilitate them to overcome the developmental hurdles and develop an experience of competence?

That applies to all children, and particularly when children are dealing with issues such as separation, loss, adversity within the family, conflict between their parents. We should help them to overcome adversity and emerge intact, emotionally and psychologically. This promotes an integrated approach to life, and when they have a family of their own, they will reference a manageable experience. This will assist their emotional regulation and capacity to maintain relationships – to hang in there!

You have covered this, but is there anything else to add about how parents can best support their children going through a separation?

Provide age-appropriate information.

Do not denigrate the other parent and their extended family and community.

Do not be bloody-minded when it comes to fairness.

Really work towards having a collaborative approach.

Provide children with an environment where they experience mutual respect, so that they can trust their carers. Promote a sense of goodwill.

None of us is perfect, particularly when it comes to parenting. So, we need to forgive. To forgive each other. Our children and ourselves.

It is not about fairness, whose turn it is, or the capacity to bring a contravention application.

> Take any opportunity to approach your circumstances with goodwill. Wherever possible, communicate in a respectful manner with your co-parent so that problems (and there will always be problems) can be solved in the best possible way. Bear in mind there are no absolutes. There are many paths. Search for flexibility.

The aim is not to create a perfect environment. Without challenges, children don't develop. But the challenges need to be manageable. Overcoming adversity is an integral part of life.

> The aim is not to provide a perfect environment but, rather, to provide one that is good enough...

To provide children with a rich developmental experience, which prepares them for the world ahead. We should think about the next generation and beyond.

That is really interesting. Particularly the part about children learning flexibility and how to overcome adversity. In passing, you raised the issue of parental alienation. This is something that comes up with clients who have said to me that the other parent is alienating. Do you have any thoughts about that?

I do see this happen.

The challenge for the parent who views the other parent as alienating, criticising, or undermining is to not quiz the child. Don't interrogate the child or look for evidence. Don't focus on what the other parent is doing.

Instead, focus on your own approach. Focus on your own parental and personal responsibility, so that you are doing the right thing by the child. This is within your control and will assist you in feeling less powerless and frustrated. The best way to combat such circumstances is to have a good relationship with the child. The more you focus on the other parent, the more this becomes the child's life experience.

Too often the child becomes the delegate for the other parent. If the child experiences you to be resentful, angry, and hostile, this will play into the other parent's narrative about your problematic approach to life. Should your child look into your eyes and see you frustrated and angry, this will promote any alienating dynamic.

It is really about focussing on what you're doing with the child. That the child has the experience of 'Dad and Mum are there for me. They do care about me.'

Do you have views about reform in the Family Law process?

Anything that promotes a collaborative model, that reduces the level of adversarial conduct, that focuses minds on the children's needs would be helpful. Taking an adversarial approach to such matters is problematic. An inquisitorial model is a much more appropriate approach to exploring family dynamics.

One of the problems of applying an adversarial model to an already dysfunctional family dynamic is that it serves to amplify the nature of the family psychopathology. It amplifies the lack of mutual respect, trust, and goodwill. Legal correspondence impairs the capacity of parties to communicate and solve problems, as everyone becomes reactive.

So, we have a process that promotes reactivity and a lack of respectful communication between parties.

> We need an environment that helps everyone to get together and think about the children's experience.

This will be of benefit to children and families into the future.

I would like to ask about family therapy when it is Court-ordered.

Therapy works when people are motivated. Court-ordered therapy may be necessary to bring parties together.

> It works best if parties are committed to the process and are willing
> to examine their own areas of vulnerability. It does not work if this
> becomes a venue to blame the other side.

The experience of bringing parties together to think about the children is an important step. Just being in the room together can be beneficial.

Court-ordered assessments do have the capacity to be beneficial. Sometimes, it is the first time in years that a parent has seen their child with the other parent and have the opportunity to witness that it is ok. Often, their experience is of a distressed child at handover. They may come to recognise that ...

> just because a child has difficulty in transition, it doesn't mean they
> are being abused or neglected.

Family therapy can assist parents to sit together and receive the same information from a therapist who is there to contain their emotional distress and help them refocus on the child's needs. Thus, even though Court-ordered family therapy can be challenging, it can be very useful.

I wanted to raise something I have noticed in my work as a family lawyer. There still seems to be this concept that the only real abuse is physical or sexual abuse, and there's this very confused attitude towards psychological abuse.

Psychological abuse can be more damaging than physical or sexual abuse, particularly if it's enduring.

It can be difficult for Child Protection Services and the Court to delineate psychological abuse. Psychological abuse Is underdiagnosed because of the lack of evidence. It is challenging to determine, as people's behaviour behind closed doors will be different from their public face.

We know that people behave differently when assessed. The underlying security of the attachment will be more important than a single episode of substantiated physical abuse. That said, psychological abuse will often coincide with other forms of abuse as there is a lack of 'good enough parenting', care and control.

If, occasionally, things get out of control, perhaps under the influence of alcohol or other substances, or during a transient disordered mental state, this may not be representative of the child's general experience. The provision of scaffolding and specific supports may be more effective than long-term removal in such circumstances.

Do you have any tips or words of wisdom for solicitors?

Please help your clients to think about the totality of their children's experience.

Parties come along in the heat of the moment. If you take an approach that magnifies their adversarial stance, this will be detrimental to children.

Promoting a more balanced approach to children's developmental experience, be it within the family, school, or social network, will be helpful. Please ...

> encourage the parents to take a developmental-
> rather than rights-based approach.

It is not about fairness. Parents often become preoccupied with this. It's about how to best assist your child as a responsible parent attending to their developmental needs.

Please limit the focus on allegations, as every allegation, every legal letter, preoccupations with breaches, will amplify the parental conflict.

Look for opportunities for collaboration, and encourage the client to understand that both parents should remain core figures in their children's lives.

We discussed psychological abuse. Are there any other psychological concepts that are misunderstood in Family Law?

A motivating factor for me as a court expert, educator, and therapist is to translate what I see from a psychiatric and psychological perspective, to inform the Court and the parties in their understanding.

The developmental trajectory children and families follow is influenced by numerous factors: organic and biological factors within the child, psychological and developmental factors within the family, and their experience within the broader community.

Importantly, things change. An absolute, categorical approach to diagnosis and treatment is inevitably flawed because things change. Things change for children, for families; things change within a child's brain. The challenge is not to take a black-and-white approach, despite the Law's need to, at times, impose specific outcomes.

> The strengths and weaknesses of each family, each parent and child, should be considered.

The adversarial legal process amplifies the stigma of mental illness. In my assessments I am looking for insight and reflectivity which enables vulnerabilities to be addressed. Mental illness need not impair parenting capacity if strategies have been successfully implemented. But we need to overcome denial to achieve this outcome.

At times I witness the Court place onerous restrictions on contact beyond that typically imposed by child protection authorities. In different jurisdictions, different tests and interventions apply. Balancing safety and risk is challenging. We seek to protect children, yet avoidance will amplify anxiety. Where possible, there should be continuity of contact between children and both parents.

I am concerned that once contact is suspended this may become prolonged. Whilst the Court tests the allegations, pathological dynamics may be reinforced by the lack of contact. Of course, safety comes first, but if possible contact with both parents should be maintained. Recurrent experiences of separation and loss are detrimental to a child's developmental experience. This will be a cause of psychological harm.

Alison O'Neill

Clinical psychologist and expert report writer

Allow children to have a childhood

Alison O'Neill is a clinical psychologist and PhD candidate with a Master's degree in Clinical Psychology. She conducts clinical and forensic assessments for children, adults, and families in the criminal and civil domains. Her core practice is the assessment of families and provision of expert reports for the Children's Court, Federal Circuit & Family Court, and the Supreme Court of Australia. Her reports address a range of referral issues, including child sexual and physical abuse, neglect, surrogacy, adoption, relocation, family violence, the impact of substance use and mental illness upon parenting capacity, and when children reject a parent.

She is an Independent Expert on family violence for the Department of Immigration and Border Protection (DIBP), an Authorised Clinician for the Children's Court Clinic, and a member of the Fertility Society of Australia (FSA) and the Australian and New Zealand Infertility Counsellors Association (ANZICA).

Additionally, she is a guest lecturer at UNSW for the Forensic Master's Program and she regularly presents at conferences and training seminars. She was previously a Regulation 7 Family Consultant for the Federal Magistrates and Family Court of Australia and an Authorised Report Writer with the NSW Victims Compensation Tribunal (VCT).

In this interview Alison demystifies the process for preparing an expert report, from what happens at the actual interviews with the expert to how the report is prepared and submitted. Importantly, Alison also addresses how a report can be challenged, and gives practical tips for parents about how they can best support children through a separation.

⁙

Firstly, can you describe your work? In particular, how does what you do fit into the overall Family Law Court process?

My role as an expert psychologist is to assess the parents and the children, and to explore their relationships with a view to what is in the best interests of the child, or children. I then prepare a comprehensive report which can be used as a tool to help parents achieve settlement and/or assist the Judge in making findings about what is in the children's best interest if the parents cannot come to an agreement.

Can you please describe the process for preparing an expert's report? Can you explain what actually happens when you meet the parties?

Experts conduct the assessments in different ways. Personally, I choose to see the family for an entire day. I spend a few hours interviewing each parent (and their respective partner, or parents, if relevant). Understandably, many adults feel nervous during the interview, but relax once we start talking. The interview is lengthy and detailed, but always aimed to not only better understand the individual parent but also the impact on the dynamics of the relationship with the other parent and the child, or children. I also administer special kinds of tests that psychologists use, called psychometric tests, which may investigate the parent's mental health, drug use, or the children's psychological issues (depending on what issues are relevant to that particular case).

Additionally, I spend time interviewing the children and observing the children with the parents and siblings.

Again, many adults feel nervous about their child being interviewed alone and also observed. However, the children are rarely nervous and my role is to support and assist the children, so I am mindful not to distress them in any way.

> Most children actually enjoy talking and
> having their views listened to.

They also enjoy spending time in my playroom.

To assist in the preparation of the report, I am provided with documentation to read by the Court, which typically consists of Court documentation, such as affidavits and orders, along with material provided to the Court from the school, mental health practitioners, the police, or any other independent source that the lawyers think might be relevant to helping me understand the matter. The report takes many days to prepare, especially to write a formulation/analysis, giving my opinion about what is in the best interest of the children, and how the family can move forward. When the report is completed, I send it to the Court and the Judge decides how and when they distribute the report to the parties.

One thing I have come across in speaking with litigants who have been through the process is a feeling that once the expert report is prepared, it is definitive. Can you describe how an expert's report can be challenged?

The expert's report can be challenged and it is important that they can and are tested. After all, the report is only one piece of evidence that the Judge has to assist them in decision-making. The reports can be challenged in cross-examination where the expert is asked to clarify or justify the basis of their opinion. They can also be challenged by having another expert comment on the report, which is referred to as using a 'shadow expert'.

The process of challenging a report is designed to test how useful the report is, and how much consideration the Judge should give the report in making their decision.

What matters would require an expert report?

Frequently I am asked to prepare a report when there are allegations of family violence, that one or both parents abuse alcohol or drugs, or that one or the other has physically or sexually abused the children.

I am also asked to prepare reports when the child, or children, reject one of the parents and refuse to spend time with them.

In other words, in any case where the parents cannot agree or where there are concerns about the parents' functioning or the children's wellbeing.

I have noticed that reports are also often prepared when there are allegations with regards to a parent's mental health. What are the kinds of mental health, or personality, or other issues that individuals you interview might suffer from, and how can such issues affect a person's parenting capacity?

The main kinds of mental health issues I am asked to comment on are mood disorders (including major depressive disorder and bipolar disorder), schizophrenia, substance use disorders, borderline personality disorder, and narcissistic personality disorder.

I think it is important for parents going through Family Law proceedings to understand that ...

> the key question is not whether a person has or does not have a diagnosed mental illness. Rather, what is important is the impact their psychological issues have on their parenting capacity.

For example, a father may have suffered a severe depressive episode in the past but he sought treatment, is compliant with medication and therapy, and has achieved stability. Further, he may have a clear understanding of the impact his depression had on his day-to-day functioning and his parenting, and he may be aware of warning signs and ways to prevent another episode. As such, there would be minimal risk to the child in his care.

On the other hand, a mother may have borderline personality disorder, is unable to sustain relationships, has a fractured sense of identity, has a long history of self-harming, suicide attempts, and substance use, and is unable to consistently prioritise the child's needs. For example, she may falsely believe that her infant is crying to annoy her and reacts with anger, or she may react negatively to the child having fun with others because she takes that to be a rejection of her, and engages in self-harming behaviour. Her attitude and behaviour towards herself and the child in these examples may leave the child at an unacceptable risk of harm in her care.

In addition to cases where a parent has a mental health or personality disorder, I have noticed children's interests are often compromised more generally when there is Family Law litigation going on. How can parents remain child-focussed and best support their children when they are going through a separation?

Parents can best support their children by allowing them to develop and maintain close relationships with both parents, as long as there is no risk of harm to the child.

It is important for the parents to separate their feelings about their ex-partner as a spouse from their feelings about them as a parent.

Ideally, they should remain child-focussed, reassure the child that they are safe and loved by both parents, and shield the child from adult issues and conflict. At all times, the parents should speak positively about each other because the child's own identity and self-esteem is informed by what they hear about their parents.

For example, if a little boy grows up hearing about his father in negative terms, then he may question whether he possesses those negative attributes, and he develops a negative view not only of his father but also of himself.

Saying nothing about the other parent is not the same as speaking positively. Children pick up the obvious and not so obvious messages and take them to heart.

In addition to remaining child-focussed, what other advice or tips would you give to people going through the Family Law system?

Some tips would be to:

- Remind yourself that the ultimate goal of both parents is to maximise love and care, and to minimise stress and conflict
- Speak positively about the other parent – they are part of your child's life and identity
- Act in the child's best interest, not your own
- The children's routine should allow them to have a childhood, including doing sports and having playdates with friends
- Protect the child from being exposed to conflict
- Allow school to be a safe haven from any conflict
- Seek out information about what is in the child's best interest from books, literature, and experts
- Settle the parenting matters as early as possible, as children (and parents) are adversely affected by ongoing litigation

Do you have any views about possible reform to Family Law?

Ideally, there would be greater consistency in the quality of expert reports and more specific training for experts.

I also think that it would be beneficial for families in high-conflict situations to consult with experts earlier in the process so that intervention could assist the children by preventing problems rather than treating them.

As it is, many families are not seen by a social scientist with expertise in Family Law until five years after their separation, by which time the children have been adversely affected and the relationship dynamics become quite fixed.

Linda Campbell

Family consultant, expert report writer, family therapist

Permission to love the other parent

Linda Campbell currently works at the Relationspace in Sydney and is a well respected Family Consultant and expert report writer in family law Court matters. She graduated with a Bachelor of Social Work (First Class Honours) from the University of New South Wales in 1990. Linda worked for the NSW Department of Family and Community Services (FACS) for over 20 years. Linda has extensive experience in working with clients whose children are at varying levels of risk resulting from parental mental health issues, substance abuse, and family violence.

In 2007 Linda was instrumental in setting up the first specialist team in FACS to respond to children and young people with high and complex needs in out-of-home care. In 2010 Linda began working as a Family Consultant, using her expertise and experience in her child protection career to her assessments of children and families in family law. Linda's practice focuses on the preparation of comprehensive, outcome-focussed, and strengths-based family reports and the provision of therapeutic child-inclusive mediation services to families who seek to resolve parenting issues in a collaborative, child-centred framework.

Throughout my years as a family lawyer, I have found that clients often complain of what they perceive as bias from the Family Consultant or expert report writer. In this interview Linda discusses in detail the issue of bias and the strategies she uses to guard against it. Linda shares her tips for supporting children through separation and also her ideas about where to go from here, with her supporting a more collaborative child-centred approach in Family Law matters. I particularly like Linda's point that children need permission to love the other parent. It draws attention to the fact that often in divorce, somehow even quietly a message can be given to children that they cannot freely love the other parent.

Thanks for speaking with me today. Could you please describe what it is you do?

I work in the Family Law system as both a Regulation 7 family report writer, and as a single expert report writer. I also provide therapy services to separated parents who are experiencing high levels of conflict in their co-parenting relationship.

The difference between family reports and single expert reports is that the former are allocated through a central process after being ordered by a Judge, and the costs of preparation of the report are borne by the Court. In the latter, the preparation costs are borne by the litigants and/or legal aid.

The single expert reports that I do often look no different to a family report in that the matters covered are often very complex and multi-faceted. As a social worker, I do not do single expert reports where a mental health diagnosis is required. I do, however, make extensive enquiries into a person's behaviour and assess the impact of this behaviour on the children's safety, welfare, and wellbeing, as well as how it contributes to the parental conflict.

How did you come to do this work? What is your background and experience?

I came to this work in 2010, after spending 20 years in what is now the NSW Department of Family and Community Services (FACS), firstly as a child protection caseworker and then many years managing caseworkers and running clinical teams. This means that my areas of expertise are in parental substance use and mental health, family violence, and attachment relationships/parenting capacity.

In my experience as a family lawyer and mediator, I have often found that a fair bit of controversy surrounds such reports. What are some of the issues with family reports or single expert reports as you see it?

> After reports are completed, many litigants form a view that the report writer has been biased against them in some way.

Please elaborate on this issue, as I have found that clients often perceive bias in the report.

A common theme is that a report writer is for or against mothers or fathers, and that they have been charmed or seduced by one parent to take their side against the other.

I cannot comment on the work of others, but in my work, I realise that I need to be highly vigilant about possible bias. This is a complex process that is hard to describe but, in essence, it is about always generating alternative hypotheses (about what you believe has happened or is happening) and testing these, asking both parties hard questions, and maintaining an individualised focus (as distinct from applying formulas about x behaviour = y outcome).

The most important way to guard against bias, however, is to always 'be hard on your opinions'. I always tell litigants that while they might not agree with my recommendations, it will always be very clear to them why I think what I think.

My hope is that this transparency assists litigants to understand that my opinions are based on 25 years of cumulative experience in working with children and families, rather than a belief system that, for example, mothers are more important to children than fathers, or that mothers are routinely obstructive in trying to prevent fathers from having a relationship with their children.

Given your 25 years' experience working with children and families, any thoughts on how children can be affected when parents separate? And things mums and dads can be mindful of?

One of the most common issues I see with litigants is that they experience a lot of difficulty in separating their children's needs from their own needs. They may feel very wronged by the other parent, who may have behaved very badly prior to or at the point of separation. They struggle with the idea of supporting the child's relationship with someone they abhor (often with good reason). They view everything this parent does or says through this lens, and they will often draw the child into this by asking them pointed questions about the other parent.

This emotionally loaded atmosphere often means that the child feels obliged to provide the 'right' answers to their parent. Ultimately, this becomes a self-fulfilling prophecy, where the parent gathers information that supports their view of the other parent.

Unfortunately, the child gets caught in the middle of this. They feel that they don't have permission to love and care about the other parent.

When they have positive experiences with this parent, they feel conflicted about this and struggle to resolve these (unresolvable) contradictions.

This is an exceptionally negative experience for a child and if it continues over an extended period of time, it can cause immense problems for them, emotionally, psychologically, and socially.

I would ask parents, then...

> to be acutely aware of the need to put aside their own issues with the other parent and to ensure that they are genuinely supportive of the child's need to have the best possible relationship with each of their parents, if they want this child to do well in life.

Given, as you say, the importance of being child-focussed, do you think this is achieved in the current system? How can we be more child-focussed, and do you have any ideas with regards to reform here?

In regards to Family Law reforms, my view is that the adversarial nature of the process needs to fundamentally shift to a collaborative, child-centred approach.

This could include that at the point of a dispute being identified, the parties have access to professionals who can assist them to identify the needs of their children (based on developmental psychology) and coach and educate them about how to best meet those needs in the context of co-parenting with someone they may not like or trust. This must always be a child-inclusive process to ensure the centrality of their needs, views, and experiences in an objective manner.

> Lawyers need to facilitate, not obstruct, the process of resolving the matter in a child-centred way.

Having said this, my view is that an entirely different process needs to apply in cases where there is coercive and controlling family violence, substance abuse, and/or diagnosed mental health issues. These matters, ideally, should be triaged carefully by the Court to ensure they do, in fact, have these characteristics and then managed using a multi-disciplinary approach.

Julia Nowland

Family therapist and counsellor

Working out the kinks

Julia Nowland, head of Whole Heart Relationships is one of Australia's most highly regarded relationship experts, with over a decade of experience helping families. Julia can assist anyone going through a separation in terms of individual therapy or also by way of offering family therapy.

As a qualified Family Systems Therapist, Julia also holds a Master's in Social Health from Macquarie University and a Post-Graduate Diploma in Relationship Counselling from the Australian Institute for Relationship Studies.

Regularly called upon as a relationship expert on national TV, she's a regular on Channel 9's Today Show, appears on Talking Lifestyle radio, and has been featured in major publications, including *Woman's Day* and *Psych Central*.

In this interview Julia talks about the roller-coaster of emotional stages following separation, what is normal and what is not, how former partners can reach a functional co-parenting relationship, how to explain separation to children, self care during separation. In short Julia explains how to work out the kinks.

Firstly, can you please describe your work? In particular, how does what you do fit into the overall Family Law process?

As a qualified Family Systems Therapist, I have specific training that helps me view the patterns of behaviour that have a negative impact on relationships. Working with one, a few, or the whole family in the room, I take into consideration each person's unique story and help people change the way they view the problem.

> Separation or divorce does not mean that the family has stopped existing; rather, it means that there are now two families: Mum's family and Dad's family.

This is a major transition and deserves compassion from all those involved in the divorce process.

Before separation, it is not uncommon for couples to see me to try and resolve issues in their marriage. Such issues may be relatively fresh and raw, or ingrained over longer periods of time. Individuals often consult with me if they're wondering how to go about asking for a divorce, because it's daunting to acknowledge your marriage may actually be over. A compassionate and unbiased ear brings direction and clarity.

Parents also engage with me during separation. By establishing a self-care plan and receiving increased emotional support, they feel a sense of relief. Together, we also determine what co-parenting looks like. This includes setting boundaries and defining, for example, tricky situations like Christmas.

I like that you describe how people can access you at all stages, whether together to try and save the relationship, or during separation, or individually. I know of parties who saw a marriage therapist to try and repair the relationship. Once it was clear this wasn't possible, they continued to see them for guidance and support as to how to keep co-parenting and support the children after separation. I think that's commendable. So, how did you come to do this work? What are your experience and qualifications?

With a Master's in Social Health, and major in drug and alcohol counselling, I spent just under a decade working with adolescents and their families. Their issues included drugs, alcohol, mental health, and their families. It was through this work I discovered my passion for opening up and working with a family as a whole. I would thrive on breaking through with each family member, and this was when I decided my area of expertise would become couples and families.

I taught students in the Social Welfare department at TAFE, NSW, whilst I studied Couple and Family Therapy. To deepen my knowledge, I worked for Relationships Australia, facilitating relationship educational programs, before moving to Catholic Care (also known as Centacare) alongside mediators and the Women's Domestic Violence Court Advocacy Service (WDVCAS). With this heightened level of experience and expertise, I branched out on my own, seeing clients face to face, as well as online as my client base expanded across the world.

Despite working internationally, I suspect although paradoxically everyone's situation is different, unique, that even across different nations there are many common human emotions. What are the kinds of common issues and challenges faced by the families you see in therapy?

Parents are flooded with emotions. The first emotion to present itself is often anger or rage. However, underneath that pointy feeling of rage is a deep pool of other emotions. These include sadness, fear, hurt, betrayal, rejection, loneliness, abandonment, and vulnerability.

When we're in the depths of these feelings, we can often have the mentality of 'I'm going to get what I deserve', or 'I want them to hurt as much as I'm hurting'. This way of thinking creates havoc for every person involved in the separation.

Yes, that ties into what Judge Sexton said in relation to parties being in the right mentality to sensibly discuss settlement, and how, when they are in that early stage, it can be very hard.

Parents will fight for 50/50 shared care, imagining that this means their child will do alternating weeks with each parent. This arrangement might sound easy on paper; however, it can become very disruptive to the child's routine. Take a moment to think: Have you ever gone on a holiday visiting more than one destination? You're constantly packing your suitcase and moving around. It can become tiring and lonely.

Shared care means that you both take an active interest and role in your child's wellbeing and development. That can mean paying for excursions, taking an active interest in school activities, and taking time off work when they're sick.

It's easy to get caught up in the 'amount' of time you have with your child. Parents can often fight over days, nights, and holidays. Remember...

> for your child, they want quality time with you. They won't remember how many hours they saw you for; they'll remember the memories you made during those hours.

You can make a plan on how things are going to look, but sometimes that doesn't work. It's really about working out the kinks. Your child is not a mini adult.

That is a great point. They are not mini adults.

Yes. They don't comprehend the complexity of the process. For example, 6 p.m. every night might be the only time they get to talk to Daddy until they see him. But sometimes at 6 p.m. they are preoccupied and this call has little relevance to them. Or Dad is held up at work and phones later, only to be told he missed his window today.

So, for their sake, sometimes it's about pushing your patience and growing your compassion and understanding a little further.

Fathers often complain of not getting enough time with their children. Mothers often complain the children come home either hyped up on sugar or out of their routine and are terrible to settle at night. Mums protest that they're the ones who have to do all the 'boring' stuff, while Dad gets to be the 'fun' parent. So, as you can see, it becomes a vicious cycle. Dad tries to create as many 'fun' memories in the short amount of time he has, leaving mum feeling annoyed when the kids come home. Mum feels resentful that dad doesn't do the 'hard' parenting stuff and doesn't allow dad to have as much time with the kids.

If both parents were able to see shared care as sharing the responsibility, then this fun parent–boring parent dynamic wouldn't have to be present.

What are the kinds of mental health issues you see in your work? Is it necessarily the case that just because someone has a mental health issue that their parenting capacity is compromised?

Mental health has such a terrible rap when it comes to Family Law because it can be seen as being weak. Partners can use their ex's mental health as a way of discrediting their parenting ability. In doing so, they manipulate the custody arrangement they're seeking.

Yes, some of the people I've interviewed who went through the Court process have said this.

The World Health Organisation (WHO) declares that health is a state of complete physical, mental, and social well-being, and not merely the absence of disease or infirmity.

I like to think of the Complete State Model of Mental Health, proposed by Corey Keyes, when working with clients. This model looks at mental health symptoms from absent to present on a continuum, and mental wellbeing on another continuum from low to high. These continuums intercept each other.

You can be low on the continuum for the presence of mental illness symptoms, yet you also have high mental wellbeing. That is, you have been functioning well, despite your illness. You haven't relapsed, you have a great care plan in place, and you regularly attend support.

On the other hand, you can again be low on the mental illness symptoms continuum but instead of having high mental wellbeing, this could be coupled with being low on the mental wellbeing continuum. Therefore, you don't look after yourself very well. Perhaps you drink one to two bottles of wine every night, due to stress; your work load is huge and you don't emotionally connect with your children. You don't have a great care plan in place and you don't have any support.

The question shouldn't be: Does this person have an absence of illness (and therefore does this make them the better suited parent)? Rather, it should take into account the person's ability to take responsibility for their own health and capacity to care for their child. A parent is often penalised for seeking help for their mental well-being when they should be praised. Regardless of any issue a parent has, or once had, as long as the child is safe, their emotional, physical, and mental needs are being met.

It should not matter if Mum once suffered from postnatal depression. Or if Dad had anxiety during his last job. However, it can be taken out of context during divorce.

Well, what are the real ways in which parents do (often albeit unintentionally) cause psychological harm to children during a bitter separation? What are some of the common issues for children when their parents separate?

First and foremost, it's important to dispel the myth that separation impacts children's mental health – it doesn't. What we know, through research, is that the continual high conflict of parents is what impacts a child's mental health.

Depending on the age of the child, there will be different concerns. Who will they will live with? Are they still loved by both parents? Is it ok for them to still love both parents? Was it their fault?

I'll never forget one of the most moving exercises we used in a group. You can try it now. We asked parents to write on a piece of paper how they would describe their ex-partner. They were to place the paper under the chair until the end of the group session. Before they left, we asked the participants to write on a new piece of paper how their child would describe their ex-partner. Then they compared the two pieces of paper.

The difference between the two papers would be shocking for some. Parents need to understand that their child will still love both of them very much. The child is often conflicted, because they don't want to upset either parent by loving someone that one parent disrespects or is angry with. Children can appear to adapt to situations in order to cope with the conflict between the people they love very much. However, they are bottling up their emotions in order to please their parents.

> It's important for the parents to keep the children
> out of the conflict.

This means not making the child the messenger; you shouldn't ask them personal questions about the other parent, and if you are going to argue, do it away from your children.

In terms of the push–pull of being (a) honest with children, but (b) not over exposing them to adult issues, how should parents broach the subject of explaining to children that they have separated?

You know your situation best, so it's important to decide together as parents who or how you are going to broach the subject.

> Let your children know that it's not their fault, that you, the
> parents, are responsible for the separation.

Remind your child that you both love them very much. Reinforce that, no matter what, they are safe and protected.

It's important to encourage your child to talk about the separation in their own time. Let them know that you feel sad about the separation, but that you are ok. They should be told that things will get better.

Let them have their own feelings about it. Some children will be angry; be compassionate and give them time.

You did raise this a moment ago, but can you detail more how does witnessing parents' conflict affects children?

What we know through research is that high conflict affects children's mental health. Children are very good at adapting to situations in order to keep a parent happy. It's important that I note I am not talking about family violence when I'm using the term 'conflict'.

Children can often become overwhelmed by their feelings of sadness, confusion, anger, and fear. As they are unable to deal with their feelings, they will often show their feelings through behaviour. These include: clinginess, Regression, over responsibility, self-blame, sleeping difficulties, difficulties at school, such as poor concentration or general misbehaviour, fussiness, aggression, and separation problems (from parents).

Again, you have raised this earlier; but in specific detail, how can parents best support their children when they are going through a separation?

It's important for children to have a safe and stable home. Even if there are two homes, they need to feel that one is a stable base.

Try to stick to your child's routines to make things predictable for them. Even if they're not spending the majority of the time with you, make sure they have a little space of their own, where they feel the most comfortable, and where they feel they belong.

At the same time, it's important to lower the expectations that your ex-is going to parent the same way as you do.

There is more than one way to parent; they might not do what you would do, but that doesn't always mean how they do things is wrong. Try to plan things and make decisions in a way that doesn't cause stress on the children. This is what we call parallel parenting.

You might find it hard to cooperate, but you can agree that you will both parent responsibly.

Talk to your child about their feelings. Make sure you're not trying to make them feel happy by saying things like 'Don't cry. I don't like it when you cry.' Allow your child to express their feelings. If they're sad, you can just sit with them. It's also important to continue using healthy discipline, as this creates limits and, again, reinforces safety.

They may want to ask you questions about life, now that there are two homes. Answer their questions as best you can.

*It's vital that you don't speak disrespectfully
of your ex-partner.*

Nor is it helpful to ask your child to 'keep secrets' whilst they're with you about how they spend their time. This puts them in a compromising position, especially if they mention that they have a secret but can't tell anyone.

During changeover isn't the best time to bring up issues you have. Nor is it ok to ignore your ex. Your child will pick up on your tension and become distressed on the way home.

*Introducing new partners can also be
distressing for children.*

They may not show it to you, but this is because they don't want to disappoint you. It's important to introduce them slowly. Take time for your child to adjust to the separation of the two most important people first.

I think what you just said there is important. I have been involved in matters where there really was a lack of sensitivity to how new partners were introduced and things were moving at warp speed. I also want to ask: What are some strategies for how parents can continue to co-parent after separation?

Depending how far along you are in the divorce, co-parenting can seem like a fairy tale. That's because of the level of emotional intensity and investment you have with your ex-partner.

Let me explain. When you're in love, living together raising a child or children, you have trust, respect, positive expectations and experiences. Your emotional investment and level of intensity is high and positive. When your relationship is in distress, you have the same level of intensity and investment; however, the level of emotional investment and intensity is now negative.

The trick is to bring the level of investment and intensity down, and, in doing so, become less reactive to your ex-partner. Have you noticed that friends or co-workers can say something that annoys you, however, your response is different, depending on how close they are to you?

Depending on how distressed the relationship is between you and your ex-, start looking at the relationship as a business relationship.

And how can a businesslike relationship with your ex-be established?

I would suggest trying the following:

- Prepare yourself emotionally
- Lower your expectations as to what your ex-partner 'has' to do or say
- Make sure that you communicate clearly, directly, and non-judgementally; watch your tone, pitch, and level
- If there's a problem, don't push it to one side and say it's their problem; help look for solutions
- Work towards a compromise, not a 'win'
- Keep the topics to common interests or concerns; don't expect your ex-to divulge what's going on in their personal life, and you don't have to talk about your life either
- Pick the timing of when to talk, i.e., during work isn't always a good time

Something I was interested to ask you about is what are, when a relationship ends, the stages a person goes through?

The end of a marriage is a death of sorts, and it's normal for people to grieve.

Not surprisingly, the person who asks for the divorce has had more time to ride the rollercoaster of emotions and may not appear to be as affected as the person who didn't initiate things. Don't take it personally if your ex-partner doesn't seem to care.

Grief is personal and unique to everyone; there are no hard facts when it comes to grief. However, people often say it takes about two years for the emotions to settle and for them to feel at ease with things. The first year can be a bumpy ride.

Here are a few things you might be experiencing:

- Anger, sadness, betrayal, confusion, rejection
- Fantasy about revenge (Please note there is a HUGE difference between fantasy and acting out revenge. Fantasising about getting the new partner deported is different to keying their car, which is a crime.)
- Crying at unexpected situations or feeling teary a lot
- Fear of the future
- Wanting to frequently talk about the separation
- Difficulty concentrating, and often drifting back to thinking about the separation

This is something I am passionate about. How can parents best take care of themselves and their own mental health when going through a separation and the stresses of the Family Law process?

Everybody has a stress vulnerability threshold; that is, everybody can handle a level of stress before their mental health and wellbeing becomes impacted. Depending on how much stress you have in your daily life, you could be dealing with stress in a healthy and productive manner. However, adding overwhelming stressors such as divorce, death of a family member, loss of a job, or relocating could push you past your threshold into your vulnerability zone.

Looking after your mental health and wellbeing is vital

...in keeping you down below your threshold. This is where you feel more comfortable to go about your daily routine, regardless of the added stress of a divorce.

The first thing is to look at the basics, such as:

- Good sleep hygiene; getting at least seven hours of sleep each night - and turning that phone off
- Eating regular, healthy meals and drinking plenty of water
- Getting moving; exercise is an awesome way to shake off the stress

It's important to ask yourself: What helps me to relax? What can I do that helps me feel alive? What can I do that helps me to switch off?

What kind of activities could these be?

Well, the answers could lie in activities such as: joining a dance class, yoga, gardening, surfing, trail bike riding, going to the gym, painting, reading, and massages.

A well-rounded self-care plan should include a mixture of all of the above: the basics, activities that help you to relax, and a strong support network.

Lastly, what services or supports are available for people going through a separation?

Depending on where you live, services such as Relationships Australia have many programs on offer, from groups about parenting after separation to counselling and mediation.

Other not-for-profit services can offer family support, mediation, and counselling. These include Catholic Care, Uniting Care, and Anglicare.

If your circumstance involves domestic violence, there is also the Women's Domestic Violence Court Advocacy Service (WDVCAS) NSW. They help support and advocate for you when there is domestic or family violence involved.

Jakki Schwartz

Children's contact supervisor

Without seeing their children

Jakki Schwartz is a rising star in the field of child contact supervision. She is currently the Director of Holding Hands Children's Contact Service, which she started in 2017. Having graduated from UNSW with a Bachelor of Social Work and undertaking postgraduate study in the area of Social Work Field Education Supervision, Jakki has spent the last 14 years in the social work sector.

Jakki started her career in Out of Home Care at Barnardos before deciding to focus her energy and skills in the field of child contact supervision. Having spent five and a half years working as the Coordinator of CatholicCare's Sydney Children's Contact Service (in between taking time off to start a family of her own), Jakki's dedication to child-focussed practices has contributed to the success and continuous growth of the service.

In 2016, Jakki left CatholicCare to start her own private children's contact service, together with her husband, Benjamin. Holding Hands was conceived out of a belief that a better success rate for families post-separation could be achieved from establishing a high quality supervision service undertaken in the community rather than in a centre. Holding Hands' early successes are a result not only from the focus on improved outcomes from court-ordered supervised visits but also in contact supervisor standards, supervision, and training.

Looking to the future, Jakki continues to focus on the growth and success of Holding Hands by continuing to research improved service outcomes, better quality supervision standards, and innovative child-focussed practices.

Jakki's passion for improving the standard of supervision was evident in her interview, in particular in her discussion of how we need to pay more attention to children's voices and experiences of supervised contact. In addition, Jakki discusses some of the myths surrounding supervision, including the purpose of supervision reports and the fact that, in her view, supervision is ideally not a final destination.

⋮⋮⋮

To start, what are the services that Holding Hands offers? How is this service different to a contact centre?

Holding Hands provides contact services to parents who have been court-ordered to have supervised visits and changeovers, though we also work with parents who have a parenting agreement through mediation or an agreement they've come to themselves. From their first interaction with us, we aim to find pathways with them, with the end goal being self-managed contact arrangements where the parents are able to communicate and plan their child's visits in an appropriate manner without the need for outside supervision.

We differ greatly from a contact centre in that we facilitate visits in the community – in parks, playgrounds, libraries, and in wet weather we might head to shopping centres, indoor play centres, and museums.

> Community visits allow interactions in more normalised environments and across different venues.

This not only helps the child and their parent in that moment but I think it also creates a foundation of confidence for the parents and child once they begin to plan and undertake their own unsupervised visits. So, a parent and child who have had supervised visits in parks and shopping centres will be more likely to continue to have successful visits once they've progressed to self-managed visits than those parents who have only had visits with their child inside of a contact centre.

How does someone access the services at Holding Hands? How long does it take between applying and using the service?

Our clients predominately get referred to us by family lawyers; however, there are a number of parents who have either done their research or heard about us through a friend or co-worker and come to us directly. If a parent wants to use our service, they can just call us.

The first step is always an intake assessment with both parents. This sounds so much more daunting than what it is. I conduct numerous intakes each week and, really, I am just trying to obtain background information on each parent and their particular matter.

From there, the next step is a child familiarisation session, which takes place in the child's home and allows them to become familiar with their allocated Supervisor prior to visits starting. There is so much going on for the child, and by giving them a chance to build a little rapport with the Supervisor in a familiar setting before the first visit, we reduce their anxieties and enable them to feel more secure and comfortable once the visits start. This process usually takes around a week, but if we have the available resources, then sometimes it can be done sooner. We take the view that the sooner we take you into our service, the sooner we can progress you out of the service into self-managed visits - which is our ultimate goal.

How did you come to work at Holding Hands, and what is your background and experience?

I have a Bachelor of Social Work from UNSW, worked at Barnardos for my final year university placement, and then was employed there as a Foster Care Worker/Case Manager for four years. Whilst there, I found a passion for supervising visits, and gained a lot of skills and insights into the dynamics between children and their parents' relationships.

Most recently, I was the Coordinator of the CatholicCare Sydney Children's Contact Service (based in Redfern) for five and a half years. My role was to manage the scheduling of visits, provide direction and supervision to a team of Supervisors, provide case management to client families, and introduce many child-focussed practices. Leading that fantastic team and being able to develop and evolve the program over the years was an invaluable experience.

I've also provided Professional Field Education Supervision for social work students from UNSW and CSU completing their university student placements, which I find rewarding as I have an opportunity to meet the future of our industry.

What kinds of things are commented on in the supervision reports?

Our reports are the backbone of our service and, generally speaking, document the observations of the supervisor, from the very beginning of visits, including the initial greetings, all the way through to the farewells at the end. It tends to be a very comprehensive document. The reports also document any interventions or involvement from the Supervisor, any concerns raised, and what the highlights and positives of the visits were.

I think supervision reports are often seen in a very negative light, that they are used as a vehicle of criticism and failure.

Yes. I was going to ask about that. I have had matters where clients have been concerned about this.

Holding Hands tries to discourage this view right from our first conversation with the parents...

> as we feel that the reports are important aids to help parents move towards visits without us. The aim is not to catch out the visiting parent but, rather, to assist them for future visits...

as one of the roles of the Supervisors is to role-model positive parenting behaviours.

In taking this approach, we are able to map the improvements in each parent's capacity over time.

The reports also serve as an important tool in our staff meetings. By discussing different situations and concerns in a group forum, our Supervisors are able to assist each other in formulating strategies for future visits.

Many of the interviewees have mentioned that the delays for contact centres are problematic. Is it possible for someone to use your services whilst they wait for a spot in a contact centre?

Oh absolutely! In fact, we encourage this. Often when parents contact us, they have already gone for several weeks or months without seeing their child, and they are desperate to just see them. I do encourage parents to put their names down on government-funded children's contact services' waiting lists, and use us in the interim. One parent actually described Holding Hands as a 'buffer service', and I like this analogy.

Do you have any tips for someone navigating the Family Law system? Particularly for someone using supervision services?

It's important for parents to understand that there are ongoing lengthy delays in the Courts, and it's very easy to get frustrated, so it's important for parents to keep things in perspective and remind themselves that there is nothing more important than their children.

We employ a child-focussed framework at Holding Hands and my advice would be to seek professional support in the form of counselling or therapy for children (depending on their age and development). This could be art therapy, sand therapy, school counselling – any type of intervention that will help to support the child through this process.

I often see children who struggle to self-regulate, struggle with anxieties before and after visits, and children whose behaviour regresses once visits start, as there is often uncertainty about the contact arrangements.

As adults, we have many support systems and mechanisms to understand what's happening around us. However, children are too young and, developmentally, they don't understand the system – nor should they!

From your perspective, are there any reforms that you believe should be implemented to the Family Law system?

I think children's voices should be heard a lot more than what they currently are. Over the years I have worked with hundreds of children who have gone through supervised visits and changeovers, and because a lot of supervised contact services view the parents as their clients, the children's thoughts and feelings can go unheard and unnoticed.

Holding Hands has recently begun long-term research into the experiences of children going through children's contact services, as we believe this will not only give us valuable insights into what this process is like from a child's perspective but also reveal how we can further assist them to navigate through this turbulent time.

Property Matters

Court experts and other professionals

Brian Pickup

Specialist forensic accountant and expert business valuer

The complexity within

Brian Pickup is a Chartered Accountant who has been in practice for over 30 years. Brian practices as B Pickup & Co in Sydney CBD. Prior to this, Brian was a partner at Deloitte Touche Tohmatsu.

Brian is a specialist Forensic Accountant; however, over his career he has had experience in other accounting areas, ranging from auditing public companies to acting as the accountant, tax adviser, and management consultant for small family businesses.

For more than 15 years Brian has provided specialist expert reports in Family Law matters. The expert reports include the valuation of all types of large and small businesses, companies, trusts, and superannuation funds. Brian has also prepared expert reports detailing the taxation implications of the movement of assets between parties and entities as a result of a property settlement. Brian is regularly appointed as a single expert providing evidence to the Family Court of Australia and the Federal Circuit Court of Australia. On occasions, Brian is also engaged as an expert critiquing other valuation reports and providing adversarial evidence in Court.

Brian's professional qualifications include a Bachelor of Economics (University of Sydney), membership in Chartered Accountants Australia & New Zealand, registration as a Company Auditor and Tax Agent, and holds Chartered Tax Adviser status with the Tax Institute of Australia.

Brian's opinion is well respected by clients, solicitors, barristers, and the Courts. He regularly speaks at legal seminars on financial aspects in Family Law matters, as well as the financial implications of the structure of certain settlement orders.

In this interview, Brian breaks down the anatomy of expert reports that can otherwise seem confusing and overly technical. He talks about his process for preparing a report and the choice of methodologies a valuer has, providing clear and practical tips for lawyers and clients. Echoing Justice Rose's observation, Brian discusses how the complexity within property matters has increased, in particular with regards to business structures. He also shares his practical tips for anyone separating when a family business is involved and what options are available to best manage this.

⁘

Describe what it is you do? In particular, how does your work fit into the overall picture of the Family Law process?

My job in the Family Law process is to assist the parties, their legal representatives, and the Court with financial issues within a Family Law matter. Often, there are businesses and structures which have evolved for many reasons over a long time. My job is to review these and bring clarity and certainty to an often confusing area.

In actual reality, what would this involve?

This can involve:

- The valuation of an entity such as a company, trust, partnership, sole trader or a self-managed superannuation fund
- Assessing the potential taxation impacts (current and future) of the eventual movement of assets between the parties

- Interpreting financial statements and financial reports to assist the parties, their legal advisers, and the Court to understand them
- Determining whether assets have been removed from the asset pool by any of the parties

Quite often I am appointed by both parties to act as the single expert. On other occasions I am appointed as an expert to assist one party in their case.

So how did you get into doing this particular work as an accountant in Family Law?

I have been a Chartered Accountant for 35 years. My formal qualifications include: a Bachelor of Economics, Membership of the Chartered Accountants of Australia & New Zealand, the Tax Institute qualification as a Chartered Tax Adviser, ASIC registration as a Company Auditor, and registration as a Tax Agent

More importantly though, I have been in public practice for 35 years, working for clients ranging from small businesses to large multinational companies. I have had intimate exposure to businesses and transactions in all circumstances.

The ability to be able to interpret financial statements, and understand the implications of transactions, has been developed during my time as an adviser to clients.

I came to the specialist Family Law area approximately 20 years ago when I assisted a barrister for one of my clients who was involved in a Family Law dispute. I found that I was able to communicate the various financial aspects involved in the matter at a level which was understandable by the client, the barrister, and the Court.

So what kinds of matters would require a report prepared by you?

I prepare reports in matters where:

- a business is one of the assets of the parties and it is required to be valued as part of the process to prepare a listing of the parties' assets

- there are possibly taxation issues as a result of the movement of assets between the parties
- there are company or trust structures owned by one or both of the parties and these require an explanation to be properly understood by the parties, the legal representative, and the Courts

Can you provide, in a bit more detail, some examples of the kinds of matters you have been involved in?

I have been involved in varying matters which include:

- The valuation of all types of professional businesses (financial, medical, legal, investment, and so forth) and trading businesses (manufacturing, construction, trades, retail, wholesale, and so forth)
- Determining the most tax-effective methods of moving corporate assets between parties
- The tracing of funds through tax havens around the world
- The valuation of the interest of a movie producer in movies previously made
- Discretely determining the net worth of high-profile individuals
- Determining the value of self-managed superannuation funds and advising the advantages and disadvantages of keeping the funds within the superannuation environment
- Reviewing draft Family Court orders to determine if there are any unforeseen taxation or other liabilities which may arise as a consequence of the orders

Are there challenges in explaining the technical concepts in accounting to lawyers and Judges that have a legal and not an accounting background?

There can be difficulties in explaining technical aspects; however, I find many lawyers, barristers, and Judges are able to grasp the concepts when I explain the issues in less technical language.

Describe the process for preparing a report. More specifically, I would like to know more about the different methodologies that can be used to value a business.

The process to prepare a valuation report commences with an engagement letter, where I provide the terms of the services, the scope of the report, my estimated fee, and also request the preliminary information.

Once the documents are received, I carry out reviews and analysis to determine the best valuation methodology to adopt.

The four main methodologies include:

1. **Discounted Cash Flow (DCF).**

   The DCF method calculates the value of future cash flows expected to be earned from the asset (in most cases, a business) being valued. The methodology relies on accurate long-term business budgets which detail future profits and cash flows of the business. Although it is seen as the most accurate valuation methodology, most small- and medium-sized businesses do not have this information available, and thus it is rarely used in Family Law matters.

2. **Capitalisation of Future Maintainable Earnings (FME).**

   The capitalisation of FME is regularly used in Family Law matters to value profitable small- and medium-sized businesses.

   The methodology firstly involves determining the future core business earnings (after adjusting for abnormal income and expenses). This is referred to as the FME.

   The FME is then multiplied by a capitalisation rate to value the business. This capitalisation rate is a reflection of the return which would be expected by a notional 'hypothetical willing and able buyer' if that buyer was to acquire the business. The calculated value of the business includes the tangible (for example, say, equipment, working capital) and intangible assets (such as goodwill).

   Any surplus assets not employed in the core business are added to the value, and debt is deducted, to arrive at the value of the entire entity.

3. **Industry Rules of Thumb**

    Within certain industries or for certain types of businesses, there may exist certain industry benchmarks (commonly referred to as 'rules of thumb').

    Although these can be seen as a 'shortcut' method, rules of thumb used in regular market transactions cannot be ignored when assessing the fair market value of a business.

4. **Net Asset Backing Basis**

    This method requires an assessment of the estimated realisable value of the entity's tangible assets and liabilities. It is commonly used when the entity is not trading (such as an investment entity), or when the entity is operating a business that is not earning sufficient profits to generate a value above the core net business assets.

    When adopting this methodology, the values of assets and liabilities are restated to a going concern (or fair market) value.

Taking you back to the process of preparing the report, what happens after you prepare the report?

When I complete a report, I provide it to the instructing party. That could be one party, or in the circumstance where I am appointed as the single expert, both parties receive the report simultaneously.

The Family Law Rules allow the parties 21 days to request further clarification of my report, if required.

If the matter proceeds to Court, both parties have the opportunity to cross-examine me on my report.

In speaking with Judges, they discuss how matters have become more complex. Have you also noticed such changing trends in matters you are involved in?

Yes, I have. The types of matters that I am involved in has not changed; however, I agree that the complexity within those matters has changed.

The structures which have evolved (mainly due to taxation consider-ations over many years) have grown in complexity.

Additionally, director/shareholder loan account issues have become more prevalent. This can involve the dissection of loan accounts, or loan accounts being deemed as dividends due to non-compliance with taxation rules.

Almost everyone I have interviewed has talked about how delay is one of the main issues in our current system. Are there any specific issues with regards to Court delays and reports needing to be updated or becoming out of date?

To provide expert advice in a matter or properly value a business entity, current financial statements are required. It is therefore important that the parties have prepared and provide the expert with current information.

After completing my report, often there is a delay before the matter is dealt with by the Court. Over the course of time, my report may not reflect the actual circumstances at the time of the case. Generally, an update is requested. This requires the parties to keep up-to-date records and financial statements over the period until the Court date so that unnecessary prepara-tion delays are not encountered when compiling the update.

I know this is not your role per se, but just as an observer, are there any tips you would give to litigants involved in a dispute where there is a business involved?

Where there is a business involved I would advise the litigants to:

- Prepare up-to-date financial information
- Provide a commentary which is agreed by the parties on the business performance over the years, and the future prospects of the business
- Where there are areas of disagreement between the parties, these should be detailed
- Provide honest and complete information to the expert so delays will be avoided

- Provide prompt and complete answers to requests for additional information
- Listen to the advice of the legal representative who have been through the process many times and understands what is required

And any words of wisdom for the solicitors?

Clients are involved in the day-to-day managing of their financial affairs, plus dealing with all of the aspects of a Family Law litigation, often for the first time.

The advice that I would give to solicitors is to urge their clients to give prompt attention to the information requests of the expert, even though it no doubt will seem unnecessary and disrupt their normal daily routine. The quicker the complete information is supplied, the quicker the expert report can be finalised.

Additionally, it can assist in certain matters to have the solicitors jointly contact the expert and confer on any areas which are difficult or lengthy to explain in writing.

What are some of the key issues that occur when a couple separate but were previously involved in a family business together? Do you have any observations here?

There are a number of issues that occur when a couple separate and were previously involved in a family business together. Many of these derive from whether both partners stay working in the business or one leaves the business. This can affect the efficiency of the business, staff morale, and the financial independence of one or both of the parties.

Questions arise such as:

- Where one partner leaves the business, how is that partner to be supported after leaving?
- Can the business afford to employ a new employee to carry out the duties?

- How will the partner who left the business ensure that the earnings of the business are not 'adjusted' by the partner who remains in the business?

> I have seen instances where both separated partners remain working within the family business. This can cause tension for the parties and the employees who may relate better to one partner over the other.

It can result in the mixing of personal and professional tensions, resulting in a poor working environment. In these circumstances, my advice is to try and resolve the Family Law matter as soon as possible.

In other cases, I have seen instances where one party leaves the business. However, prior to leaving the business, an agreement is reached regarding additional controls to be employed in the business and a regular reporting requirement of the party who stays in the business. This reporting is made to an independent accountant engaged by the party no longer in the business. Although not foolproof, it does provide a level of comfort over the running of the business until the matter is resolved.

David Bird

Expert real property valuer

A human element

David Bird is the Director and Principal of Kohler Bird Valuers, founded in 1990. For more than 20 years, Kohler Bird was a broad-based valuation practice of up to 12 valuers, with an affiliated office in South East Queensland.

David has worked solely as a property valuer since 1983, covering Sydney and coastal and country NSW, and has gained extensive experience in all areas of real estate valuation, ranging from residential through commercial, industrial, investment, and tourist/entertainment properties. He continues to hold registration as a valuer in Queensland, where his expertise lies in coastal and prestige residential property.

His personal area of specialisation is in litigation and expert witness valuation and this is now the main focus of Kohler Bird Valuers.

David is an Associate of the Australian Property Institute (formerly the Australian Institute of Valuers and Land Economists) and is a Specialist Retail Valuer under the API Listing. David has carried out valuations for litigation purposes for over 30 years and has appeared as an expert witness in the Family Court of Australia, Federal Circuit Court, NSW District Court, Supreme Court, Land and Environment Court, the Consumer, Trader & Tenancy Tribunal, and the NSW Civil & Administrative Tribunal.

In this interview David talks about the nuts and bolts of how property valuations are performed and provides some insights on the problem of Court delays, given the sometimes galloping pace of real estate prices. He also provides practical tips for lawyers and litigants and explores innovative ideas about how we could use property valuations in Family Law differently. David acknowledges that property valuation is an inexact science and that there is a human element in trying to determine the 'intangible appeal' of properties.

⣿

Briefly, please describe what it is you do? In particular, how does your work fit into the overall picture of the Family Law process?

I am a property valuer, and my role in the Family Law process is to provide a full and comprehensive valuation report, which covers all relevant aspects of the subject property, and at its essence asserts a 'current market value' of this property for use in determining the total value of the asset pool.

What is your background professionally? And how did you come to do this Family Law niche work?

I have over 30 years' experience as a property valuer in New South Wales and Queensland. I was initially employed in a mid-size valuation firm in Sydney where, as is typical of most junior valuers, I did mortgage valuation work for banks and other lenders.

I established my own valuation firm in 1990, and whilst overseeing a team of valuers carrying out predominantly short-form mortgage valuation reports, I personally became more and more involved in the Family Law and litigation valuation sphere. This grew to the point where, in 2010, I divested my mortgage valuation practice to a larger, national-based firm, and focussed on the Family Law and litigation valuation.

What kinds of matters would require a report prepared by you?

I prepare reports in matters which require the establishment of the value of real property, which can extend to its rental value, retrospective value at any point in time, the apportion of value attributable to specific actions (for example, renovations or repairs) or any hypothetical scenario relative to a dispute over the property.

What are some of the kinds of matters you have been involved in?

The whole range of real property, such as vacant residential land, cottages, apartments, off-the-plan purchases, commercial/industrial holdings, air space, major rural holdings, primary production properties, open-space zoned land, easements, and the like, to name just a few.

Any thoughts on the challenges in explaining the technical concepts of property valuation to lawyers and Judges?

Yes, this certainly can be the case. In particular, arguments or discussions on the more technical points or means of comparison between two expert valuers can often be difficult to convey to lawyers and Judges.

To overcome this, we can generally try and work through the issues in layman's terms and more simplified approaches. But, in reality, it is often difficult for concepts and analysis we would take as understood to be determined in Court.

How would you describe the nitty-gritty of the process for preparing a real property valuation report in a Family Law matter?

Firstly, initial searches are carried out to establish property details, zoning/planning issues, and the like, and any aspects arising are clarified. With the current available databases, usually a quite clear picture of the property to be valued can be formed at this stage.

Then, initial drafting of a report may well take place and comparable sales or appropriate evidence of value is initially formulated. An arrangement for a full internal inspection of the property is made and carried out, photos taken, and any surrounding issues checked.

Following this, further drafting and refinement of the formal report is undertaken, and analysis and refinement of comparable sales or other evidence takes place, working towards an end value. When the report and valuation are finalised, final overseeing takes place and the report is issued.

What happens after you prepare the report?

The report is typically delivered by email, in PDF format, simultaneously to all the legal representative-instructing parties. If required, an affidavit is usually prepared by one instructing legal party and provided to the valuer for swearing and signing.

What is the range of fees that a registered valuer would charge to prepare an expert report in Family Law litigation?

My fees generally range between $1,500 and $5,000, plus GST, for a full and comprehensive valuation report.

What are some of the common issues with such reports?

Unfortunately, given the expense of the valuation exercise, costs are sometimes cut by instructing less experienced valuers at lower rates. This can often lead to poor-quality reports, as valuers cut corners and are not mindful of the absolutely critical role the valuer plays in determining one of the most significant financial situations of a person's life.

So, the adage 'You get what you pay for' could apply?

Yes. These,

> low-cost reports by less experienced valuers
> can often be challenged and defeated,

in effect adding significant cost and heartache to the process. In my opinion it is always worth paying for experience and reputation.

Valuation is, however, an inexact science, and there is usually no particular correct answer, so the valuation is an attempt to determine a fair and reasonable assessment of what view the market in general would take of a particular property on a given day.

You mentioned that reports can be challenged. What are the ways that an expert's report can be challenged?

From my point of view, queries can be directed back to the expert under the Family Law Rules, or, going further, an adversarial valuation expert can be instructed to critique a report and, if necessary, provide a full adversarial valuation report of their own.

Have you seen changes to the kind of matters you are involved in?

Not in particular, though reports for mediation or as-if-for-litigation are becoming more common, to attempt to solve disputes outside of actual court appearances.

What changes have you noticed in the Sydney property market since you first began work as a registered valuer?

The Sydney property market has become increasingly sophisticated since the early 1980s, and the availability of information in terms of sales evidence and details has been perhaps the most significant aspect.

Property investment has become far more widespread through all ranks of society.

Of course, I have worked through at least three boom-and-bust cycles, the global financial crisis (GFC) when interest rates for borrowings were a high of 15%, and down to current all-time lows around 4%. In simple terms, I have seen values for many typical suburban family homes less than $100,000 to very few now less than $1 million.

In particular, was there an issue with regards to how quickly property prices were rising in Sydney recently?

Sydney is a constrained market in terms of supply, and is the major centre for high-earning employment in Australia.

There is, and will continue to be, a surplus of demand over supply, particularly for residential accommodation within the inner to middle ring suburbs, and thus values will rise.

Other than a complete collapse of the economy, the likes of which we have never seen, values will continue to rise over any medium- to longer-term scenario, whilst still experiencing mini boom–bust situations.

Given this sometimes astonishing rise in prices, does this amplify the issue with reports becoming outdated, given Court delays?

The market, over time, does, of course, give rise to issues with valuations being outdated.

A very general rule of thumb says:

valuations are probably reliable for, say, three months,

however, in the heat of a boom, even this can be questioned.

I find myself in many cases updating valuations over the course of one to two years and beyond, creating significant extra burden in costs to the parties.

Delay is an issue certainly. What is working well with how reports such as yours are prepared and used in the Family Law system?

Full reports appear generally well considered and provide an understanding of how the valuation is arrived at. Any issues should be flagged and can be queried. As alluded to, valuation is not an exact science, and we are trying to provide an insight on how the market in general would treat any property.

However, as is common knowledge and well reported each week, auctions and sales are reliant upon a human element which is almost always difficult to particularly define. As valuers, we are trying to determine the intangible appeal of a property and make a judgement call by referring to similar, however never identical, pieces of evidence.

Are there any changes you think could or should be made with regards to how reports are commissioned or used?

I think generally the system is reasonable; however, maybe there could be a mechanism for the parties to provide written submissions to the valuer – as laymen, not as property professionals – with full disclosure of any issues they believe relevant to the valuation of the property.

Homeowners in general usually have an extensive knowledge on their own property and neighbourhood, which can assist in the valuation process. A valuer, as a professional, will readily be able to identify relevant information as opposed to that with particular bias or of a less useful nature.

Are there any other reforms that you believe should be implemented to the Family Law system?

One reform which could possibly be explored is whereby the formal valuation report process is reduced to having the valuer provide an initial opinion, working from a desktop or database situation, with regards to a property.

It may well form an initial base for negotiations, mediation, or other alternative dispute resolution, and if both parties can find some common ground in this opinion, there is the potential for a significant reduction in valuation costs.

The valuer involved would have to have a proven track record and experience in Family Law litigation, and perhaps be sanctioned or recognised by the Court as being able to provide this very specific and skilled service. The Court may only recognise a handful of such long-term and highly experienced valuers as having the necessary qualifications and skills to carry out such a task.

Following on from this, I also believe there may also be a place for such a valuer in the Court or mediation room, at a preliminary stage. At this stage the valuation issues of some or a whole portfolio of properties could be worked through to give a baseline of an overall value, prior to the expensive work of individual inspections and formal reports being carried out.

Given the amount of database information, sales details and the like able to be called upon by a suitably skilled and experienced valuer from a computer desktop, and adding to this their local or property knowledge gained from years in the field, I consider there is a real opportunity to provide valuation information within the day, for example in a Court or mediation room. The process could be transparent and in front of all parties, who could also have continued input, rather than weeks and months, with the associated considerable expense.

What tips would you give to litigants involved in a dispute where there is real property?

My initial tip would be to try and reach some agreement on value between themselves.

Guidance from local, reputable real estate agents is becoming more and more professional, particularly if the reasons for it are set out up front and clearly, without the hidden agendas of a low/high appraisal.

Agents are increasingly professional and regulated, and are being made more aware of their professional responsibilities, so this is becoming a better path than in years past.

As valuers, we are simply trying to determine the market's view of a particular property; there is no secret formula or approach. We are doing the same as buyers out there in the market, interpreting the advantages and disadvantages of any given property.

Look at your property objectively, through the eyes of the general market in a typical selling period. Try to exclude your personal bias, thinking along the lines of 'What could be if I renovate/repair?' etc. We are valuing exactly 'as is', as we see it on the inspection day.

If a reasonable value range can be considered by both parties, there is at least a starting point for negotiations.

If a formal valuation is required, there are at least hopefully some realistic expectations.

Present the property to a good and neat standard on inspection day, and allow the valuer time and access to fully and properly inspect all areas. We are, however, not building inspectors, surveyors, or structural engineers; we are viewing and making judgements as property professionals.

Are there any things couples buying property should be mindful of, in case, say, they were to separate in the future?

It is difficult to offer any reasonable advice here, as who plans for a separation!

My only thoughts might be along the lines of clearly documenting monetary and time/labour contributions if renovations/repairs are being undertaken.

If a property is already owned and brought into the relationship, it may worth consider documenting value, or at least condition, at this point.

The relative advantages in Joint Tenants versus Tenants in Common may well be worth discussing.

Also, family loans or contributions should be clearly and unequivocally documented and, if necessary, registered on title as a mortgage or the like.

Any words of wisdom for the solicitors?

I find, in general, the experienced Family Law solicitor provides a very professional and knowledgeable approach to instructing valuers. Those with less experience in what is a very specific field would do well to be guided by their experienced peers. However, generally, I strike few significant issues.

I would strongly recommend against looking for cheaper or low-cost alternatives. Valuation in this sphere remains a matter of getting what you pay for.

> Instructions to valuers should be relatively simple, though do disclose issues or contentions up front. It is better we be told rather than having to search or, in fact, not discover matters.

Valuation is a significantly involved process when producing a full report for Family Law litigation, with numerous searches and matters to be investigated. The more time to prepare and schedule our work, the better. Also, the more informed they can make their clients about the process, the better.

Tristan Oddi

Real estate agent

Fully informed

Tristan Oddi is a fully licensed real estate agent with over 10 years of experience. He specialises in the sale of residential real estate in the eastern suburbs of Sydney. He works for the leading agency in Australia, Phillips Pantzer Donnelley. On an annual basis they transact over $1 billion worth of real estate and also handle a large rent roll.

Tristan focuses on the Kensington/Randwick area and has a vast and large knowledge of the local area and the community. He has personally transacted over 100 homes in his career.

In the preceding interview, court expert and registered property valuer David Bird raised the fact that, increasingly, parties can rely on market appraisals by real estate agents in Family Law matters for the purposes of negotiation. Following on from this, in this interview I discuss with Tristan the process for preparing market appraisals in Family Law matters and also ask about some of the challenges of acting for a separating couple.

⠿

When do people involved in the Family Law process require assistance from real estate agents?

I have been asked on a few occasions to facilitate a sale for people getting divorced. For me, it's the same as any other family looking to sell – some may require more attention or more updates, but in essence it is the same process, with the same goal.

What are the kinds of issues that arise when a couple separating have to sell the family home? How do you address these?

The most common issue is disagreeing on price and sale process. This can be handled by sitting down with both parties, separately or together, and explaining the best way to go about getting them the best result and helping them move on with their lives.

Are there issues with both parties perceiving an agent as neutral when there is a sale during separation? How do you manage these?

Yes, this is usually the case, and can sometimes be the case in a normal sale. The best way to manage these is constant reporting and face-to-face meetings so that both parties are fully informed at all times.

In my experience, clients in the Family Law process often seek out the assistance of real estate agents to prepare market appraisals of properties. Please explain how real estate agents prepare such market appraisals.

Most clients usually get between three and five appraisals and then make a decision on an agent. The preparation for the market appraisal usually takes around 20 to 30 minutes, and then we present the information to the client.

What is the usual cost?

There is no cost to the client for the initial appraisal. If, though, they then select you, the usual fees apply, i.e., marketing cost and commission.

Another issue in Family Law matters is that often clients do not have access to the property, as their former spouse is residing there. Is it still possible to prepare a 'drive-by' appraisal?

Yes, I have had this many times. We can usually conduct a drive-by appraisal, but we also request photos and/or a floor plan from the owners, if they have them.

If the property is a stock standard home, then it's usually fine. If it has something unique about it, such as a unique waterfront, then we always request an inspection before appraising it.

Charlie Viola

Wealth management adviser

Emotions have ruled reality

Charlie is a partner of Pitcher Partners Sydney, the head of its Wealth Management, and an executive board member. Charlie was named as number one on Barron's list of the Top 50 Financial Advisers in Australia. He has over 20 years of advisory service experience and specialises in attending to the needs of high net worth individuals.

He personally manages about $1 billion of client assets under advice and administration. He sees himself as the genuine 'trusted adviser' across a client's whole situation.

His clients range from wealthy families, self-funded retirees and pre-retirees, and listed company executives. He has a wealth of knowledge in investment management, structuring, employee shares schemes, superannuation, and the overall planning space for these groups of people.

While not a core area of business, he has good experience in dealing with families going through separation, and has become highly experienced in helping couples work through how to split their assets in a practical and feasible manner, ensuring longer-term goals are met.

Assisting in valuations, asset splits, structuring advice, and future cash flow planning and goal setting, Charlie ensures he can both educate and assist all clients who are going through a property settlement.

In this interview Charlie discusses the importance of thinking methodically and strategically to avoid the common post separation pitfall he has seen: when 'emotions have ruled reality'. In particular, Charlie urges clients to understand the application of a Family Law settlement in practice. That is, what is it you will actually receive as a result of the division of assets? What is the mix of assets you will receive, and also the tax consequences of any division of property? Charlie also enlightens us about why superannuation may be an untapped gem in terms of tax effectiveness and how it could be lot more important than you realise.

What role do you play when clients have decided to separate, and how do you assist them?

Given it tends to be a very emotive time, for both sides, in the early stages, the best thing we can be is the genuine trusted adviser. Best as we can, we do it for both sides and as independently as possible. In most occasions, we continue to do work for both parties after the finalisation of the split.

As we generally have full knowledge of the financial affairs of the couple – that is, we know what the assets are, who owns them, why they bought them – we are in a good position to help them understand what their financial life will look like after any asset split, and in the context of their situation, who is best to get what asset, or what assets should be sold.

> The most important thing that we do is
> have them re-assess their financial goals.

For lots of people, their financial goals were wound together as a couple, and some of those goals were just assumed.

For slightly younger people, we make sure they are across all the real expenses they have, especially school fees, mortgages, etc., ensuring that whatever goals they had are either still achievable or, if not, how would they replace it.

The older they get, the more it becomes about what they will do with their spare time in retirement.

Previously, the blind goal may have been that they expected to retire and travel together, so we ask them to reassess those goals post separation.

Not to labour the point, but it's about context. It's about trying to ensure they are genuinely planning ahead as they consider what life holds and what they will need to do to finance it.

Our role, in the main, is to counsel them through the situation and end up in a position where they can articulate their actual goals, so they can make the best of a bad situation and, importantly, educate them as to what they have and what it means for their future.

Do you often see lots of anxiety about the financial side of things?

The financial discussion is very often filled with angst and anxiety, which is mainly driven by one of two emotions, either:

I just don't know how I will survive... or *I worked so hard and I am now 20 years behind again...*

We try and put a lid on this by working through what they actually mean, and building it back up into a set of goals, and try and put some real numbers beside these.

We look at how best to take the settlement – that is, is it super, cash, or the family home, etc. – and how to ensure it's fair and tax effective, but, above all, aligned with their overall goals.

What are the financial pieces to consider when going through a property settlement?

There is a heap of considerations, in reality: superannuation, tax and capital gains tax, valuations of assets, what structures (like companies and trusts) are already in place, stamp duty, land tax – the list goes on.

And then, so they can meet the new goals they have now set, how should it look in the future, and therefore how should they take the assets.

Sometimes, especially when we take the client on who is going through the separation process, our job is to educate the spouse who has been less involved in the family's financial affairs as to what it all looks like and how it all works.

We have found, over the years, in lots of cases they own assets in their own name they weren't overly aware of, were beneficiaries of trusts they didn't understand, or were party to debts they didn't know existed.

The issue is heightened where lots of the family wealth is tied up in a family business.

So, how do you do that? How do you educate the spouse who has been less involved in the family's financial affairs?

Giving them some comfort on how it all works, how much money is actually there, and drawing them up a simple balance sheet and structure diagram of the family wealth, and how it all interrelates – this often removes a fair bit of anxiety.

The overlay of that is the tax planning considerations and the access to capital. It becomes an education process, ensuring that anything they end up agreeing to is fair and in their best interests.

People need to understand what assets they are agreeing to hold, and how accessible those assets are and what level of revenue those assets might actually produce. They also need to be aware of how any two assets might be compared in terms of tax outcomes and risk.

Splitting an asset 50/50 with someone, like a share portfolio isn't often fair, especially where those shares have differing cost bases. Work has to be done so that the net or after-tax outcome is equitable, not the pre-tax number. Understanding the tax position becomes important, as Family Court asset splits often have their own rules which need to be played out.

The same issue exists for stamp duty and stamp duty exemptions on the changing of property ownership as a result of Family Court asset split.

What people need to understand, though, is that some of these protections offered by the Family Law Court in an effort to provide fairness don't extend to other entities (like trusts, companies, or superannuation), so understanding the real impact is important.

There have been times where emotions have ruled reality. There's no point in seeking to take all the settlement as the expensive family home and then have no way to pay the costs of upkeep, or, as sometimes happens, take the home and a good portion of debt, often as a means of not disturbing where children live, but have no means of repayment.

Once a settlement has been reached, it is important to consider how far those assets will stretch, and how they should structure them to get the most from them. It's important to work through the options available and ensure that despite reducing the asset base as a result of separation, they are structured efficiently and working towards their main goals.

What about superannuation?

The biggest issue, outside of the family home, is often superannuation. Superannuation is the most tax-effective and advantageous structure we have, but it comes with more complex rules around access.

Often, people will overlook super in favour of other assets because it hasn't been front of mind, but, especially for older people, the difficulty in getting money into that environment often means taking more of the super, as on an after-tax-weighted basis, they will be better off financially.

> The older the client, generally,
> the more we want them to have in super,

... or to consider a super split. Everybody, of course, needs their own specific advice on this, as it becomes complex, depending upon age, investment balance, and the type of super fund used.

In your experience, what traps do clients fall into, post separation?

What you work out quickly is that while money wasn't generally the reason for the separation, it sometimes becomes the weapon to attack the other party with, following separation. It becomes the basis on which parties try and 'win' over each other.

My experience of people going through this is that they do become very myopic; they can't see past the trauma that they are experiencing.

Our advice is to, as much as possible, in terms of financials, anyway, try and look past it and see the context of what two, three, five years ahead might look like.

I made the point about the family home earlier, and it's an important issue. People often overlook the costs associated with the upkeep of big houses, and if a good percentage of any settlement is taken up by the award of the full ownership of the family home, then it's important that the spouse who has taken that property on has the financial means to support it.

Equally, no great point in being 42, and being awarded all of the super assets in lieu of other assets, expecting to be able to access them now, as access won't come until at least age 60 in the vast majority of cases.

Looking forward and doing cash flow planning for the next few years is very important in my view, and we seek to do that for everyone so they can see what the future might hold.

I think the biggest trap, though, is not getting advice, so they can really understand the impact of decisions from a financial perspective, to ensure that their own goals can be met.

You have touched on superannuation a few times. Tell me about the specific considerations people need address for superannuation.

The main considerations are, firstly, access to the capital. Moneys in super-annuation are preserved until you reach the prescribed age. Generally, for anyone born after July 1964, this is age 60. To then gain access to the money, whether in pension form or lump sum, they would need to cease a role they were gainfully employed in.

This becomes a real consideration for how much younger people take in super, and will, of course, be dependant upon their overall situation.

Secondly, contribution restrictions – there is a finite amount that can be contributed to superannuation over someone's lifetime. Given that super is the most tax effective of all arrangements, as people get older we generally like to see a bigger bulk of their wealth in super.

If someone elects to split away a majority of their super to enable them to keep other assets, then they need to be mindful of the restrictions and limitations of getting money back into the superannuation environment. Too often people think they will just sell other assets later on and stick the whole lot in super. At present, people are restricted to making personal after tax contributions to super of $100,000 per annum (a person under age 65 can pre-pay the following 2 years as well, meaning at one time they could put a maximum of $300,000). If they are over 65, they are both limited to the $100,000 per annum limit, but they would need to meet a work test for moneys to go in.

Thirdly, tax benefits – people often overlook super, but they need to realise it's the most tax-effective environment we have available in Australia.

When in the accumulation phase, earnings are only taxed at 15%, and capital gains 10% where an asset has been held for more than 12 months. When in pension phase, earnings and capital gains are tax free.

> Assets in super have the potential to be of greater value than assets outside of super because of the tax benefits.

And lastly, updating beneficiary details and insurances. Reviewing your super after a split is finalised is also very important. Most super funds these days have insurance policies and beneficiary nominations attached. It's important to review those to ensure that if you do pass away, you haven't bound the trustee to pay assets to your former spouse.

Again though, we would urge everyone to get specific advice on how it impacts them, their position, and their goals.

You mentioned tax issues previously very briefly. What specific tax issues need to be thought about in terms of a Family Law settlement?

I think the main considerations need to be capital gains tax (CGT) and the real value of an asset.

When someone takes on an asset as a result of a Family Law split, they in effect 'inherit' or take on the cost base of that asset. They need to be mindful of the real value of that asset on an after-tax basis.

Using a really simple example, let's say a couple splits, and the husband takes a $1million share portfolio, which has a cost base of $400,000 (what it originally cost to buy). Meanwhile, the wife takes an investment property worth $1 million, which has a cost base of $600,000.

If either were seeking to sell these, they would end up with differing outcomes. The property is potentially worth more, as less CGT would be payable.

Should there be consideration for different types of assets?

Yes. Notwithstanding the structuring discussion about whether assets are in super or out of super, people need to consider what type of asset they agree to take on. While cash is simple enough, others may have some idiosyncrasies that need to be considered. Using my earlier example, where the husband takes the shares and the wife the investment property, they need to consider:

- Costs of holding and maintaining the asset – a property is more expensive to hold than shares
- Income the asset will produce – generally, shares will generate a better cash flow than a property
- Liquidity – shares are easier to cash in, and can be done so in part, unlike a property which is expensive to sell and it takes a good period of time to realise the actual cash.

People need to ensure that from a Family Law property settlement they get a fair mix of assets, or at least assets that are in line with what they are trying to personally achieve.

How is the transfer of property dealt with in the case of a Family Law settlement?

As I noted before, for an investment, the main one is that the cost base of the asset is carried across and the new owner takes it on. There is no tax to pay at the point of settlement; it simply remains deferred until a real sale event occurs.

This is only the case when assets pass directly between those splitting. The rules are different if assets are held by super, a trust, or company.

In terms of actual real property, such as the family home or an investment property, the transfer occurs without stamp duty. Where the property has to go from being in joint names to one name, or one name to the other as a result of the orders, an event that would usually incur stamp duty, it is exempt.

Mark Lipson

Specialist forensic accountant, expert business valuer

The numbers don't tell the whole story

Mark Lipson is a director of Forensic Accounting at Hall Chadwick Forensics, a division of Hall Chadwick Chartered Accountants. He is a Fellow of the Chartered Accountants in Australia and New Zealand (CAANZ) with over 25 years of forensic experience.

Mark provides forensic accounting services in Family Law matters involving forensic valuations of businesses, companies, and trust structures as well as shares, units, and other equity instruments as a single expert and as an adversarial expert. The work undertaken by Hall Chadwick Forensics also includes complex family-law forensic investigations to trace the movement of family assets prior to the breakdown of marriages and relationships.

Mark appears as an expert witness in the Family Court in Australia (Victoria and Tasmania) as well as the Federal Circuit Court regarding both Family Law valuation opinions and his findings in forensic investigations. Alongside his experience in forensic accounting for Family Law matters, he also receives instructions regarding a large range of commercial disputes that require expert forensic evidence.

Apart from his forensic expertise, Mr Lipson has recently completed a 10-year appointment as a Lay Member of the Victorian Civil and Administrative Tribunal (VCAT) in the legal practice list. This appointment provided an opportunity for him to sit with both County Court and Supreme Court Judges to hear and assess written and oral evidence and determine matters before the Tribunal.

In this interview Mark talks about the difference between a single expert and an adversarial expert, and how he approaches both engagements in much the same way. He also cautions against cheaper inexperienced accountant reports and talks on the issue of hidden money and tax fraud. Lastly, one of Mark's most interesting insights is the emphasis he places on face-to-face interviews and having a visceral feel for the business premises, and his view that the 'numbers don't tell the whole story' in business valuations.

⋮⋮⋮⋮

What is it you do and how does that fit into the picture of Family Law?

With regards to Family Law, what I do is act primarily as a single expert, either appointed by consent by the applicant and respondent or directly by the Court.

The purpose of the engagement is to value a business and/or an interest in the business if that business isn't wholly owned by the wife or husband.

I also take on engagements as an adversarial expert where manifest errors have been identified in the single experts report.

How is your role different when you are an adversarial expert?

Well, in my view, there's no difference. Whether I am a single or adversarial expert, I approach the engagement with an independent, objective mind with an overarching duty to the Court. It makes no difference to me. Fortunately, referring solicitors who instruct us know that.

I think that's a good point because the word 'adversarial', when referring to an adversarial expert, could suggest you're on the side of one party, but

what you're saying is that you have a duty to the Court and have to approach it objectively.

Yes, objectively and independently. I make that very clear in my engagement letter, that I will only prepare forensic valuation reports consistent with the Family Court Rules and APES 215 & APES 225, which are the accounting professional standards relating to forensic accounting and valuations. I also state in my engagement letter that I have a primary obligation and duty to the court.

What is the difference between a forensic accountant versus a normal accountant?

I think the most important difference is a forensic accountant, who has had a number of years' experience, has a better understanding of the litigation process.

An accountant who has little or no experience in forensic matters, that has come from an audit or business services background is more likely to be an advocate for the party that's instructing them. I clearly state that I will express an independent and objective view as to the value of a business.

What is your background with regards to work in Family Law?

I have been preparing valuations in family law for over 25 years, and have completed between 2000 to 3000 Family Law valuations. I have appeared in the Victorian and Tasmanian registries for the Family and Federal Circuit Court.

My background was as an educator. I taught accounting and economics at TAFE and university. I spent nine years as an academic and educator, and those skills of communicating to reduce complex concepts to simple elements stem from that background.

I left education in 1987 and joined the accounting profession, and in about two to three years I began preparing reports for family law matters. I am now the director of the Forensic Accounting practice at Hall Chadwick Melbourne I have five full-time chartered accountants working with me. All of them have been trained and have been involved in a number of family law and commercial law matters. With every engagement, I have direct supervision over all of their analysis and reports.

You and your team have a lot of experience and are used to preparing reports in the Family Law setting. Have you seen other people prepare such reports who don't have that expertise? And what issues can occur when people are trying to skimp and save here? What are the problems that can arise?

I have reviewed a number of valuation reports in the Family Law framework from accountants who would not be considered forensic but are, instead, tax accountants or family accountants for their clients. Their opinions suffer from a range of issues.

Most of the reports don't comply with the rules of the Court in regards to expert evidence, so they are prepared in a manner which may not be admissible.

A further problem is the language used isn't neutral. Emotive language can identify the accountant as being an advocate for their client. The result is that upon reading the report, it is clear to the Judge that this report is directed towards supporting the client and not providing the Court with an unbiased, objective opinion on value.

So, there are some traps that one can fall into. In your opinion, is it worth paying for a forensic accountant with years of litigation experience to prepare a report?

Absolutely, because once a report is prepared by an inexperienced accountant, there is a strong possibility that it may be subject to an adversarial response and this adds to the cost for the parties.

The property settlement inevitably is delayed, either for a final hearing or mediation.

When do you come into the process?

There's no set time or stage in the litigation. I have been instructed prior to a matter being filed in Court and I have been literally rung up by barristers who have said, 'I'm in Court. Can you take on a valuation?' It could come at any time.

What I say to anyone who asks, though, is that I will always undertake an engagement using the processes and methodology, and not take any shortcuts simply because the matter's already in Court.

What are the methodologies that you use?

On the facts, I determine what valuation methodology is appropriate initially. Throughout the analytical processes (and keeping an open mind), I may change the methodology, because one methodology may become inappropriate based on the facts.

What are some of the main methodologies you might use?

If it's a business that is a going concern, I initially look to value that business on an earnings basis. There are a number of variants on an earning methodology that I could adopt. I use an EBIT (earnings before interest and taxes) definition of earnings or an EBITDA (earnings before interest tax depreciation and amortisation) depending on the facts. Under some circumstance, I will adopt a discounted cash flow basis, again depending on the nature of the business that is being valued.

If the business is running at a loss, or if there is considerable likelihood that there is no going concern for this business, or if the business makes a bare profit, a small profit, or a thin profit, then I would probably look towards an asset-based valuation.

The last thing that I would use – and I would only use it if it is appropriate as a secondary valuation to support our primary valuation – is the rule of thumb. Certain industries have certain rules of thumb. I don't adopt that valuation method as the primary valuation method, but I will look at them in order to support the orthodox approach using one of the earning valuations methodologies.

Is there any issue with – and I am making a comparison with real property valuations – how although you can say a business is worth x value, ulti-

mately the value is what someone is willing to pay for it, while usually if the business is being valued, this means it isn't going to be sold, so that actual real life valuation can't be realised. I mean, is it a bit of an art as well as a science?

It is a mixture of art and science. The science relates to the objective facts and analysis. The art refers to the valuer's experience relied upon when determining a valuation opinion from the facts and the analysis undertaken.

I should point out that:

> there is a difference between value and price.

Price is determined by the bargaining process between the buyer and seller, where they agree on a particular price to transfer an asset. But in circumstances where that is not going to occur, I have to determine the value using a market-based assessment of that business as if there is a hypothetical buyer and seller who are prepared, but not anxious, to enter into negotiations for that business.

I suppose this is also when it is important to have those years of experience, to have a real feel for what something would sell for.

I think it is absolutely critical. The Courts expect an expert witness, who is a forensic accountant, to bring to the matter that level of experience and expertise.

Often, I have had situations where one party has been less involved in the business and may be anxious that there is hidden money, or the books have been 'dodgied up' and that there is a lack of integrity with regards to the records records of the business. Is a good forensic accountant pretty quickly able to sort that out?

Over the years that I have been undertaking Family Law forensic investigations, I have, on occasions, come across matters where money has not been properly disclosed, either in the financial statements or to the ATO. In cases where I have been instructed to investigate these allegations, I undertake a process to determine if these allegations can be made. These engagements are complex and difficult. What I say to clients is that I will undertake various processes to trace money through a range of bank accounts held by a number of entities over a defined time range. This type of forensic investigation can be extremely costly. In all these types of investigations my objective is to give the referring party certainty as to whether those allegations can be made. That is the ultimate objective I should have as a forensic accountant; to state that, on the analysis of the facts, I can't find evidence of that allegation, or I can find evidence of that allegation and quantify it.

So, basically, you have to follow the money trail. I imagine that would be very complex.

Correct - that is what my experience has led me to do. By using various processes and systems to undertake an analysis, I am able determine if there is any basis to the allegation of the hidden money.

So, that is the other part of your work - investigations, in addition to valuations?

Oh, very much so. I look to identify if there are, not just hidden monies, but hidden assets and whether assets have been transferred as a result of the family law action or if there has been an underreporting of income and profits, not necessarily for family law purposes but to defeat the taxation office.

That leads me to something else. As you are aware, the Court has cross referral powers which means they can refer parties to the ATO. Just anecdotally, have you been involved in matters where that has happened?

I have seen it happen, and I have been involved in those particular cases.

What happens is that I identify that there has been a fraud against the Commonwealth. Normally, I pick that up quickly and early in our processes. I ask a whole series of questions of both parties around my findings, prior to preparing the report. The parties quickly become aware that there is a risk that the Court proceedings may be derailed, as the Judge may refer the matter on to the ATO or the DPP.

I suppose the lesson there is to be squeaky clean.

Well, you should always be squeaky clean.

Of course. Sometimes a Family Law matter brings to the surface behaviour that is noncompliant with the *Income Tax Assessment Act*. That might not have come to light had the parties not separated, is what I mean.

That's correct. What you tend to find is the spouse that doesn't control the business makes the allegation. As a consequence, if the allegation is made, because my primary duty is to the Court, I certainly have to investigate it.

In some matters you also have a matter where both spouses are very heavily involved together in a business which can become very messy upon separation. Any thoughts?

I don't give any strategic advice on how they can move forward. I strictly limit myself to valuation services or investigative services.

Well, if I can phrase it this way: What are the different ways you have seen parties cope with this situation?

Well, commenting only as an observer, I have noticed the non-business-controlling spouse is often made aware, by their solicitor, to keep the business going because it is the primary source of income that will provide ongoing support for the children.

You mentioned that fees for a forensic accountant are expensive. What is the range of fees you might charge for a valuation?

I approach every valuation on the basis that I don't cut corners. I don't accept an engagement for a discounted price – I don't believe a discount approach is in the best interests of the Court or the parties. I charge on an hourly basis and prepare a fee estimate prior to being engaged. I put that fee estimate in writing and wait for the parties to approve this, and then I move to an engagement letter.

I have been in matters where it was a fairly simple process and the fees were $8,000 to $15,000. But, I have been in very complex matter with interconnected equity holding of very large groups of companies in trusts where the fee has been in excess of $350,000.

There's no standard fee. It depends on the circumstances and structure of the business.

You would be aware the Attorney-General has commissioned a review of the Family Law system.

Over the last 25 years, what I have observed is that forensic accountants have moved away from being advocates. I think the single-expert regime has made it easier for forensic accountants to be independent and objective in the way they approach their engagement and conduct themselves.

I have observed an enormous improvement over those 25 years.

Today, in Victoria, the experienced forensic accountants I deal with in joint conferences of experts to produce joint reports, have worked independently in accordance with the Family Court Rules. Whereas, if I went back prior to the single expert rules, business valuers tended to prepare valuation reports that were inclined to support the views of the party that was paying their fee.

I think there has been a vast improvement in how forensic accountants are much more aware of what their primary duty is to the Court.

However, I think we will always get those inexperienced accountants who act in their client's interests, rather than the Court's interests. In my view, the professional dedicated forensic accountants that I know, take their primary duty to the Court very seriously.

Have you noticed any changes in how matters are run in the many years you have been working in the courts?

In the Melbourne registry, I have observed that instructing solicitors look towards settling property matters in mediation or a conciliation conference prior to final hearing.

When I first started providing forensic accounting services, solicitors were more inclined for the matter to go to a final hearing. Today, nearly every solicitor I deal with in Melbourne, would certainly and respectfully look towards mediating a settlement rather than taking the matter to a final hearing.

Are there issues with delays in the Melbourne registry and, if so, do these create issues with experts' reports, for example, frequent updates?

There are delays. But I don't fully understand the causes for them. Consequently, I can prepare valuation reports or investigative reports for the Court and the matter isn't heard for 12 months or longer, and I often have to prepare an updated a report.

What is involved in preparing an updated report?

For the inexperienced accountant, the trap they fall into is to simply add to their existing analysis and calculation an additional 12 months of data. I don't do that. What I do is I analyse the additional data for any changes in trends that may require any further investigations. That is an essential element to the update process of any valuation.

Inexperienced solicitors also often fall into that trap and they say, 'Oh, it's just putting in another financial year'. But if you analyse that data in relation to where that business was trending, you might find that there are issues that have arisen in the last 12 months that require independent and objective analysis in order to update the report for the Court.

Once you prepare the report, that isn't the end of your work. If the matter goes to trial, you will be cross-examined.

If I am appointed as a single expert and the matter goes to trial, both sides may accept the valuation. But, where the report is not accepted by one or both sides and the matter goes to final hearing for a Judge to determine, yes, I am ready to go and be cross-examined.

In terms of cross-examination are you willing to change your opinion if new evidence comes to light?

Yes. This is where your primary duty to the Court comes to the fore. And it has happened to me that in the process of cross-examination, additional financial material has been presented to me that wasn't disclosed at the time of preparing the report. I have been asked, 'now that I'm aware of this new information, does this affect my valuation opinion?' I am duty-bound to look at that information, and if it has an effect on my opinion, then I should express to the Court that the additional material may have an impact on my opinion.

I know, anecdotally, some clients have felt the expert was unreasonable in not willing to move on their opinion in the face of new evidence. I mean, there is more than one consideration when deciding which expert to engage: there is the report, and the quality of their report, and also what their approach is when they are cross-examined.

For every engagement I take on, whether Family Law or commercial litigation, I automatically assume I will be cross-examined. That is how I approach every new engagement.

I stress to my experienced forensic accountants who assist me that it is not my fight. As a consequence, if it's not my fight and if I am provided with alternative information that is robust and factually correct and affects my valuation opinion, I am duty bound by the rules of the Court to alter my opinion.

What is the point of difference with Hall Chadwick versus other accounting firms?

When I conduct a valuation, I always go out and interview the business controller and their accountant, and I always go onsite to see the business.

A lot of experienced forensic accountants will also go on site to interview and view the business. However, there are also a lot of forensic accountants who are chained to the desk; they do phone interviews only. They don't go out and see the business. They don't walk around and see the offices, or warehouse, or manufacturing process, and that has an enormous difference in terms how you perceive that business as far as a valuation is concerned.

So, you think seeing and meeting with the parties involved and seeing the premises can make a difference to valuation?

Yes. It can either support the opinion or question the opinion you're starting to develop.

It's interesting, because normally these interviews go for several hours, depending on the complexity of the business. Often, when you sit in front of the business controller and you're asking set questions that you've generated from your analysis and you talk to them, they become quite candid after 10 minutes. It's very difficult for people to maintain an attitude of minimal disclosure after about 10 minutes, because they are quite proud of their business and they have an audience, so they want to talk about their business.

What I find is, it generates a whole series of new questions in relation to what the business is doing and what it will be doing in the future. These questions and answers may have an effect on how I perceive the business for valuation purposes.

Do you record these interviews?

No, I don't, for one simple reason: When I interview the husband or wife who controls the business, and/or their accountant or financial controller, I want a free flow of information. When you put a tape recorder in front of someone, it creates an inhibition to that free flow of information or exchange.

I always conduct the interviews with one of my forensic accountants, who takes notes. I record it in written form and when we get back to the office, the first thing I do is write a detailed file note as to the information and the answers to not only our set questions, but the answers that have been generated by that free flow of information.

That sounds quite significant, and I must say, most forensic accountants don't do face-to-face interviews.

Well, I am fortunate that my practice tends to value substantial businesses. I started off valuing smaller businesses (because you have to start somewhere). I still value those businesses, I might add, and we still go out and talk to them, face to face.

But when valuing a business that could be worth $100 million or more, you can't do it at a desk. You've got to go out there. You have to talk to the financial controller. You have to talk to the managing director, be it the husband or the wife. You have to talk to the key staff and you have got to walk around. You've got to look at the conditions of the place of business. How tidy it is? Are there are appropriate systems and processes in place? As you're walking around, you're asking the business controller, 'What does this person do? What does this department do?' And so on.

> When you visit the premises in person, you get a strong feel and a visual understanding of how the business operates, and I think that's absolutely critical. Because the numbers don't tell the whole story.

Individuals
who have
navigated the
Family Law system

*Please note that individual's names and other identifying features have been changed

Simone

I never had that

On being a child with parents who are going through bitter
litigation about parenting

Simone was only five when her parents first separated. She recalls being
initially relieved when they separated, as she thought this meant an end
to witnessing her parents fighting. Little did she know the 'mind games'
were just about to begin.

In her own words, Simone has 'met with every single person and
expert in the Family Law process and gone to every single facility on this
earth'. For Simone, she felt this was overexposure, and she still continues
to resent this.

What struck me personally as I listened to her story was the sense
of grief, of having had a childhood essentially stolen from her. Simone,
herself, says she 'missed out on the chance of a better childhood'. The last
thing Simone said to me, when talking about how she now supports her
friends if their parents divorce, was 'I never had that.' To me, those last
words sum up hers as a story of grief, loss, and lack. She never had a proper
childhood, because, as the oldest child, she had to parent her younger
siblings and also was cast in a role of monitoring her father's drinking,
pursuant to Court orders. She lost the possibility of a close relationship
with her father and sister She missed out on a happy Christmas due to
changeover in the middle of the day, and lost hours of precious playtime
with friends that would have allowed her to feel more 'normal' in order to
speak to countless experts in the Family Law system. Lost innocence, lost
time, lost relationships. And all of these so very present in their absence.

Her's is both a real story and a parable to parents to remember that a tower of pain in childhood can cast a long shadow into adult life, when there are often frantic and misguided attempts to try and fill this void formed in childhood. For example, Simone talks about her sister's attempts at being 'self-medicated with various concoctions of whatever's making [her] feel good that week, whether that be sex, drugs or alcohol'. When we talk about parenting and how to best support children through a separation, it is not just about what kind of childhood our children are having, but what kind of adulthood we are setting them up for.

⁚⁚⁚⁚⁚

Thanks for doing this interview. Just to start, can you please give me some background on your family?

I am the eldest of three children, all aged about 18 months apart. I was about five when I first began to notice Mum and Dad fighting, and they separated not long after.

Since the divorce, I have gained a stepmother (whom my father has since divorced, yet I remained close to until recently – despite his best intentions) and just recently a stepfather which brought along various new siblings. However, my stepfather's children are twice my age and have their own children, so I will still be subject to the duties of being the oldest of my siblings, which from about five meant parenting my younger sister and brother.

Do you have many memories of your parents together before they separated?

They are limited, as I was quite young when they were driven to separation. The majority of the time Mum and Dad didn't fight as intensely until after putting the kids to bed; however, while my siblings slept, not knowing the hostility of the situation, I would be sitting at the top of the stairs looking down into the living room on my parents screaming and yelling. Watching them interact as they did, it was difficult, if not impossible, to believe they ever loved each other. They drove each other crazy, which was only emphasised when alcohol became involved. At five years old, I could see how toxic it was, so I wondered why weren't they doing anything about it.

Do you remember your parents telling you they had separated?

I don't remember how Mum and Dad originally told us they were separating, but I'd figured it out for myself before it had happened. I don't think I ever had a formal introduction to the legal process, but as it went along, I put two and two together and figured most of it out for myself. As we got older, Mum became a family lawyer, so I was relatively exposed to all the processes from observing her work.

Strangely, I had no concerns or fears at the start of the separation. It sounds sad, but,

> I was actually happy when my parents separated, because I thought that meant the fighting would end.

Funnily, most people my age whose parents are now separating can barely cope with it, but I was elated.

> Little did I know things would just get worse – everything became a mind game once they separated.

How did the separation affect you?

The entire separation, both between Mum and Dad and Dad and Step Mum, was hostile and my entire childhood felt like I had to walk on eggshells.

I felt condemned to a life of listening to one parent complaining about another and trying to coax you into agreeing with them to feed their own ego. I also remember McDonald's car park changeovers, never being able to commit to plans because you don't know whose week it is, and eventually when one parent moves cities, not being able to participate in co-curricular activities with friends because the school says you must commit to 75% of games. In my case, I could not commit to this 75% because every second weekend I had to travel two hours to see Dad, who only saw us every other weekend, so, somewhat understandably, he didn't want to sacrifice his time with me. On the other hand, he also never bothered to come down and watch me participate in co-curricular activities, whether that be because he had other plans or because he didn't feel welcome because he thought mum has spoken badly about him to either the school or other parents there.

School was also difficult. It's embarrassing and traumatising having to think which parents are going to cause a scene today. Often,

> I think parents can get so caught up in their own anger and frustration, they don't realise how much damage they're doing.

Another event of note in my dad and step mum's separation is when she had been a big part of our lives and they had only recently separated within the month, and she took me and my siblings out for dinner with our cousins on her side for my birthday and my dad showed up to the restaurant drunk, causing a scene and accusing her of kidnapping. Totally horrified, I was under the table of the restaurant, crying and embarrassed. I had just wanted a nice celebration and he couldn't even hide his hatred for one night – he had to drive to the restaurant and cause a scene. Later that night, my step mum took us back to her parents' house to sleep there, where later the police turned up about the alleged kidnapping.

Everything about the separation was unjustifiably malicious. There were so many occasions of unpleasant behaviour from all of them throughout the whole separation process. There was never a changeover without a snide remark from either of my parents. I can understand they were angry and didn't want to be around the other person, but I do feel anger over this. Is it really that difficult to pull your heads in for two minutes so your child doesn't have to have panic attacks the entire car trip there, thinking about the hostility of the situation? It should never have been so difficult.

How did your parents resolve matters? Did they go through the Court process?

For my family, with both separations, most issues had to be resolved in Court, and it is my honest opinion that they would not have been able to do it any other way, as they are all very stubborn people.

My parents went back to Court a few times. It went from Mum and Dad 50/50, week on, week off, to not seeing Dad for six months, to supervised visits with Dad, to moving cities with one parent and only seeing the other one every second weekend. We grew up living out of bags, McDonald's changeovers in the middle of Christmas day, which meant we weren't allowed to bring our presents to the other parents' house or go away for Christmas.

All of which sounds like such first world problems, but that is the world we're living in. It's not that I am having a constant meltdown over not going away like all my other friends, whether it be Europe or even just a beach an hour away, but I'm also not going to apologise for being upset and feeling like I might have missed out on the chance of a better childhood.

For parents that fought so much to see us, though, we spent a lot of time in after-school/holiday care. I understand parents have to work - especially single parents - but I resented that I was always one of, if not the, oldest one there.

Did you meet with any court experts or other people in the Family Law system?

I think, as a child, I met with every single person and expert in the Family Law process and went to every single facility on this earth regarding Family Law, and I hated it.

Yes, you have a job to do, and while I believe strongly in doing things with the child's best interests in mind, nothing about this process was in my best interests. Imagine missing out on recess and playing with your friends, one of the only times you get to feel normal and forget how dysfunctional your real world is, to meet some expert. This time is taken away from you because you have to go to yet another family psychologist or another Children's Lawyer. Maybe it works for other people who are younger and more naive, but a lot of people I know with parents getting divorced while they're younger have to grow up before their time and find no pleasure in drawing photos of their dysfunctional families or sitting in a hand-shaped chair, being treated like a child yet answering questions that are going to affect you like an adult. By the end of it all, my siblings and I were so over it.

One day we travelled three hours to go to the Court-appointed psychologist. We spent the whole day between his office and waiting room, taking it in turns to go in by ourselves, then with Mum, and then with Dad. Not only were we trapped in a tiny office space for 10 hours with two people who couldn't stand each other, but we were kids, and we were kids who wanted to be anywhere but there. We started mucking up around lunchtime because we were so exhausted and over it, and everybody could see that, except this Court-appointed professional who also gave the Court a deranged report on the day and found no problem with the child having to be the one to report back about Dad's breach of court order (that is, his drinking habits). To this day I resent the entire experience.

> I never felt like I was being listened to or that they
> felt my opinions mattered.

What primary school kid should have to have their lunchtime spent not with their friends but with a psychologist or ICL talking about how broken their life is? Children already feel isolated and different to their friends. Don't take away their playtime, their chance to feel normal and have fun.

You mentioned your father's drinking. Was this an issue?

Yes, it was. Before and once divorced, Dad's drinking was still an issue. It became part of the Court orders that he was unable to drink 24 hours prior and during our time with him. When I'm on a diet, I'll put a sticky note on the fridge saying, 'Don't eat it.' How's that piece of paper going to make me accountable for my actions though? Honestly, in my experience, a Court order like that is not much different. When we were with him, it was just the three kids and him. I can't stop him from drinking his 'tea', especially if he is an aggressive drunk. If the only way someone would find out if he had been drinking was if either my siblings or I reported it, how is that order effective? Turning the kids into having to betray their own dad just does not work. Every night he would pass out on the lounge from this magical 'tea', burning the dinner, leaving the oven on, leaving me to mother everyone like I'd been doing my entire 'childhood'.

Did you ever confront your dad about his drinking?

When I was in my late teens, I decided I'd had enough of Dad's drinking. I was no longer going to feel guilty about telling someone, because I wanted him to stop. I was sick of how he treated me when he was drinking. It may not have been physical abuse, but emotional abuse still hurts.

I stood up to him that night, and called him out for his 'tea', and we had a massive fight, and my sister even threw a bowl of pasta at my head to prove to my dad that she was the loyal one and she deserved all his love and attention.

I left Dad's house that night and didn't talk to him for two years.

While my siblings who remained were lavished with gifts for the years to come, I, on the other hand, only received a birthday card about rappers who 'didn't make it'.

What is your relationship with your siblings like now? Also, do you feel you or they have been affected as adults?

I am now able to overlook the continued emotional torment. As for my siblings, my brother and sister haven't handled everything so well. One has mental health issues; the other is self-medicated with various concoctions of whatever's making them feel good that week, whether that be sex, drugs, or alcohol.

What would you say to parents about how they can best support their children during separation?

> Parents need to remember that if you're going to
> sit down and talk to children during a separation,
> don't lead their answers.

Almost 90% of the time their answers are going to be biased towards the parent they're talking to because they don't want to hurt their feelings. Looking back, I am angry about that manipulation. I can say that now, but as a kid I felt guilty and I'd try make my parents feel ok.

People talk about 'child's best interests' but personally, to me, that would mean not dragging them through the court processes and appointments they resent going to.

I think during mediations or court proceedings, all parents need to stop being so selfish with what they want. Yes, you want to see your child; so does the other party. Yes, you may be hurting, but so may they. It's already an unpleasant process; it doesn't need to be made worse by being so malicious.

Remember:

> Mum and Dad hating each other isn't going to make the child's life
> better. It's just going to damage them.

I think my friends are thankful for me now. Their parents have gone through divorces as they've gotten older (I was one of the first out of my friends). Because I have such vast experience with the entire Family Law system, my friends who have parents divorcing find me really helpful to talk to. I never had that.

Nina

A vague, but powerful painful perception

On being a teenager, protected (yet not) throughout her
parent's separation outside of court

Nina was 11 when she first realised there were 'cracks' in her parents'
relationship. Following that, a mysterious pain covered her childhood, and
she talks in terms of the details being 'blurred' about what her 'impression'
was, what she had a 'sense' of, and what she could 'glean'. Essentially,
despite her parents appearing to have tried to protect her from Family Law
issues, Nina had a 'vague, but powerful painful perception' due to 'nothing
in particular' that she, her brother, and her mother were 'leeches' with
regards to needing financial support.

Although her story is not dramatic or striking, or something that would
be 'clickbait' in the media, to me it is still important in the way it makes us
consider how do we really protect children from the potential hostility of a
divorce? Is this ever really possible? Or, like Dr Milch raises, is it merely a
case of choosing the least detrimental path? I am also reminded of clinical
psychologist Alison O'Neill's insight, that 'Children pick up the obvious
and not so obvious messages and take them to heart'.

Perhaps Nina's story is a lesson in how the less obvious, the vague, and the
'nothing in particular' can still cause a deep wound. In Nina's case the wound
remained as an unspoken, unresolved resentment between her and her father.
It seemed she had never really confronted him about her true feelings, and a
silent distance remained in their relationship.

⸭

When did you become aware that your parents were separating?

I was 11 when I first became aware of serious cracks in my parents' relation-ship, which had been long-term de facto since my accidental conception.

How did you become aware of this?

The details are blurred. I remember about three years of uncertainty before it came to a complete end, and a couple more on top of that before their financial and legal separation was finalised in the late '90s with the sale of the family house (a prolonged and emotionally fraught process, not without drama). I remember my dad brought his new girlfriend (who I perceived as the catalyst for my parents' separation) to the sale of our family home, which caused havoc.

During this time I remember overhearing embittered, mostly hushed bedroom arguments and phone conversations involving lawyers, though I think both my parents had a mutually agreed-on policy of 'protecting the kids' from the messy details as much as possible.

Were you aware of what was in dispute?

I was able to glean that there was a dispute about how to divide their shared wealth, accumulated through many years of living, working, and raising two children together. Dad worked full time and mum worked part time, but then full time once both me and my brother were both in school.

She did the domestic work, with bits and pieces filled in by babysitters and the odd fortnightly cleaner. It wasn't a high priority for her so our house was generally a mess, but it was a fun, stimulating environment, and very open to our friends. I don't remember my dad cooking, aside from prepar-ing tomato soup out of the can on Sundays, which was something of a ritual. My mum prepared breakfast, lunch, and dinner on an everyday basis, in a hassled way – I think it was a bit of a thankless task, in retrospect.

My overriding sense was that in the legal battle, her domestic labour was somehow devalued during the separation, perhaps more by gendered societal expectations than by my dad in particular.

I remember there being an issue around the fact that they were de facto not married, and my impression was that this gave my mother significantly fewer automatic rights to their shared assets.

Were parenting matters in dispute between your mum and dad?

As far as I'm aware, custody was not a significant issue in my parents' separation. As a teenager in the final years of high school, I was given a choice about whether to split time between two homes, once they had each found stable accommodation in rented, semi-detached houses.

My brother, who is four years younger, would stay with my dad and his girlfriend (to-be wife) on alternate weekends, and some weeknights on a semi-regular basis, and there was some chronic tension around the practical and emotional difficulties involved.

> I loathed spending time with them (my dad and his new partner) as a couple, so I declined to ever spend the night and rarely visited. My dad had rented somewhere deliberately close to my school and bought me a classic wooden desk to study on, but I don't think I ever used it.

It sounds like your relationship with your dad became quite difficult during and after the separation.

> Well, I was also aware that the amount and length of child support was a particular point of contention, which was the most painful and confusing aspect for me.

This issue didn't go away for many years, as my mother was annoyed that my dad wanted to stop paying child support to her as soon as we turned 18, despite the fact that we lived at home with her, and were arguably still 'dependents' for all intents and purposes, throughout university. He wanted to pay me directly, which my mum found offensive and frustrating.

I had the impression my dad felt 'gipped' because I spent significantly less time with him, and was at times openly hostile towards him. I imagine he resented the ongoing financial expectations on him partly because of this.

How did you feel towards the rest of your family?

On a few occasions, relatives on my dad's side weighed in with strong, loud opinions on the financial split.

I felt highly protective of my mother, partly as a result of this, because I perceived her to be under attack and relatively under-supported by her family, whom she was less close to.

> I remember feeling defensive of my brother, and of myself, for being made, somehow, by nothing in particular, to feel like we were leeches. It was a vague perception, but a painful and powerful one.

Kris

Unconditionally

On being a child with parents litigating in Court

In Kris's interview, I again found it telling that he could not remember the details of what happened, and yet he is affected by them. The memory of the actual events of what happened to him as a child are unclear, yet Kris finds himself cautious in relationships as an adult. So, while the actual narrative of what happened is vague, its effects are felt. He can't tell the story, but the story tells him, as psychoanalyst Stephen Grosz discusses in *The Examined Life*: 'When we cannot find a way of telling our story, our story tells us – we dream these stories, we develop symptoms, or we find ourselves acting in ways we don't understand'.

So often, when I speak to other adults who were children when their parents separated, they also describe the vague memory of it in terms of an aching fog. Yet one thing that is often very clear is the unconditional love children have for their parents, as discussed in this interview. This again echoes what I found as a Court appointed Independent Children's Lawyer – that whilst people often talk of the unconditional love parents have for their children, it is actually children who love unconditionally, who never give up on their relationship with their parents, and who ceaselessly forgive, forgive, forgive.

What are your memories of when your parents were together?

I have really pleasant memories of my brother and sister and me, of when my parents were together. I can recall several family holidays and outings.

What do you remember as leading to your parents' separation?

I was 11 when they got divorced and not fully aware of the true reason for their separation. But what I do recall is them fighting a lot and having many a yelling match. I think they simply had had enough of one another and became quite abusive towards each other.

Did your parents resolve issues between them in Court or outside of Court?

They went to Court. The outcome was that we spent five days out of the 14 with Dad and the rest of the time we resided with Mum.

How much exposure did you have to the process?

I remember speaking with a lawyer, the Children's Lawyer, and they asked me some questions about my mum and dad. I can't recall exactly what they were, but it had something to do with who I wanted to live with.

> To be honest I think I have blocked large parts of the entire process out. A lot of it is a blur.

Did your parents discuss with you and your siblings the situation?

They sat us three down and told us that they were going to separate. They didn't really explain the Court process or what to do. I don't believe they felt we would have been involved with the process.

Did you meet with any other experts or professionals during the Court proceedings?

Yes. I met with a counsellor on several occasions to talk about my feelings and thoughts about the whole process. This lasted for several months.

Do you have any specific memories from your parent's separation that have stayed with you?

Yes, I remember both Mum and Dad talking negatively about the other when I was in one or the other's presence.

> I remember being terrified of being in Court. I wouldn't wish that on any child. The whole experience was very traumatic.

What were your feelings when your parents separated?

I suppose, like any child, I didn't want my parents to separate. I was concerned that I wouldn't be able to see them as often as I'd like. I was also torn between the two of them.

I think my siblings were also quite affected. They are both younger than me but I know it has mentally scarred both my brother and sister.

What was the relationship like between everyone in your family after your parents separated?

It had changed. However, your parents are always your parents, and children will always love parents unconditionally – even if they have done the wrong thing.

How is your relationship today, years after the divorce?

Currently, actually, my relationship with my family is better than ever. I have amazing relationships with Mum, Dad. and my siblings and couldn't be happier. I think it was a choice I made, and it was a conscious effort to keep these relationships strong.

Now, looking back at your parents' separation, do you have a different perspective on what happened?

Yes, for sure. Now, I can see the past events from an adult's point of view and truly believe that they should have got divorced. It's unfortunate that it had to happen, but I feel it has made me stronger as a result.

Have there been any long-term negative effects?

Yes, I feel that I am very cautious with my own relationships and it has made me jaded when it comes to commitment.

In light of your own experiences, what are your views about how children should be involved in the legal process of their parents' separation?

I personally think children under the age of 13 should not be involved in the legal process, as they are completely unaware of what's happening or their surrounds. They aren't at an age where they can make a big decision like that.

The legislation says that children's best interests are the paramount consideration in parenting matters. What does 'children's best interests' mean to you?

I'm sure that whilst children's best interests are what the courts have in mind, when parents are fighting over kids, they lose sight of that!

What's best for their kids is most likely the last thing on their mind, and they are more interested in who will be getting the bigger payout.

Children's best interests, to me, is that they should be sheltered from the situation and should live 50/50 with both parents, if possible.

I think it is always going to be difficult in getting a result which all parties are happy with. My advice is to let children live equally with each parent (as long as both parents are of sound mind), and to keep the children as far removed from the conflict as possible.

Any advice for parents separating about how to keep their children's best interests in mind?

My advice to all parents is:

> Don't blackmail your ex-partner in front of your kids, and always put them first, even if that means you don't like the decision.

> If the children want to spend time with the other parent, don't deny them this privilege.

Noah

Terrible things

On being a child when his relationship with his
mother fractured

::::

Noah was a young child when his parents separated and a bitter divorce
played out in Court, following which his mother relocated from Sydney to
the South Coast.

What I found interesting about his experience was the fact that it was
not the separation that upset him but the way his mother processed the
separation and the effects of it on his relationship with her that were most
detrimental. As an adult, Noah has chosen to move overseas to another
country to 'escape' the relationship with his family.

Who is in your family?

Mother and a brother, along with a brother and sister from my father's
second marriage.

What are your memories of when your parents were together?

Not much. I was happy as a child, prior to the divorce.

Did your parents resolve issues between them in Court or outside of Court?

Both, I think. There were a lot of difficult arguments between them over stuff. I can't remember the details of what was argued over in Court.

Mum relocated with us about two or three hours drive away from dad after the divorce.

How much exposure did you have to the process?

My only exposure was my mum complaining about it to me and bad-mouthing my dad – a lot.

Did your parents discuss what was happening?

In terms of explaining what was going on, only my mum really discussed it with me, and this only really amounted to 'Your dad is doing terrible things', or something to that effect.

What were your feelings when your parents separated?

The thing I remember the most is a significant change in my mother's mood and temperament. She was very angry after the divorce and quite a changed person, I would say.

> I can't remember being upset over the actual divorce. I think the actual hard part was mostly related to how my relationship with my mother changed after the divorce

...it had a very toxic effect on our relationship.

I'm sympathetic to my mother, as I always have been, but it's a shame it had to wreck my own relationship with her.

Do you think you have been affected by your parents' separation as an adult?

I have definitely been affected by the separation.

I think my relationship with my mother turning toxic at the age of
four was quite traumatic for me at such a formative age.

One of the reasons I've moved to live in another country is to be able to
escape my relationship with my family, which is not the best.

Brooke

Two lives

On being a mother with a child who is self-harming
in Family Law proceedings

Brooke's matter is an example of how being in the Family Law system on and off for years without any real end can unfortunately be an ongoing state of affairs for some families.

Her matter illustrates the effect of delays on families and how, even in a case such as hers, where a child is self-harming, it can take months or even years for orders to be made on an interim basis.

Brooke's experience also forces us to question if currently the system is actually focussed on the children's best interests. Brooke tells of how her son is self-harming, yet the matter is not prioritised, and of how her son has not been given an adequate voice in the process. In Brooke's view, the focus on equal shared parental responsibility eclipses the ability to actually see a situation that is detrimental to a child. It has, from her perspective, created a situation where her son leads 'two lives'.

▦

What is the background to your Family Law matter?

I met my future husband while travelling for work. Therefore, we met when we were living in different cities, but we seemed to make it work while we were dating. We spoke on the phone every night and I thought we got through a lot of important topics that way.

After we married my husband seemed to have less interest in travelling on weekends. I began travelling more to make sure we saw each other. Eventually, it was clear that he was worried about his career and that he was not making plans to transfer cities (even though his company had an office in my city).

My husband did not move to actually live with my son and I until several years into the marriage. I later found out he only moved in with us due to financial stress and not being able to afford his own mortgage.

When did you start to realise the relationship had serious problems and what led to the separation?

In hindsight, my husband had a mid-life crisis. He was depressed, although I didn't realise it at the time.

He would have a lot of energy some days, staying up all night working on his computer. On other days, he slept most of the day and didn't realise when our son and I had gone out and come home. He became very unhappy about my career and things I did with friends. He put down my profession and told me that I needed to take a suburban job so that I could have another baby. When I said that I worked in a corporate job and had no experience that would allow me to take a suburban job, he told me I was being selfish.

He began to put down our son and tell him to 'man up'. At age five, my son started wetting the bed again and he was afraid of his dad, who smacked him. It was at this point that I decided I had to separate from my husband.

What issues (including legal issues) were in dispute with you and your partner when you separated?

My husband was very unhappy that I separated from him. He blamed me for breaking up a 'perfect' family. As a result, we could not agree on parenting or property matters and he brought proceedings against me within a couple of weeks of our separation. His approach has been to make every interaction, whether in person or between the lawyers, difficult.

I don't think I would have changed my mind about commencing my separation, given my beliefs and convictions, but...

> I do now understand why many women return to their husbands
> and bad situations, because the process is very difficult.

How was the dispute between you resolved?

We initially settled parenting after going to Court for three days and agreeing orders on the last day of the hearing. Our agreed orders were for my ex-husband to have care of our son for four full days every fortnight, starting the previous night and so covering five nights.

However, my ex-husband has breached the orders a number of times, including an order which restrains him by injunction from approaching me. Alternatively, he interprets the orders in an unintended way and uses this to justify keeping our son in his care longer than allowed. I have had to commence a new set of proceedings to seek new orders.

So, there were issues with the orders given, and you have had to commence new proceedings. Can you tell me more about the original orders?

I agreed to the original orders because I was advised that this was the likely best outcome of a Judge-decided matter, and it could in fact end up being worse than this.

I did not think that this would be good for my son who was only six years old at the time and did not have a good relationship with his dad. His dad had been away so frequently, even before we separated, that our son called his dad by his first name.

In hindsight, I have been right, as my son has developed anxiety as a result of having to spend time with his dad. He self-harms when he is in his dad's care and I have had to seek treatment for him.

My ex-husband is in denial that our son self-harms or has an anxiety issue.

How have you found the Court system? I mean, do you feel your matter has been prioritised, given your son is self-harming?

Delay and lack of resources is a problem throughout the entire system.

In a way, I feel that my matter presents as a middle-class matter, with no drug, alcohol, domestic violence, etc. issues. As a result,

> our matter hasn't been prioritised, despite the fact it is clear that our son is self-harming and is at risk.

> I have been very surprised at the lack of urgency demonstrated by the Court in a situation where a child is self-harming.

This has been demonstrated by long waiting periods to obtain hearing dates, changes of hearing dates after they have been set, and a tendency for the Court to refer the matter to other avenues rather than to make an interim order.

The main professional we interacted with during the process was the independent psychiatrist for a single expert report. Again, the demand on his services means his availability is severely affected.

What are some of the problems as you see it with the current Family Law system? In particular, just the actual practical problems you encountered?

There are quite a few things I have observed as problematic.

There is a complete lack of adherence to Court deadlines. In my experience, parties with proceedings in the Family Courts do not respect Court deadlines for filing Court documents. There is a general acceptance of this by Family Law practitioners, and parties use this to surprise the other party with evidence late, or to reduce the amount of time for analysis. Judges easily grant extensions to file documents. This adds to delays in proceedings and extended costs.

Obviously, another issue is a lack of resources. On many occasions, a date has been set for a hearing of our matter and we have then been notified that the date has to be changed to a number of months later due to resourcing changes. I have tried towards the end of a year to have a matter resolved, which would impact on the start of the next school year, but been told that I needed to commence proceedings 12 months prior.

On a recent Monday in 2018, when our matter was scheduled for a mention in the Family Court, our Judge was the only Judge sitting in that court that day which is in a major Australian capital city.

Yes, that is partly why I am doing this book – to draw attention to just the practical, actual real-life problems we are facing when you are a litigant in the Courts. I am glad you mentioned this.

Yes, I noticed that the ALRC is looking at more, wider issues, such as gender, and other thematic issues. However, I really want there to be a focus on the actual nitty-gritty practical problems, like how is it possible that there is only one Judge sitting in an entire Court on a Monday in a major city?

Another concern I have is that my ex-husband has used the delays to superficially deal with the issues I have raised in the proceedings. This means that by the time we return to Court, he has some evidence that he has modified his behaviour, which adds to the Court's reluctance to make a decision adverse to his rights. When this risk has passed, my husband then reverts to his previous behaviour.

Amidst all of this, there is a difficulty in obtaining interim parenting orders. I am told Judges are reluctant to make interim parenting orders because of the precedent it sets for final parenting orders. As a result, it took two years on the first occasion to obtain parenting orders for our son. It has so far taken 18 months on the second occasion.

Do you have any views about whether the best interests of children are currently being achieved in Court?

I think there is too much of a focus on parents' rights.

I have seen that the Family Law currently seeks to ensure that both parents can share in decision-making in relation to a child and have caring responsibilities. There is a presumption that responsibility should be shared equally, and the onus is on the parties to prove how this 50/50 outcome should be marginally shifted one way or the other. The reasoning is that this in the best interests of the child. On the face of it, I agree that this reasoning, and approach is logical and fair.

However, my lived experience is that Judges and single experts become too focussed on the 50/50 outcome to the point that they fail to see evidence that should change this outcome and fail to seek to understand what the child wants and is in their best interests.

It has been a struggle for our son to live according to the court orders. He effectively leads two lives – one with me, where he can express his interests and decide what extra-curricular activities he wants to do, and another with his father, who insists he does different activities in the week our son is in his care.

As a result, our son can only attend science and chess clubs, and participate in the school choir, every second week. He is only helped with his homework and cello practice every second week. He is not allowed to bring anything from our house to his father's house, so he has to remember to take his much-loved Fitbit off and leave it at my home. Our son still cries every night before he has to go into his father's care the next day.

How was the process with regards to his representation in Court? Did you feel the Court took notice of your son's views and perspectives?

No, not really. In my experience, the Family Law system has, and wants, limited interaction with the child. By way of an illustration, I was shocked when, one day while talking about my son in conference with a barrister about to represent me, the barrister told me she did not want to see a photo of our son because it was irrelevant.

The Independent Children's Lawyer has only met him once for 30 minutes, although she has acted on his behalf for nearly a year.

The judges we've had have twice ordered for our son to be seen by a single expert as the means for his best interests to be assessed, with the single expert meeting him for only one and a half hours each time in a clinical environment. I have been advised that it is not appropriate for my son to write a letter to the single expert about how he feels, regardless of whether the letter is sent beforehand or presented at the appointment.

I don't think that any of these processes have been adequate to understand our son, what he wants, and what is in his best interests.

Our son is a quiet, respectful child. It takes a while for him to develop the confidence to speak openly to an adult, let alone to a stranger, and I don't think that he has been given the time or environment to fully express himself.

Given your experiences, are there any reforms that you believe should be implemented to the Family Law system?

Matters involving young children should be prioritised so they can be addressed by the system faster.

I can see from my matter how many societal issues are created from Family Law situations.

I also think children appear to easily fall between the cracks in the AVO framework.

While my ex-husband's behaviour towards me has been sufficient to justify an AVO, his careful behaviour towards our son has prevented me from being able to extend an AVO to our son.

The system needs to be improved to be able to provide protection to children quickly. If is it proven that one parent's behaviour is generally unacceptable, it should be sufficient evidence to be able to move to protect the child.

How has the service been from lawyers?

I have changed lawyers twice. Each time it has been by referral by friends or other lawyers. This has been important to ensure technical ability, as well as to find a lawyer who has an approach to my matter similar to mine.

I have changed lawyers twice because of lack of capacity to run my matters. The chief indicator of this was failure to lodge documents by Court due dates even though I reminded them and pre-drafted responses for them. The lawyers in this area of the law are terribly under-resourced based on my experience of other areas of the law.

And how did you fund your legal fees?

I am paying cash, on time, rather than pay at the end. Frankly, I think this gives you access to better lawyers, but it does mean you need to be able to afford to do so.

In addition to the issue of delay, are there any other observations you would make about the Family Law system?

The process has been obviously adversarial, and the lawyers for my ex-husband seem to have run this as an adversarial matter without considering what is best for our son. I think this matter could have been concluded sooner, and wasted less money, if it had had a different approach.

In relation to the process being adversarial, I also note I am legally trained and financially secure in my own right.

I feel that if I had not been legally trained, I would have been more daunted by the process and probably settled for a lesser outcome.

If I had not been financially secure, I am sure that I would not have been able to afford the lawyers that I use and that my husband would have financially frustrated me to force a suboptimal outcome.

Following on from this, I think it could be said that the system is biased against women who don't have a legal background and don't control their own finances.

Do you feel this experience has changed you as a person?

The adage that what doesn't kill you makes you stronger is definitely applicable! The experience also gives you better perspective on what is important in life.

Jacqui

Subtle, quiet abuse

On how the court process facilitated ongoing abuse
from an ex-husband

Jacqui's story is particularly important in the way it shows how Court delays negatively impact individuals and families.

In her case Jacqui found the length of the Court process meant her former partner had an extended opportunity to subtly bully her through the Court process. I think this highlights one of the interesting paradoxes of the Court process, and the law more broadly. People come to the law seeking redress to a problem. Yet so often there is something about the legal process that (unconsciously) replicates the harm or trauma they are there, ironically, to remedy.

In this case Jacqui found the 'subtle' abuse she was subjected to in the relationship only continued during the Court case. At the same time, the law (eventually) corrected the situation in terms of outcome. This shows there can be a difference between outcomes and processes. It also raises the question: How can we prevent perpetrators of family violence using the process as a vehicle to continue abuse or violence?

▦

Can you please tell me about what led to you and your former husband's separation?

Without going into huge amounts of detail my ex was reckless with money, spent thousands of dollars of savings that had taken me years to build up and repeatedly lied about finances. One day I was on a work trip and came home to find messages on his phone between himself and another woman which indicated that he was involved with her. This was the absolutely final straw. I told him we were getting divorced. He suggested counselling, which was tried for a few weeks, but it was futile.

I found another apartment, and I was transparent about my intention to move out. A week before I was able to move into the new apartment, he threw me out of the house, took my car, and told me that if I didn't agree to 50/50 care of the kids (then aged three and six) that he would just keep them.

I was due to have surgery in three days and was traumatised by his behaviour. I moved out, got my car back, and was able to set up a home with help from friends. The 50/50 arrangement was set up, but I didn't feel it was in the kids' best interests, so I was working to arrange mediation.

That sounds incredibly traumatic. As the matter progressed, what were the legal issues that arose?

After about a few months of 50/50 and mediation that was going nowhere, my ex-demanded to change the children's schools and daycare, even though he still lived in the marital home, which was in the catchment for my daughter's primary school. He had unilaterally enrolled my son in a different daycare centre and was sending him there on alternate weeks but denied this when asked, and would not tell me where the daycare centre was.

The children had been told to keep it secret, but my three-year-old let it slip. I received a phone call from the principal of my daughter's school saying my ex-had turned up and told them he intended to transfer her to another school. I wrote to both schools and told them I didn't consent to her enrolment being changed. The schools proceeded anyway.

> Because he knew that I would just return the children to their normal schools when they returned to me, he refused to return them at the end of his week, and sent a letter via his lawyers demanding I agree to certain terms.

I spent the next week frantically working with my lawyer to draft an application for interim orders. It was filed one week from the day on which he refused to return the children. An interim hearing was listed 10 days from the filing date. There was no financial application as we had no assets to divide, only a self-managed super fund which I was able to extract my funds from after about two years of disputation.

My ex-seemed to think he should be able to unilaterally make arrangements for the children while lying to me or concealing from me what he was doing, and that if I didn't agree, he would use withholding access to the children to coerce me into agreement. Whilst there was no physical violence, there was coercion and other forms of psychological and emotional abuse.

Given this history, I can imagine it must have been difficult to amicably resolve things. How did you ultimately resolve the dispute?

Mediation failed; negotiation via lawyers failed.

On the first interim hearing date, the Judge indicated that he took a very dim view of my ex's behaviour and would not make orders in his favour. However, it still took over seven hours to negotiate a settlement. The kids were returned to their schools, the arrangements were changed to 10 nights with me, four nights with him, and I was given sole parental responsibility.

My ex-still wanted to press the issue of the school, and a further interim hearing was set. At the hearing his barrister refused to run the school argument, and the consent orders from the first hearing date were upheld. My ex-proceeded all the way to the full hearing on the issue of seeking 50/50, a return to shared responsibility, and to change the kids to the school he originally wanted. The final hearing was held late 2017 and we still have not received judgment. The matter had been in court since early 2015.

Just weeks after the hearing, my ex-moved from a house next door to the school he wanted to change the kids to, into the same postcode as myself.

You mentioned child support was also an issue?

The child support assessment was subject to an objection by him. He was complaining that $320 a month was too much to pay for two children. He went through two internal CSA objections and an AAT hearing. The final assessment following the AAT hearing was that he should pay $1,170 per month. Over $16,400 is outstanding.

The child support appeal process, while it significantly increased the amount he was assessed to pay, offered him a small concession at the final stage, which is likely to mean that every assessment will have to go through the entire objection process up to the AAT stage.

How did you find the Family Law process?

I knew the Court was overburdened, and it was expensive, but the reality of it is shocking. The long delays and costs are appalling. The courts are overstretched and somewhat unpredictable.

> The process, being so lengthy itself, offered my ex-a long period in which to engage in abusive behaviour which was very damaging to the children and myself. The process lent itself to significant financial and emotional abuse.

I was fortunate to have a very compassionate lawyer, but the costs of the process are extortionate and prevent many people from pursuing their rights.

Despite the Court's policy that each matter should have a single judge, we had five different judges over a two-and-a-half-year period.

I was pleasantly surprised at the outcome of the interim hearing, but I am awaiting the outcome of the final hearing five months after it concluded, so I can't comment on that.

I think I was better placed to understand the processes than most people because of my legal knowledge. However, the emotional toll was extreme, and the financial costs of the process are astronomical.

It doesn't protect people from the more subtle, quiet forms of abuse. The stress is incredibly damaging to parents and children. Unfortunately, *the way pre-Court processes are set up, the more powerful partner tends to get away with bullying,*

and this is only rectified at the Court stage, so people who should be going to court to protect their children and their own position probably can't afford to do so.

This is horribly detrimental to post-divorce families. The delay causes trauma and ongoing damage to parents and children and cripples the parents financially. The process can be unpredictable (it wasn't in my case but I see that as being partly due to luck) and it is hopelessly ill-equipped to deal with the highly emotional people involved.

Can you detail any of the ways the process allowed your ex-husband a vehicle to, as you say, continue his subtle emotional abuse of you?

On the day of the hearing, I was presented with a case outline sent to my lawyer at 10 p.m. the night before. It contained copies of pages from my personal diaries and notebooks which my ex-husband had kept when he ejected me from the marital home.

The extracts from my personal diaries (dating back to years before I met my ex-husband) were used by my ex-husband with the intention of humiliating and embarrassing me, and to insinuate that I had a mental illness or drug problem. My treating psychologists' notes had been subpoenaed and were available, but these were not tendered. These extracts were not included in evidence in chief, and their use was highly improper.

To object to their inclusion in evidence would have pushed us beyond our two-day estimate and resulted in us being only partly heard. Obviously, there would be significant further costs involved in this strategy and I had already incurred significant debts in paying for the hearing. I had to submit to humiliating cross-examination on these extracts, despite the fact that both my barrister and the ICL's barrister argued that this was highly improper, that they should not have been in evidence in chief, they were an abuse of process, and that the prejudice outweighed their probative value.

What is your relationship with your ex-like now?

Largely non-existent, but at least not actively combative at the moment. Since the final hearing was concluded, my ex-partner has moved to the same area and his behaviour seems to have stabilised. This seems strange as I don't understand why you would behave badly when under scrutiny and threat of court proceedings, but normally when that threat is finished. Regardless, that is how it is.

And your relationship with your children?

It has definitely improved after the hearing, as I think the stress was affecting all of us. I have a close and loving relationship with the kids. Also, they seem to have a close relationship with their father.

Did you retain a lawyer?

My lawyer has been a truly wonderful lawyer, a gentleman and a friend, and he was extremely kind and compassionate throughout the process. He also compromised his fees to an extraordinary extent. I was profoundly lucky.

> During the process, my lawyer was my closest confidant. We worked together, he was always available, and always had time for me. I still consider him to be one of the finest men I know and I will always appreciate what he did for me, as it was, by far, above and beyond the call of duty, or the fees that I paid to him.

It is good to hear you had a good experience in terms of legal representation. How did you fund your legal fees?

My lawyer compromised his fees to an extent that he probably shouldn't have. He wanted to see the matter through for me and he only charged me what he felt I could afford, which was probably 20% of the work that he did, if that. It was still expensive.

If he had not done this for me I would probably have had to self-represent, but dealing with my ex-and the numerous interlocutory proceedings could easily have jeopardised my employment due to days in court and preparing paperwork, let alone the stress and effect on my mental health.

What other professionals and experts did you interact with during the Family Law process?

I had a private mediator, and he wasn't great. The Child Dispute Conference seemed to be a waste of time. The family report writer was great. The mediator for Legal Aid was great. And the Independent Children's Lawyer was amazing.

The barrister/advocate for the ICL was, by far, the best practitioner on the day and she was truly extraordinary. I felt the people involved genuinely cared about the children.

Do you feel the process has biases against certain people?

The process has certain underlying biases which probably can't even be articulated – about what it means to be a 'good' parent and how people are supposed to behave, which are unrealistic. It is incompatible with the level of emotional turmoil the parties are experiencing. Also,

> like any litigation, it is biased in favour of the
> person who has the most money and resources,

which is usually the male partner in the relationship for structural reasons. The delay and cost work against those in poverty who have suffered financial abuse or domestic violence.

Do you feel there were any long-term negative consequences from the experience?

Yes. Despite the fact that the costs were lower than they would have been, the financial consequences leave me with a difficult financial future. Emotionally, I think I and my children will be scarred to some extent. I have been hurt and traumatised beyond anything I had ever anticipated. I have also had to become extremely strong. I have difficulty trusting people, and I think it's unlikely I will have a relationship again for a long period, if ever.

Did anything positive come out of it at all?

My time with the children increased from 50/50 to 10 days a fortnight and this was a huge positive for me. I received a lot of support from a whole range of people, which was lovely. I found that I was stronger than I'd thought.

Reflecting on your own experience, do you have any thoughts about other support services that you think could exist to support people going through a separation?

Psychological, legal, financial, and emotional support are all needed, along with support for children's mental health, and child care to assist parents with establishing a new life.

Most people are in financial distress and can't afford the services they need to get through the process. They just try to survive any way they can.

Are there any other reforms you believe should be implemented to the Family Law system?

Having been through the Administrative Appeals Tribunal (AAT) system for child support, I wonder if this style of forum would be better for resolution of Family Law matters. It's less formal, requires no representation, has fewer interlocutory steps which delay the process, and would lower the cost. It was much less stressful than going through court.

There needs to be a much greater understanding of and training in child development, domestic violence, and psychological, emotional, and financial abuse in the system.

The system should be set up to help separated parents establish functional new lives for themselves and their children, not to give them a forum to attempt to destroy each other, which is what the current system does.

Michael

We've got to stand up for the blokes

On being a father and survivor of domestic violence
and misuse of child support

Michael is currently facing a final hearing on parenting and property matters with his ex-wife. His is a tale of love lost to financial difficulties and emotional abuse at the hands of his wife. In Michael's view, the current Family Law system is biased against men in several ways. When he informed the child support agency of the true parenting arrangement, he says his wife retaliated by suspending the children's time with him. During the process, Michael felt that his situation of being a victim of family violence was not really understood.

Although he does not use these words, he seems to say there is not yet a discourse around men as victims of family violence. Is it the case that not only women, but men too, are limited by traditional ideas about gender? More specifically, perhaps the refusal to perceive men as victims of family violence is the shadow side of the old idea that men are stronger and more masterful than women. On a related point, even during his relationship, Michael recalls his former partner would taunt him daily saying "you're not a real man." Paradoxically he was both terrorised during his relationship by ideas about how gender should be performed and after his relationship ended these same ideas about gender led to his situation not being understood.

::::::

Firstly, please give me a brief background about who's in your family, and what the current proceedings are about.

Currently, things are ridiculous. We are arguing over custody of the children in Court when we've largely had an agreement in relation to who had the children for ages.

For months I was overpaying on child support, but I was afraid if I made an application to change the child support payments to reflect the actual real parenting arrangement she would cut off access. So, I kept on overpaying. However after many months, I thought it'd be fairly transparent that if she did something to deny access to the kids, it would have been tied to child support.

When I made an application to change child support within days she cut off the children's time with me or some completely fabricated reason.

So you felt, in a sense, her letting you see the children was really tied to money that you shouldn't really have to pay, given that you were paying over what you should be paying for child support. It sounds a bit like having to "rent the children", in the sense of paying for time with them.

I overpaid thousands of dollars in child support based on incorrect information about the living arrangements to the Child Support Agency. I paid it because I wanted to see my kids and I was fearful she would cut off my time if I stopped. Which is exactly what happened. Because of that I had to file in the court urgently so I could see my children again. I also think the fact my ex wife found out I had re partnered around the same time as me changing the child support also added to her cutting off the time out of spite.

Eventually the Court saw through what she was doing and an arrangement was made for me to spend lots of time with my children thankfully.

Okay. And are you self-representing?

I've got a lawyer and counsel. I've spent thousands and thousands in legal fees. Frankly I have spent almost as much on legal fees as what we are arguing about, in terms of property. She's trying to represent herself. Partly, she's trying to represent herself I think she was encouraged to do this by a counsellor from one of the family support type centres who led us both to believe family law is easy and anyone can run their own matter. This has been a disaster because she hasn't filed any of the documents that she's supposed to file.

So, you don't actually know what she wants, really, in terms of what she's seeking?

She hasn't said what she's seeking, and indeed she hasn't put in an outline of argument for anything to the Court like we have.

Coming back to the child support overpayment, where you overpaid on child support so your ex would let you see your children, is that a wider gender issue, I suppose, with dads having to essentially overpay child support to see their children?

What I have seen with other dads I have known is that, generally, the female in this particular situation will make an application for a domestic violence order to get custody, because then they've got custody of the child automatically and they've excluded the other partner from having contact with the child. And then they go to the child support agency, and the father is forced to pay child support and denied access to their child. It's a double whammy.

And then if they can't afford to fight it through the courts, and couldn't defend the application for domestic violence order and then defend the matter through the Federal Circuit Court, or the Family Court, they're basically screwed. And that's when you see very high incidences of suicide amongst fathers who have been denied access to their children. Often, they're in financial difficulty too.

I've just learned very recently that while I left with about zero money and frightening amounts of debt, meanwhile, she had a hidden stash of money that I didn't know about. At the time that we split up, I didn't know she had any money, while I'm desperately trying to cover our debts partly from a giant credit card bill that she ran up. I have since heard that this is not uncommon. That someone in the marriage is dishonest about secret money or assets that they have hidden away. Once one of my children said, when a friend of mine was talking about arranged marriages, 'but that would mean you don't know the person when you marry them.' I thought afterwards, 'It is the same in our culture too- only you think you know the person, but you don't really.'

So, is financial stress what led to the separation?

Firstly, money problems were huge as our property lost value and also my wife's spending, and then also the way my ex-treated me – it would be regarded as family violence. I wasn't being punched or being physically hit, but I was being constantly being bombarded with mental abuse.

I was told I wasn't a real man, and a roster of other really abusive things I can't repeat and that I was useless on literally a daily basis, several times throughout the day. Constant abuse and being put down, and 'You're not a real man.' All this abuse. And it went on and on for months and months. I am not talking about a one off incident. This was daily, many times a day.

She always took the view that all of the debt was my responsibility because I'm a man and I must provide for her.

She would go through cycles. So, it was a lot of screaming and shouting, putting me down, and she'd be really angry, before calming down a bit, and there'd be a bit of an apology or 'I love you, really' sort of thing, but then it would build again. It's basically battered wife syndrome, but against the husband.

> I wasn't being beaten up, but it was emotional,
> which was almost as bad.

Probably as bad, actually. I would have rather just been punched in the face. But she wouldn't abuse me in front of anybody else. Nobody else knew. Also, and this is really hard to even talk about,

> she tried to persuade me to commit suicide
> for the life insurance money.

I mean she literally explained why this was a good idea and tried to convince me in all seriousness. I was pretty disturbed by that. I spoke to my family and they encouraged me to leave. I wonder, if I had been a woman going through the family law system, if I would have been treated different in the process.

Along the way I have raised these issues and nothing has been offered to me by way of support for the psychological family violence I have been subjected to. The thing is all of us, men and women, we are all still people. Someone going through what I went through (regardless of if they were a man or woman) deserves support and to have what has happened to them recognised.

And I'd seen a psychiatrist at that time because of stress over the financial situation and how my ex-was constantly compounding it and making it worse, constantly saying it was all my fault. My psychiatrist also said, 'She's a psychopath, and she's a narcissist, and you need to get out'.

So, they said she's got a personality problem.

Yes, I think I would say that, without any hesitation. So, she lied in the court proceedings several times. She has committed perjury repeatedly.

Frankly, I'm nervous for our kids in her care.

So, do you feel like, in terms of family violence, that your situation has been understood in the legal system? Or not really?

No, it isn't understood at all. The number of magistrates I've heard saying, 'You've just got to man up' – I'm not quite sure what that means. You are just treated as the bad guy, and

there's a presumption of innocence in relation to the woman and a presumption of guilt in relation to the man.

It is not as black and white as there being violent men and poor victimised women.

There are plenty of male victims of domestic violence. I think it tends to be more sort of psychological.

Obviously, domestic violence of men using their sometimes superior strength over their partners to bash them up is appalling and disgusting, and anything we can do to stop it is obviously important. However, there is a percentage of the female population using the system to prevent access to the other party out of spite, and to get the child support.

So, if there's anything you could say in terms of reform and changes to the Family Law system, do you think there should be better understanding of men as victims of family violence?

There is bias against men in the system. When I spoke to a former colleague who had been through a really nasty divorce, he said to me, 'Your children will be used as a weapon against you. It's going to be very difficult.' And he was absolutely right. The kids are being used and manipulated and twisted, and access to them is being denied for money.

> The child support agency is a major problem, because it usually incentivises women. They deny access to the children for money.

So, what would you say to a dad who's, say, in a situation like yours?

The thing to do probably is to get legal advice. See a psychologist and see a good family lawyer before you decide to do anything. I'd say be very careful about what you do or what you say. It's widely known that a domestic violence order is a quick solution to the problem. The child support agency comes in and the bloke is completely screwed.

And, also, the sense of injustice is basically like you're being accused of committing criminal offenses, and denied access to your children, without there being any kind of trial or anything. Because a domestic order will generally get granted. The allegation is raised, the order gets granted immediately, even in the absence of the person – they just get told about it subsequently, and then it's up to them to come to court and say, 'Okay, well, I want to go to trial on this; I want to prove my innocence.' So there is a presumption of guilt, and you're basically told to get out of the house. The person is basically told to get out of the house, and the police will come in and pick up some clothes and things, and then they're gone. And their access to the children is cut, and access to anywhere to live is gone, and they've got to try and find somewhere else. They may not have the money for a bond.

The entire system doesn't work. The Family Law system is very, very expensive. It just heightens animosity and the cost involved with it. I spent months working on my matter and nearly every weekend for months and months. I don't know how many hours I worked in it, but probably thousands of hours have gone into this matter.

So, you think there is some sort of not genuine, not authentic use of perceptions around male physical violence?

Politically, it's a little bit awkward to say that, because there is a concern that people might look like they are somehow excusing domestic violence against women, or that they're saying there isn't a problem when clearly there is one. But there is also a problem of using domestic violence orders to gain the upper hand in property and parenting matters.

So, I know that it happens. It's just that it's politically not something where anyone really wants to stand up and say, 'We've got to stop this happening. We've got to stand up for the blokes.' Because, traditionally, all the sympathy has been in the quarter of female victims of domestic violence.

> I'm not trying to detract from female victims of domestic violence, because there are genuine female domestic violence victims. But there are also genuine male victims of domestic violence, many of whom are just blokes suffering in silence.

How can we support these male victims of domestic violence in the Family Law system?

Awareness of the problem would be helpful – changes to the way the current systems operates.

> There should be consequences for false accusations in relation to domestic violence.

There needs to be more understanding of the fact men can also be victims of violence, particularly emotional, verbal, and psychological violence, from women.

Ryan

Getting on and off at various bus stops

On being a self-represented litigant in property proceedings

A significant proportion of the parties before the Court in Family Law matters are self-represented. Ryan sheds light on the experience of having legal representation and then representing oneself in Family Law matters. For Ryan, it was the lack of communication between the lawyers and what he viewed as wasted legal fees that led him to the decision to represent himself in Court. Interestingly, although Ryan did ultimately represent himself – including at final hearing – he still advocates for parties to at least initially obtain legal advice so they understand the range of reasonable outcomes in their matter.

In Ryan's case, he offered his ex-wife a settlement that he felt was within this reasonable range, and two years of litigation later, she eventually accepted this initial offer (or rather an offer that was 1% worse for her). This illustrates another important point – that sometimes parties agree or do not agree to offers for reasons and agendas that have nothing to do with law. Sometimes it is not a matter of the content of an offer but timing. Even though, in theory, litigants want to resolve matters at the earliest opportunity, at other times the litigation can be a subconscious way of keeping the conversation of the relationship going, even if it is a dysfunctional or argumentative one.

Interestingly, the tipping point for sacking Ryan's lawyer came after a conciliation conference, when the other party approached the conference as not being willing to negotiate. Ryan felt the conference was 'doomed to never get anywhere', as his lawyer had not called the other side to 'see if settlement was going to be possible' yet charged $10,000 in preparation. This situation illustrates the usefulness of barrister David Blackah's proposal for a compulsory phone conference between lawyers in the days immediately before Court events to 'see what can be agreed, what procedural orders should be made, and what should happen next'. Processes such as this, which open dialogue and narrow what is disputed, could be helpful. In Ryan's case, a simple telephone call could have prevented time and money being wasted.

▦

If I may go into this, I would like to know what caused the separation.

There were a lot of illness and health issues that I don't want to delve into. Also, in relation to her spending, I felt that was often unreasonable. So, basically it was health issues, spending, and so many other little things that happened. There were lots of little things, but when you add them all up... It was over everything and nothing at the same time.

Was it mutual?

She was shocked. I had said things needed to improve in certain areas or that I might not be able to continue with the relationship, but when I actually left the relationship, she was shocked.

Since I had been thinking about the relationship ending for some time, I had actually already given thought to the fact that we would need to come to an agreement about property and parenting.

I had discussions with her father because my ex- wasn't prepared to have discussions; I think she had her head in the sand. So, I presented him with a spreadsheet of the assets and what I felt was a fair settlement. From there, they weren't that happy with what I presented, but rather than talk about it, they filed an application in the Court and with an affidavit that was very long, full of opinion, and a lot of it would have been struck out. They served that on me just before Christmas.

Happy Christmas, I suppose.

Yes, like a kind of a nice Christmas present. I was stressing out about all of this and then I took it to a lawyer.

How did you choose your lawyer?

The lawyer I originally chose was a lady who was a friend of my father. I remember the first interview was free, but then there was conflict of interest as she knew my father well and my ex- had made certain allegations about him in the affidavit. So, I then went to a large Family Law firm in the city and I was very happy with them.

How did you find the legal process? I mean, I know you have a legal background, but did you find the process made sense or was it confusing?

Even though I have a legal background, I knew nothing about the Family Law system.

> In the initial meeting there wasn't a discussion of the actual practical steps; I felt a little bit in the dark about the process,

even though this was one of the best lawyers at one of the best firms in town.

Were you aware of the other alternative ways a matter could be resolved?

At that point, since the other party had filed in Court, that is what I thought had to happen. I was aware you could settle the matter, but I didn't feel my lawyer was coming up with creative ways to try and settle it.

It was more like he was taking me from one step to the next and when I went to that step, I wouldn't necessarily understand what was involved in each step or what the purpose was. It was akin to getting on and off various bus stops. That's how it felt.

So, it was just like 'Now we are going to do this, and now we are going to do this', and so on, like going through the motions of various processes without a real understanding of why and what the overall picture was?

Yes. But it is very costly. I used a city lawyer and the bills just racked up.

I ended up self-representing after the conciliation conference, but at the conciliation conference my bill was $30,000. When I went to the conciliation conference, we were in the Family Court and my lawyer had gone on long service leave and had got another lawyer from his firm to represent me. I hated that because he knew everything, then suddenly I had this new person who didn't know the background to my matter and had been briefed at the last moment. Then, at conciliation conference, my ex- didn't even want to negotiate and I was, like, 'Well, did you even speak to the other side on the phone before the Conciliation conference and ask them what their position was? Or find out if they were even prepared to negotiate?'

I was prepared to negotiate, and did at the conference, but she wasn't, at all. The registrar said to her, to my ex-wife's face, 'You're not going to get that'. And she said, 'Well, I don't care'. It was all about keeping the house for her, and in Family Law matters you either often buy the other side out or sell the house, and she couldn't afford to buy me out, so it was, like, let's sell it.

I tried to come up with ideas throughout the process about how maybe she could keep the house, for example, through some sort of long-term loan arrangement. I thought she could perhaps pay me back, or whatever it might be. I thought I was coming up with ideas, but my lawyers weren't thinking creatively.

Then, when I got the bill for the Conciliation conference for that one month and it was $10,000, I thought, well, we were doomed to never get anywhere because he never even rang them to see if settlement was going to be possible.

Yes, where's the dialogue with the other lawyer to see where the matter is at?

There was none. Basically, I said thanks, but I feel I can do this by myself because all you are doing is taking me from A to B to C. So, I represented myself and hired a university graduate to research some things for me and we ran the case ourselves.

Did this become almost akin then to a part-time job in terms of the amount of work?

Well, there was a lot of time put into it. But I had a business where I had time to do this. This lawyer was paid $50 an hour to help me. As it turned out, I made my ex- an offer of 61/39 in her favour about 18 months before we settled, which would have allowed her to keep the house. In the end, the funny thing is, we settled for 60/40, in her favour. It went through to final hearing and I had to read up about contributions, future needs, understanding a balance sheet, and they wanted add backs. It was very involved. The result I got essentially what I had offered her.

In the end, at final hearing, she had barristers and a lawyer and it was, like, 'Why are you doing this?' It didn't make sense to me that she went all this way and then settled for what I'd originally offered her anyway.

What was it all about then?

Yes, exactly – what was it all about? Because we ended up doing a deal similar to the one I had proposed via my lawyer nearly two years earlier.

It included loans that allowed her to retain the property for years and have the children stay in the property. I remember the Judge said this was quite creative and a good way to do it.

In a way it is good, but were you also thinking that if you agree to it now, why did it take two years to come around to this?

She would have spent over $150,000 in legal fees to get to the same point as I originally offered her. I saw what she spent, because we ended up sharing those legal fees, which I now know doesn't normally happen.

It was a good experience in that I got to see what lawyers do and how it could be done differently.

Another thing I was upset about was how so much information had to be transferred by way of disclosure. I would have to give the information to my lawyer, who would give it to her lawyer, who would then give it to my ex-wife.

It was moving from hand to hand to hand.

Yes, from there to them, to them. A lot of double-handing in this whole process. It would have been better if I had just prepared the information and sent it direct to the lawyer on the other side. When I was self-represented, I could give the information directly to my ex-wife's lawyer.

So, you had quite a positive experience self-representing?

Yes. I learnt a lot about the process, for one, and that increased my interest in Family Law, and I got a good result for me.

It doesn't sound like, if what you ultimately ended up with was quite similar to what your lawyer originally sought, that being self-represented disadvantaged you in terms of outcome.

I don't think I was disadvantaged, but I think I was able to do it in a way that a lot of self-represented people don't. For example, I had help from a law graduate, and I had my own legal background, and I was happy to put time into it, whereas I felt my lawyer was not making a real effort to settle anything at all.

I was often asking my ex's lawyer: How can we get a settlement? I remember her saying she wouldn't settle it, that she wanted to get the house.

Sometimes whether you can settle something is about who is on the other side. You have a registrar saying, 'You are not going to get that', and my ex-wife saying, 'I will just keep going anyway'. I almost felt like my ex-wife's lawyer should just stop representing her, because they were just lining their pockets to fight a losing cause. When it settled, it justified the original position I alluded to at the beginning.

It sounds like maybe she just wasn't psychologically ready to settle.

Yes. I think that happens in a lot of Family Law matters. They are not mentally prepared or are just fixated on one particular outcome, and they don't care; they just want to have it litigated. And, yes, it's a mental thing; it is a psychological thing.

Do you feel, overall, it was a fair outcome?

Yes, I think so.

What happened with your children?

We didn't litigate regarding kids. We had an arrangement from when we separated and have kept to it to this day. We had some issues about holiday time, but apart from this it has worked out pretty well and remained the same as it was years ago. I have a great relationship with my children and my ex- has never gotten in the way of that. We never litigated and never needed to.

So, it was really just the property side. Is there anything about how property is looked at that isn't working well?

You can have different Judges look at the same identical facts and come up with different results.

Discretion, you mean.

Yes, it is a discretionary area with regards to deciding how property is divided. There are no hard and fast rules, but there is a subjective element and I don't know how you get around it.

I think that, in a lot of situations, husbands or fathers who work think they would be entitled to everything, because they have earned the money, as compared to, say, their wife. I think there needs to be more explanation about how contributions work and what contributions really mean: How the breadwinner contribution can be valued the same as what a primary carer or homemaker does, and that bringing in property or earning money isn't the only contribution of value.

> I think as a self-represented person, you do receive a lot of spoon feeding from Judges.

Do you think they treat self-represented people differently?

Totally. Probably necessarily, because they don't have an insight into how the system works, so they need to be coached a little bit more. That works against represented people.

I find self-represented people are told by the Judge what they need to do and how to do it, and I suppose there is a bit of favouritism there.

They are sympathetic to self-represented people?

Yes, they are sympathetic.

So, you felt supported in the process by the Judge in your matter?

Yes, I think so. Having been through the process from the other side now, working as a family lawyer, I have seen that as well.

> The problem is that dealing with self-represented people often takes longer than dealing with a family lawyer, and your client has to still pay for your time in dealing with their [self-represented] ex. It can double the bill.

> It isn't fair on your client that the other side is self-represented, that they are asking for things they shouldn't and have no knowledge of the process.

But how do you really remedy that? I mean, you can't force people to have solicitors because not everyone can afford them.

I don't know. It is difficult.

Do you have any other views about how we could do things better, generally?

Yes, the awareness and education that you can settle matters. Focus on settlement and a plan for settlement. Explain the process, and what the steps are, and that you can get off the family litigation bus ride at any point and settle the matter.

A lot of people aren't sure of what is involved in the process, and I think just a better education would be good.

At your initial conference was there an estimate for fees?

No. I had no clue in terms of how much it would cost, say, to get to a conciliation conference.

What is your relationship like now with your ex-partner?

Pretty good. Well, I would say our relationship is fractured still, but we function as parents. I think she feels cheated still about the property settlement.

That's interesting. You feel the outcome was fair, but she feels cheated?

She said she doesn't believe the outcome was a fair one. Well, the way it was reached, it was interesting. When I went into Court on the final hearing day, the Judge had to be recused because I had put in a schedule of settlement offers. We needed to get a new Judge because she had already looked at the settlement offers.

Self-represented people causing havoc!

Well, yes, I didn't know back then you couldn't do that. Because of that we actually settled, because we had the whole day to talk about it. My ex-wife had a barrister who was very commercial. But my ex-wife thinks it was all a conspiracy, that I did it on purpose, when in actual fact I just had no clue.

I think, though, it helped that you had some legal advice at the start of your matter, so you at least knew the range of reasonable outcomes then. Perhaps what I am saying is that it was good to have some legal assistance for a while.

I agree. I think a situation where someone is self-represented who has never had a conference with a lawyer is dangerous because they have preconceived ideas about what they should and shouldn't get.

> Before I went to the final hearing I actually sat for a week at the back of Court and saw how matters were run.

I saw self-represented people pleading with the Judge about nothing related to the law. They need to understand the *Family Law Act* and they don't. Again, you have to give them the opportunity if they want to self-represent, but, yes, it can cause havoc.

So, you would suggest to someone reading this book who is thinking of self-representing to at least get legal advice at the start and an understanding of what the range of reasonable results would be.

Yes.

> I would say that if you are self-represented, get legal advice at the start and get a barrister to represent you at the end, if it goes to final hearing...

because they are the experts in presenting your case to the Court.

Robert

When the dust has settled

On being a father and ex-husband resolving
property matters outside of court

Robert had been with his wife Jess since they met at his friend's 20th
birthday party. Twenty six years and three children later their marriage
unwound, partly, Robert says, due to his having post-traumatic stress
disorder (PTSD) from his Profession. Despite a traumatic and protracted
separation and property negotiation, Robert found that when he and Jess
communicated again, they were able to agree and resolve matters.

Looking back, having re-partnered with his childhood sweetheart and
having a strong relationship with his children, Robert has very much come
out the other side of his divorce and even feels lucky. Life can be very different
after 'the dust has settled.' After all the noise and chaos a separation can be,
often there is an unexpected stillness. As writer Cheryl Strayed says, who
herself went through a divorce and the death of her mother simultaneously,
'Acceptance is a small, quiet room'.

▦

Tell me a bit about the history of your relationship with your partner.

I met Jess at my best mate's 20th birthday party. We met that evening and
had an instant attraction. We started seeing each other, and after five years
we were married, and had three children.

What drew you to Jess?

Originally, when I first saw Jess at the party, it was her good looks and long hair. As we grew closer, I found her to be very giving, loving, and generous.

When did you start to realise the relationship had serious problems, and what led to the separation?

After several years investigating all types of gruesome crime scenes as part of my job, I found myself alienating myself from daily routines, arguing, having panic attacks, feeling scared and hiding at home in my work shed, consuming excess alcohol. I was later diagnosed with 'Post Traumatic Stress Disorder' and was retired medically unfit to continue in my profession. I went through years of counselling, but unfortunately it took its toll on our marriage.

> Jess couldn't cope with my behaviour any longer and I was asked to leave the house. Excessive alcohol played a part in the marriage downfall,

...as I used to drink to hide from my memories and ugly thoughts and visions.

Initially, when I was told to leave the house for a trial separation, I did think a reconciliation would follow; however, it didn't. Perhaps this is when I should have started divorce procedures.

What issues (including legal issues) were in dispute with you and your partner when you separated?

Jess, at this time, was not working and I was living nearby in a converted garage, paying rent. Although separated, I continued to maintain the house, gardens, pay all the bills for the house, mortgage, and support Jess and the children financially.

I did this for a few years until I realised Jess was living on Easy Street. She saw this in a different light, as she was looking after the children. I informed her she had to get a job, as I could no longer continue to financially support everything.

How did you and your previous partner resolve the dispute between you?

I started property negotiations soon after, and the divorce aspect was finalised. Jess and I spoke and we agreed she would keep the house and contents, so the children could continue to live there. I saw the kids whenever I could. I paid child support until each child turned 21 years old.

What was the outcome?

Each case is different, and, in my instance, I made agreements with Jess. I kept my pension and superannuation, which was worth about the same as the equity in the house and she kept the family house and contents.

At the time, I was bitterly hurt, as I had renovated and built a large proportion of the family home, and to lose it was devastating.

As they say, you can't look back. I'm happy the children weren't uprooted from their home and they are still comfortable living there.

How did you feel at the time about the process?

The property part of divorce is long, expensive, and very stressful. Jess's solicitors were slow to reply to correspondence and any enquiries about financial disclosure. My solicitors would send them a reminder, but this was an added expense for me. Each time they wrote to them, it would cost me. I was annoyed and I'd get cranky with my solicitors; I was running out of money. If Jess and I had been able to speak directly, this would have made the process a little smoother. Ultimately, when we finally did speak, that is how we reached an agreement.

I couldn't anticipate what was going to happen in the divorce process, as it was my first time. The day of the divorce case was very quick. It was heard and done within 10 minutes.

What did you learn about the Family Law process from your experience?

The family law process is very expensive. Although very stressful, our matter was quite simple, with only a few minor issues. Property settlement was agreed to by Jess and myself.

Have there been any ongoing issues with what was agreed or what was your outcome with Jess?

No, other than...

> I was very hurt giving up the family home, as I'd invested many hours and many dollars into making it a beautiful home.

Jess does know this.

Did you retain a lawyer during the process?

I had a legal firm look after my divorce proceedings. I found them by searching the internet.

I had a wonderful female lawyer whom I got on with very well. She put up with my stress, my tantrums, and was very professional. I was very disappointed when she left the firm, as I then had to deal with another member who didn't know my case as well. This increased my stress levels and the expense. But the service was still very professional.

The expenses were funded by my savings. When my original lawyer left, and I was being looked after by another member, I wasn't informed of his higher hourly rates. This came to me as a shock as I couldn't afford the final account. I came to an agreement with the firm and paid for it over time.

What other professionals and experts did you interact with during the Family Law process?

External professionals were involved for superannuation valuing and psychiatrists for PTSD issues. They were professional, but just another added expense.

Did you start a new relationship after the separation?

After my separation, I located my childhood girlfriend Elle on Facebook. We wrote to each other for a month and finally met up for dinner.

This was three years after I'd left the family home, and we hadn't been in touch for over 30 years. We are still together today, and recently married. Elle helped and supported me through the divorce and attended the divorce hearing with me.

Elle has met my three children and Jess and we all have a good relationship. The children regularly come over for dinner or a visit.

It sounds like you have come out the other side of things now. Do you feel this experience changed you as a person?

Divorce is a very traumatic thing for anyone to go through. I think when the dust has settled, it makes you a little stronger and you realise that life does go on.

I feel lucky that my children still live in their home, even though I gave up ownership in the agreement.

I also feel lucky that I have met up again with Elle, and that she supports me with everything I do.

I think you need support after the divorce, so you can realise it's not the end of the earth. Don't look back. Financially, I lost out, and rebuilding your life again in your fifties is financially tough. Elle recently made me attend PTSD classes at a hospital, and this has helped me incredibly with my previous profession and the divorce. I have learned that the past is the past and it is not happening now, it can't hurt me anymore.

DON'T LOOK BACK.

What I have learnt is marriage is a two-way street and both persons must work at it. Support, trust, and communication is the most important part of a marriage, and once this breaks down, it is very hard to recover.

Any tips for those going through a separation now?

Family law is slow and expensive. Don't expect things to happen overnight. If you and your ex-partner can communicate on civil terms, make agreements together – this makes life a lot easier and proceedings faster.

Once the divorce was finalised, Jess and I agreed that we should have communicated directly more frequently during the process. This would have saved time, money and emotional stress.

Do you have any thoughts about reform to the system?

> Family lawyers should perhaps encourage or organise more mediation between the two parties.

This may assist in the expense and time and the toing and froing of correspondence between the parties' lawyers.

Hugo

The club

On being the new partner of (and funding) a mother trying to have
orders for supervised time only reviewed

I interviewed Hugo because even though he, himself, did not directly
go through the Family Law system, his story shows how it is not simply
the person who is directly named as a party to the proceedings who is
affected. Often, there is an entire family behind each person, providing
emotional and/or financial support and who vicariously experience the
Court process.

In Hugo's case, his de facto partner Lenka was, in his view, the victim
of unfair previous Court orders that only allowed her to spend time with
her daughter at a contact centre. Seeking to help her, he funded her
attempt at getting the orders revisited by the Court. From here, Hugo
explains how Lenka and he were like strangers in a strange land, on the
outside of a Family Law club they could not access. In particular, Hugo
raises the issue of experts' reports. In Lenka's matter, I got the sense that
from Hugo's perspective, it was as if things took on a life of their own.
There was an expert report that was then adopted by the Independent
Children's Lawyer. A position was repeated and repeated, growing more
powerful with each repetition. Hugo and Lenka's story raises questions
about how power works in the Court system, and if there is a clique, 'the
club' in which truth is a construct and is owned by those who hold more
power in the family Court arena.

On the issue of 'the Truth', I think, obliquely, Hugo's story highlights one
of the inevitable difficulties of Court hearings. Findings about 'the Truth' are

made. That is simply what happens at trial – findings of fact are made. There is, in a sense, a battle for ownership of the truth, which is a zero-sum game. Conversely, in alternative dispute resolution processes, such as mediation, there can be more space for both the parties' worlds to exist.

⸬

What is the background to the Family Law matter you were involved in?

I was in a relationship with Lenka for more than a year. She is Eastern European and had lived in Australia for years, and she had a five-year-old daughter from a previous relationship. The father had obtained custody of the child, in part because Lenka had sought to emigrate back to Europe with her daughter at the end of their relationship.

Lenka had been in a de facto relationship with her partner. It came apart due to pressure caused by the father's financial and legal difficulties arising from his business. I only ever heard Lenka's side of the story.

What issues were in dispute with Lenka and her ex when they separated?

The only issue, really, was custody of Lenka's daughter. Lenka tried to go home to Europe with her daughter without fully appreciating the ramifications of doing so. In her mind, the situation with the father had become intolerable and she had no obligation to the father in circumstances where they had never been married and her daughter did not have his surname on her birth certificate.

Under the Hague Convention treaty, the father was allowed to bring his daughter back to Australia. Here in Australia, there followed a contested Family Court hearing that lasted a number of days.

What happened in the original proceedings?

The father won the hearing very decisively, principally because of a report produced by a court-appointed expert that concluded Lenka had a histrionic/narcissistic personality; that in combination with Lenka's conduct in removing her daughter from Australia, caused her to appear in a very negative light.

The barrister who appeared for Lenka in the original Family Court hearing commented to me that Lenka's case stuck very strongly in his memory because she had been such a bad witness. While giving evidence, Lenka kept smiling in a disconcerting way, which seemed highly incongruous given the gravity of what was under discussion.

I do think, however, that it is possible Lenka was smiling because she was nervous and intimidated by the Court process. I also think cultural issues and English being her second language was not really understood in the proceedings.

The outcome was that the father obtained sole custody and Lenka, who had been her child's primary carer since birth, was restricted to weekly supervised visits with her daughter at a contact centre.

And what was your involvement in the proceedings?

At the point where I became involved, Lenka was seeking to vary the court orders and obtain greater access to her daughter. She filed an application seeking review of the Court's orders.

Lenka was a public servant with extremely limited financial resources; by contrast, her former partner seemed to have access to quite a lot of money. I agreed to pay Lenka's legal costs because I thought the Court's orders had been extremely unjust, and Lenka's misery at being separated from her daughter was palpable. Lenka had had legal aid for the purpose of the original Family Law proceeding, but there was no aid for the application for review.

There was an interlocutory squabble over whether the Judge who made the original orders should determine the application. The Judge ultimately recused himself, on the condition that Lenka pay all her ex-partner's legal costs to date. Those costs were $18,000.

At that point (after I had spoken to a couple of Family Law barristers, and looked into the possibility of obtaining a new expert report) it seemed clear that when the Court came to consider Lenka's substantive application, there would be opposition from the ICL to any variation to the original orders and, further, unless Lenka could obtain an extremely strong expert report that would dislodge or discredit the Court's earlier finding that Lenka had a personality disorder, her application would have no chance of success. Because of the authority of the ICL and the expert, it seemed hopeless.

When I looked into the costs of obtaining such an expert report they seemed prohibitive and, of course, there was no guarantee that any expert report I paid for would be favourable. I told Lenka that I was not willing to fund a court action that had such limited prospects of success.

How did the decision not to fund Lenka's application affect your relationship?

It effectively caused the end of my relationship with Lenka. Lenka knew that I had the financial capacity, at least in theory, to continue to fund her application, and that I was not willing to do so. On the other hand, I felt certain that it would be a waste of money to continue.

I was never in any doubt that Lenka's daughter was the most important thing in her life.

During the period of my involvement, the legal fees that I personally paid were in the order of $30,000 to $32,000, including the costs incurred by the other side.

At the time, how did you feel about the original outcome and also the findings the Court made?

At the time I felt Lenka had been done a massive injustice. I still feel that way.

The original court decision also seemed to depend, in large part, on the Court's assessment of Lenka's demeanour as a witness. Almost everybody who works in litigation is aware of the shortcomings of conclusions reached on the basis of witness demeanour.

Having said that, I can understand how the key decision-makers - acting in good faith - could reach the conclusions they did. Any person reading the Court's reasons for its original decision would be left with a sense that the Judge approached his task in a responsible and careful fashion.

To my mind, the episode seems to illustrate the inherent limitations of the curial process in ascertaining the truth.

That it is extremely difficult for a litigant to obtain reconsideration of a Court's findings, and extremely expensive for a litigant to even attempt this, reflects policy judgements about the finality of litigation that I can understand and accept.

You mentioned the expert report findings. Can you elaborate further on how you reconciled the report with the person you knew.

I found it impossible to reconcile the findings in the expert's report with the person I knew.

Over my two years of close acquaintance with Lenka, I saw absolutely no indication that she had narcissistic or histrionic personality traits; to the contrary, she was an extremely gentle and kind person who seemed to be coping in a stoical and dignified manner with immense unhappiness.

I refuse to accept there is something unique or superior about the perspective of a person who happens to have formal qualifications in psychiatry or psychology. That would mean the expert report was more accurate than my own first-hand knowledge of the person in question. I have read the original expert report, and I did not think its conclusions were well explained.

The only practical suggestion I can make, as a result of the experience, is that the Court should not receive only a single expert report. In circumstances where an expert report contains findings that are so strong they are likely to be decisive of the outcome of a Family Law matter, I would have thought prudence would require that there be a report from a second expert.

What did you take away from the experience?

The thing I took away from the experience is a near horror at the thought that one day I might find myself as a litigant in the Family Court, with a complete stranger making decisions about how much time I'm allowed to spend with my children or what proportion of my assets I'm allowed to keep.

I don't pretend to have a better idea about how Family Law issues should be resolved when a marriage or relationship ends, but I found the whole thing extremely alienating and distasteful.

Is there any particular memory that sticks with you in regards to the Family Law process you underwent?

Two things stick in my mind. Firstly, the ICL was a woman I immediately disliked.

The ICL said she would be opposing Lenka's application but she would not explain why. She also communicated a clear sense that...

> she regarded Lenka's application as a strange idiosyncrasy, and
> that this was partly because she was not familiar with Lenka's
> lawyers and did not regard them as part of the club.

I think her approach lacked empathy for the fact that Lenka is an actual person, a mother, who was seeking to spend more time with her child than an occasional visit at a contact centre. I did not feel she really saw Lenka's humanity; nor did she treat her in a humane fashion.

The barrister who appeared for Lenka's ex-partner was a rude individual, and went out of his way to be rude to me, personally.

There was a nastiness about the whole thing, albeit one sees this in other types of litigation as well.

Marco

Suffering in silence

A single gay dad's journey through international commercial
surrogacy to have his daughter

Marco always sensed he wanted to be a father. But he probably never
anticipated just how far he would have to go to have his child. In this
interview we see the lived reality of lawyer Stephen Page's observations
about how our legal settings which make commercial surrogacy a criminal
offence, mean Australians seeking to have a child this way are forced to
travel overseas.

Although Marco's story – $150,000 and months of administrative chaos
later – is ultimately a happy one with him being the father of a gorgeous
baby girl, after speaking with him I was left wondering: Could we not make
things easier for parents and children? I can imagine it would have been
overwhelming to undergo this level of administrative nightmare on top of
all the other challenges of being a new parent. Although this certainly was
never raised in speaking with Marco, I also wonder if (in some cases) fear
about possible criminal charges prevents new parents from seeking supports,
services, resources or generally reaching out for help, which can only have
detrimental effects for children?

In my view there is an absence of public discussion about commercial
surrogacy and why it is illegal and what are the arguments for changing
(or not changing) the law. I think part of the issue is there is a lack of
publicly available stories about parent's real experiences with commercial
surrogacy overseas. As Marco says it is just families 'suffering in silence'.
An obvious reason for this is the illegality prevents people sharing their

stories and thus creates a circular secrecy around commercial surrogacy that only makes changes to the law less likely. But we cannot deal with something as a society if it is not revealed. Unsurprisingly, Marco argues for a regulated framework for people to be able to undertake commercial surrogacy within Australia.

∷

To step back a bit, can you just explain the decision that led up to choosing to have a baby via surrogacy?

It's a very long-winded process. The first time I thought about it was in my twenties. Not surrogacy in particular; I just knew I wanted to be a parent.

Twenty years later, after a broken relationship because the other person didn't want to have a child, I took a redundancy from my job, and went travelling throughout Asia, and realised it was now or never. I'd moved to Asia at that stage for the sole purpose of getting a live-in nanny, because as a single person, I knew I couldn't do it alone.

I moved to Asia, and said, 'Once I get a job, I'm going to start the process and then get a nanny.' I couldn't get a job in Asia for the type of work I do, and then the whole baby Gammy thing hit. It put a huge, dark cloud over all the plans that I had in my mind. I was told many countries in Asia either outlawed surrogacy or made it much harder.

I spoke to an agency and asked 'So, what's happened to your business now that the whole baby Gammy thing is going?' and they said, 'Oh, nothing. It's exactly the same.' And I said, 'Well, how can that be?' And they said, 'Oh, we just tell a little white lie'. They explained that to get around legal requirements, the little white lie is that you're in a relationship with the surrogate. Well, she's not really represented as a surrogate. You have to say you are in a heterosexual relationship with her.

My response was, hmm... ok, I'm not 100% comfortable with that, so I let it sit for another year or so. I can't remember the exact chronology of events, but then the state I was in made it illegal for residents to use commercial surrogacy arrangements overseas.

I spoke to a lawyer here and was told 'The door's already closed. You can't do it.' Then, to fast forward about a year, one day by a complete fluke I found an old email from the agency. I emailed them and asked how things were going, and they wrote, 'Oh, everything's fine. Everything's normal.' How can that be, I thought? Ok, let's have a proper chat about this. So we organised a Skype call. I asked them a whole bunch of questions, had it all written down, and I just didn't ask certain questions. I knew it wasn't 100% legal in my state, or overseas in the countries I was looking into.

As I approached 50, I just thought less of what other people thought, in particular my mother, and I was willing to take the risk.

> Despite the risks I really wanted to have a child and commercial surrogacy was the only real way this could happen.

So, I gave it a go. Everything happened on the first shot. I said, if I am past 50 and it hasn't happened, I'm not going to do it again, as it's very expensive (about 45,000 USD just for the agency fees). And then you have to get an egg donor, and that's additional costs. If I got a local donor, it was about $6,000 for the eggs.

Can you tell me more about the egg donor?

Well, I got a whole bunch of profiles, local profiles. I was not overly keen.

> The pictures of egg donors look like they had been touched up. They're all like this [poses with hand behind head and pouting]. I mean, it's not a Tinder date we're going on!

I asked how much it would be for an expat Caucasian donor. They told me, sent me the profiles, I saw one, and I thought she was attractive – she wasn't trying to be something that she wasn't in the pictures. She was just a very down-to-earth-looking person.

I was coming back from Africa, and my stopover was where she was living in Asia, so I met with the egg donor and I quite liked her. She was doing the same degree that I did. She was educated and intelligent. Yes.

And a little bit assertive too; she was no wallflower. She could speak her mind, not in an aggressive way, but she had self-esteem and it felt a little bit feisty, which I quite liked.

Ultimately, I am glad, because I have had a daughter. At the time I was choosing the egg I did not think I would have a daughter, but now I hope she has some of those qualities. You don't have to be a leader, but I don't want a girl to just sit back and think this is what a girl is expected to be. I kind of felt I got that vibe with the woman who was the egg donor. So, anyway, I started the process and everything just happened. It happened straight away, first go.

So, what happened in terms of gender if you were meant to have a boy?

Originally, I was meant to have a boy. You can't choose the sex of your baby in most places in the world, but in some countries you can. There's a whole bunch of tests they do. Tests for everything. And one of the by-products of that test is you can find out the gender.

How did you end up with a daughter then?

Originally, they told me all along, yes, you can choose the gender, so I thought of boys' names. I was looking at everything. My whole mental picture was with a boy. Then they did the egg retrieval from the egg donor, and I think there were about 17 eggs. From those, they got about 11 embryos when they put the sperm and the eggs together, of which ...

only two were viable, and both were female. It changed the whole mental picture. I had a meltdown, actually. Oh my God, I thought, but I don't know how to plait hair!

I don't know how to plait hair either, and I have a daughter!

There's a YouTube clip that you can do. I thought, well, which toilets do I use when I go to the shopping centre, and what... how?!' I spoke to a couple of gay friends who told me they'd originally wanted girls and they got boys, and so forth.

The agency said, 'You could do the whole process again: You could get more eggs, do more semen donation, all that sort of stuff, but you could end up with exactly the same.' That would put everything back by another few months, I knew. I'd have to go back there, it'd cost thousands more. The agency said, 'Do you want to do the transfer or not?' So I said, 'Let's do the transfer.' My friend also said, 'At the end of the day, you're not going to care. You're just going to love your child.'

Two weeks later, I get this very long-winded letter from the agency that there had been a mistake and they admitted, 'Yes, you actually have seven viable embryos.' I knew what that meant. It probably meant that amongst those seven, there were boys, and if this was in Australia, it would be a lawsuit. But it was too late.

There were boys in the other ones, only two boys, and the rest were females, so it was highly likely that I was always going to get a female anyway. So, I went over for the birth.

You were there for the birth?

I was there for the birth. The surrogate was scheduled to have the caesarean on Saturday morning, and then the process to come home.

Sorry to digress but I just wanted to ask, did you have a lawyer assisting you throughout this, or it was all just done, well, renegade, so to speak?

Well, I was told of the process, and I blindly believed the process, and it was true.

> The whole process was exactly as the agency said,
> but not the timeframe.

It was about double what it was supposed to take. It's not the agency's fault with it all; it was the Australian Embassy overseas.

And then there were the legalities and the process of getting the baby back into Australia. Basically, we were there for four months instead of two. There were countless meetings, forms, DNA tests, and lost results, and letters sent to the wrong places. I wouldn't even be able to detail it all in the space of this interview.

For the passport application, I had to be interviewed, where I was told what I had done was illegal. But what they were doing was, strangely enough, using closed questions: 'Do you know that this is illegal?'

What did you say?

'Oh?'

They asked, 'Is this the agreement you had with the agency?' They were all yes and no, so I just said, 'Oh, yes.' Make it easy, ok.

Then the surrogate also had to be interviewed. The woman said, 'Can't do it today. Too busy.' I said, 'What? You mean this empty waiting room?' 'Too busy!' she insisted. You can't annoy them, because they'll just put you on the bottom of the pile. She said, 'Come back Wednesday.' That was another five days. Just get me out of here was all I could think.

We came back in five days' time and she was interviewed. I said, 'How long is the process now?' They said, 'Oh, all the stuff now goes to the decision-maker.' No title. This person is just called 'the decision-maker'. That's what's on their business card. Not a lot of faith in this person.

I can't tell you – it was all in their hands. In the meantime, my visa had expired two times. The first time, I just had to go to this big government office to get a stamp. It took three hours, sitting there, waiting in line, and it was just a horrible exercise in bureaucracy.

The second time, I had to do a day trip to another neighbouring country, so the nanny looked after my daughter. I went to another country for the day and came back, just to get the passport stamp.

The third time, I thought, 'I can't do those processes again. It's going to look really suspicious,' and it was driving me insane being stuck in the apartment.

My daughter needed more stimulation, instead of just being in the air-conned apartment. I thought, I've got to go. I've got to get out of this place.

We were at roughly just under the four-month mark. I had expected to be there for two months. This is another one of those detail things. I kept extending the apartment for another two weeks. Two weeks, a week, another week, and then day by day. I said, 'It's coming any minute. The passport's coming any minute.' Day by day. And then I asked one more time, 'Can I extend?' And she said, 'I didn't think you'd be here in April, so I've actually let it out to somebody else.' My visa had expired. I was going crazy, being cooped up in the apartment, with the pollution and the heat, and the apartment was going to be let out within the week.

The agency said I needed to go overseas, but there had been a crack-down on human trafficking, so any single person, male or female, who's leaving is going to be questioned. Somebody who was in exactly the same position as I was, an Australian citizen leaving with a baby, got questioned, had all the paperwork with him, panicked, and was denied exit. He had to forfeit the airline ticket and everything. The agency said, 'We highly do not recommend that you go alone. You need to go with the surrogate.' However, the surrogate's never travelled before, so we need to bring someone from with the agency with you, so we all left, looking like a big happy family and a nanny.

And suddenly, ta-dah! You're straight. You're with your surrogate.

That's right! Even though she can't speak English, and I can't speak her language.

Somehow the passport comes eventually. Power of attorney picks it up on the Thursday, couriers it to me on the Friday, and we come home to Australia.

Where are you at, legal status-wise?

My understanding is that I didn't need to get a parenting order, because passport, citizenship – everything is all legitimate. I'm the dad on the birth certificate and at the time I had DNA tests done through an Australian pathology whilst overseas, as required by the law of that country. I showed I was the biological dad, so I am ok.

> I believe the only issue is that if I meet someone who then becomes
> my partner, and they want to be legally recognised as a parent, you
> have to get a parenting order.

But I would be hesitant to do that, because then you are bringing attention
to the fact that you did something illegal.

**Do you have other friends who have been through this process? What's the
range of experiences?**

The experiences vary according to each country. A friend of mine did it
in Nepal, before Nepal shut its doors. That was a couple of years ago, so
the experience now would be totally different. Going through the US, their
commercial surrogacy is formal, and the same with Canada, and so forth.
It's going to be a different experience. Mine was difficult because of all
the bureaucracy.

I know Rainbow Families just did a survey about this, but I'll give you an
example of how discriminatory it all is. A friend of mine is not an Australian
citizen, but her husband is an Australian citizen. They had a baby in the
same country where my daughter was born. I said to her, 'Oh, you're going
to have to do the DNA test, just like me. It's exactly the same.' She said,
'No, we don't have to do the DNA test.' I said, 'But why? Because the baby
you're about to have, you need to prove that it's your husband's.' She said,
'No, I don't need to. I just need to show the marriage certificate.'

It took three weeks to get her child's Australian passport, while mine
took six weeks after citizenship, because I don't have a marriage certificate.
Why should I have to do the DNA test, incur the cost, and undergo the
lengthy process and the grilling when all they have to do is show a marriage
certificate? Just because you have a marriage certificate, it doesn't mean the
baby you're about to have is his.

It's still very much that traditional world view.

Conventional family, I suppose.

Same with parental leave – it is really for the mother. Only in exceptional circumstances, apparently, do they give it to the father, but traditionally, or usually, it's for the mum. I got rejected for that.

What is the total financial cost?

Financially, there was the actual cost, but then there's the cost of flying there. You're flying in and out of everywhere, plus all the rent over there. How much do you think it'll cost you financially?

> I'm broke. I am. We are on 2-Minute Noodles until she's 16.
> I would say roughly I have spent about $150,000.

That is roughly half the amount if I went through US or Canada. That's if there are no complications and everything worked the first time.

There's obviously been a lot of administrative and, I think, some structural discrimination. Do you find, though, in terms of the actual people you come across, have people been supportive?

I have not faced any discrimination myself. The childcare's been absolutely fantastic. There's another gay dad who goes there as well. No obvious discrimination. None from Centrelink, none from airline staff, absolutely none. Mind you, I live in the inner-city bubble.

It may be different if I got further out, or if I go to another state, or yeah, outback or something like that.

Some people have the attitude that surrogacy is commoditisation of women's bodies. Do you have a view about that?

My view is, I'm pro-choice, so I let a woman choose what happens to her body, including, for example, abortion. If you're pro-choice for that, then you have to be pro-choice for choosing surrogacy. You can't pick and choose.

Listening to your experience, do you think that commercial surrogacy should be legalised and also easier to do in Australia, so people don't have to go all around the world?

Definitely, definitely, definitely. I think the reason they make it difficult is, yes, there are people who have other motives for having a child, but not everyone has those motives. We're all basically treated like we're going to be doing something wrong before we are thought of as we're going to be doing something right. I know that they're erring on the side of caution, but there should be some framework for assessing the bona fides of people rather than just a flat-out no. There should be a national law and a clear framework.

> Manage it [commercial surrogacy] and regulate it,
> rather than just say no.

I think the government just thinks it's too difficult. Now, I know they've just changed the laws on adoption to make it faster and easier, but that's adoption. That's been around for years and years and years, and they've just got to it. I don't know when they're going to get around to surrogacy. People aren't protesting on the streets about it, so it is not a priority.

> The difficulty in Australia is that surrogacy has to be completely
> altruistic. There's fat chance. I couldn't get somebody to carry
> luggage for me for nine months, let alone a baby.

The adoption route – I did look into that. At my age, you're going to get an older child. If you put your hand up for a child with developmental delays, you'll get to the front of the line. But also, some countries, as a male, you will not be given a female. Females who want to adopt can be given boys, but not vice-versa.

You cannot be more than 50 years older than your child. And then each country that you're adopting from has its own set of criteria. Thailand will only allow 20 children out of the country per year. Taiwan has a preference for Taiwanese parents living overseas. In the Philippines, you have to demonstrate your Christian faith. All that sort of stuff.

Not only do you have to satisfy Australia's laws, but you have to satisfy the country's laws.

There seems to be a lot of secrecy around it. Like I said, it's hard to get anyone to talk about it. It's a circular thing, because no-one wants to talk about it. There's not even a public discourse on it, do you know what I mean?

Yes. It's just people suffering in silence.

Possibly because of the legal issue; in some states it is illegal. That's my understanding of the law. It could be different in other states; it could be different now, but that's my understanding of it.

The other thing too, I guess, is if you want to have a family, you just want to have a family. You don't want to make it into a media circus.

Of course.

It's not something you want to make public often, unless you're willing to be the poster child for surrogacy or you're willing to fight the fight in the courts. People just don't have that patience, or the money to do that.

Sure. Once you get your baby and you've got your family, you just want to get on with life.

That's right. Now that I have my daughter, I feel like writing to the embassy overseas and saying, 'I believe a lot of that process was unnecessary, blah blah blah'. All it'd do, though, is bring attention to myself, so I won't do it.

I'm just surprised that interest groups haven't picked up on it.

Rainbow Families has done that survey. They've just completed it, or they're still going through it now. It's about discrimination against gay and lesbian people trying to start a family from overseas, exactly what I went through, to institutions in Australia, such as Centrelink. I had an easy go through Centrelink, but other people, I believe, had it more difficult. I didn't have to prove that much. No-one batted an eyelid at me in Centrelink.

The thing is, I know from my experience, having a baby – obviously they're wonderful – but it's full on, you're exhausted, you're sleep deprived, and then for you to have had this bureaucratic, administrative nightmare stress on top of being someone who's just trying to raise an infant child – it seems very counter-productive.

It's very stressful. With Medicare and private health, it was difficult to get private health insurance. It's like, because you didn't have A, you couldn't get B, but then you got B, and then B says, 'You need A before B,' and you need B before A. This sort of administrative merry-go-round isn't very fun.

Because you're on the birth certificate, there shouldn't be any issues with the schooling or anything.

I believe the bulk of it is done. At the same time, from a social perspective, I've just come back from I don't know how many months away, and I've had to adapt to being a dad, but all of my friends haven't adapted. 'No, I can't go out for dinner tonight. I can't go out for this. I cannot talk to you right now, because I've got someone who just threw up and did a poo in their nappy. I can't talk to you now. Don't ring me between four and six p.m.'

Huge lifestyle changes.

Huge lifestyle changes. I've adapted; you need to adapt. But my friends have not yet.

They don't have children?

Ninety-nine per cent of them do not.

Now that things have changed, you might find that you make more friends who have kids. I know that sounds a bit cliquey, but that does happen.

No, that's what I expect. I expect 75% of my circle of friends to step back two steps, and the other 25% to step forward. They will be really supportive, and do more, and be a lot more supportive than the 75% who step back and go, 'Oh, ok. Well, he can't go out for dinner anymore, so, ok, next person. Move on.'

It has been an amazing journey having my daughter, and I am so glad she is in my life. But it has been full on doing this largely by myself. When I did it I was not aware of the support that is available. Firstly, there are some organisations that will help you. Now, I've heard of this organisation called Men Having Babies. It's North American. They run conferences, but they also give financial assistance.

I didn't know about it at the time. But also, to get financial assistance, you have to apply, and you have to go through rounds and all that sort of stuff. I would've missed my deadline, so I had to do it my way, because I didn't want to be too old.

There are also resources in Australia. There's the Gay Dads New South Wales Group which can offer support regardless of if you have had your child via commercial or altruistic surrogacy or otherwise.

Barristers

Trevor Tockar

Barrister

Through the hoops

Trevor Tockar obtained his Bachelor of Laws degree from the University of Cape Town in 1975. After working full-time as a karate instructor until 1981, he was admitted as an advocate (barrister) to the Cape Bar. In 1997 he was appointed as Senior Counsel for the Republic of South Africa, with his Letters Patent being signed by President Nelson Mandela. In 1998 he was appointed as an Acting Judge of the High Court (previously the Supreme Court) of South Africa.

In 2001 Trevor moved to Australia and was admitted to practice as a barrister in New South Wales, with a focus on Family Law.

Trevor is also very involved in the sport of karate, having represented South Africa at international level and he continues to operate a full-time dojo (karate club) in Bondi.

In this interview Trevor brings a particularly unique perspective, as he can compare the Australian system to his experiences in South Africa. Overall, Trevor's message is clear: we currently experience much uncertainty, with too many 'hoops' to jump through, and need to simplify legislation and Court processes. Again, his perspective may be informed by his experiences in South Africa, where it seems judicial processes in interim matters were far more robust and streamlined. His view is there needs to be less legislation, fewer interim hearings, fewer reported cases, and one court that deals with all family-related issues, and that if the Family Law system were streamlined in this manner, then we might not even need additional resources in the system. Trevor advocates for Judges having more power to act decisively, without having to 'jump through the hoops' as they currently do. He admits his views are dependent on the right people being appointed as Judges, and has some innovative ideas about the way in which we should select Judges.

⁣⁣⁣⁣⁣

I'd like to ask, firstly, what's your background in terms of working as a barrister? I know you've got quite an interesting background regarding how you came to the law.

I studied law in South Africa at the University of Cape Town from 1969 to 1974. I qualified with a BA LLB degree and then left the law world and taught and participated in full-contact karate professionally until 1980. I'd been practicing karate right through my university studies and when I finished studying, I promised myself that the last thing that I was ever going to do was to put on a collar and tie and sit behind a desk, and the karate life was what I chose.

I did that for seven years. It was a really great time. I fought and trained in various countries in the world and represented my country at the First World Open Karate Tournament in Tokyo, in 1975. However, in the late 1970s I had some physical problems and, after undergoing some major surgery, I decided that I had better not rely for the rest of my life on physical ability and to go back into law.

At that time in South Africa, to qualify as an attorney (solicitor) you had to do two years' articles, be paid virtually nothing, and expect not to be treated particularly well. I wasn't up for that, so I made the decision to go straight to the Bar. In 1980, the requirement for admission as an advocate (barrister) was that you had to do four months' pupillage where you would sit with your 'master' on a daily basis and observe him or her in practice and have lectures from various judges and senior counsel and then write the Bar exam. Because I'd never been in practice and had been busy with karate all the time, I chose to do a double-length pupillage of eight months, and I then wrote my Bar exam and started practicing as a barrister.

It was interesting that during my term of pupillage, there was a shortage of barristers available to appear pro deo (where you are paid a nominal sum by the State) to act in murder and rape cases in the Supreme Court where there was a possibility of a death sentence being handed down. Because of the shortage of available barristers, they enlisted pupils such as myself to act in some of these matters. My very first case was a brutal prison murder which ran for three months and where a death sentence was indeed handed down (but not to my client, who was acquitted). I did another couple of pro deo murder cases during my pupillage and then, for a number of years after being admitted as a barrister, I was in Court basically four days a week, week in and week out, doing that kind of work. So, I was thrown into the deep end, learned a lot, and slowly worked my way up to doing things such as unopposed divorces, motion proceedings, and other (better paid) work.

After a few years of that, I was offered an opportunity to go to the 'side bar', as it was called in South Africa. In other words, I was offered a job in a solicitor's office, and I did that for two years and wrote my attorney's admission exam. As soon as I finished that, I went back to the Bar, but with the feeling that I at least had an idea of what the solicitor's world was all about. I continued at the Bar in South Africa and, in 1997, was granted silk. As a silk I was given the opportunity to take some appointments as an acting Judge of the Supreme Court (now known as the High Court), hearing all kinds of matters, from criminal matters (fortunately, the death sentence had been abolished) to personal injury to commercial to family, etc.

Then, in the beginning of 2001, I moved to Australia - having been granted entry based on my karate credentials, and not my legal qualifications. Fortunately, because of my background, I wasn't required to do any of the academic requirements, or sit the Bar exam or any other exams, except for ethics and accounts. I commenced practice in mid-2001 at the New South Wales Bar, specialising in Family Law where I'd been told that there was a capacity to make a decent living. It's not because Family Law was something that was my one specialty - in South Africa it was much more general - but I had met some of the Family Law practitioners in Australia and they'd suggested that it was a way forward. And that's what I've done ever since arriving here. Now, practicing in Waratah Chambers, I have been exclusively involved in Family Law for the past 17 years.

And you were an acting Judge in South Africa, is that correct?

Yes, an acting Judge. In South Africa, in the Supreme Court (now known there as the High Court) they used to, in my time, fairly regularly make use of senior counsel to act as Judges. It was a grooming process for perhaps a permanent appointment later, and also it was to take some of the load off the permanent Judges. Today I understand that they choose from a wider variety of candidates, not just from senior counsel but also from solicitors and academics; but certainly in my time it was mainly senior counsel who would act as Judges and become permanent Judges.

It's interesting that you raised that, in South Africa, the system there is that you don't have the specialised courts. Something that was raised by some of the other professionals I've interviewed for is this concept of merging more of the courts together. We've already seen this with the recent announcement about the Family Court merging with the Federal Circuit Court. Also, for example, some people have said that there shouldn't be separate Courts for care and protection matters and family court matters. Do you have any views about streamlining of Courts and having the one court deal with what's often the same set of people?

Firstly, I think the situation in South Africa is changing and that things are becoming more specialised. I understand that there are specialised Tax Courts, specialised Commercial Courts, and there is certainly talk there of a specialised Family Court.

But the level of specialisation in Australia is far greater than anything that I hear is happening in South Africa, and I think it's good and bad.

You walk into the Family Court in Australia and you know that the Judge knows the law, knows the cases, knows the legislation, and knows the practice. In South Africa (in my day), it would sometimes happen that you would appear before a Judge in a Family Law matter in the Supreme Court who would perhaps have a real aversion to Family Law, and you would tend to lead the Judge through the legal pathway as opposed to what happens in this country, so clearly that kind of specialisation is good. But,

> what I do find somewhat frustrating and wasteful are the different practices, different procedures in the different courts, rather than a standardised system. I think it's wasteful, and it's costly, and it's confusing.

And certainly when you're dealing, like in Family Law at the moment, with the Federal Circuit Court and the Family Court, with Federal Circuit Court rules and practices and Family Court rules and practices, it's just nothing short of crazy. I see they're now changing that, but looking at the changes, I'm wondering if they're real or if they're superficial.

And do you have a view about care and protection matters? I mean, obviously there are constitutional issues there, because care and protection matters are under the state law. But I know I was in a number of matters when I was an Independent Children's Lawyer where proceedings were started in the Federal Circuit Court, and subsequently the Children's Court, and so there was that shuffling around for the same family.

Well, I haven't been too involved in care and protection matters, but, again, it seems to me that there's overspecialisation and that the Family Court should be able to deal with all of these matters without there having to be some in the Children's Court, some in the Federal Circuit Court, some in the Family Court, some in the Supreme Court. I'm not quite sure why the Family Court shouldn't be an all-embracing court dealing with all matters relating to family, which would include care and protection matters.

Do you have any other thoughts about reforms that you think would make practical sense in Family Law?

Yes. It'd be good if things could be simplified. As we've recently heard, they're now amalgamating the courts, which is good as a single entry point, but to me that isn't the difficulty. The difficulty is that, at least in the beginning, you are still going to have a stream of Judges who were Federal Circuit Court Judges, a stream of Judges who were Family Court Judges, and you're still going to have the different rules of the two Courts as far as I understand, at least for the interim.

My view is there's just too much legislation, and the more legislation there is, the more rules upon rules there are, the more the lawyers will find grist for the mill, and the more it's going to be very confusing for clients.

Things should be simplified and the rules should be more stringently applied as to length of affidavits and time for filing of affidavits and material. And perhaps some way of limiting the endless interim applications that raise the costs, that often see people going to court, getting nothing done except spending money, followed by a further delay.

When I was in South Africa, there was one rule, Rule 43, for all interim matters in matrimonial proceedings. Rule 43 was designed to provide an expeditious and inexpensive method of deciding a number of interlocutory matters arising out of matrimonial proceedings, such as those relating to interim custody of children, interim access to them, interim maintenance of spouses and children, and contributions towards costs. These were all dealt with under one rule where a very short affidavit from each side was allowed, where limited time to address the Court was allowed, where fees were capped and where judgement was usually ex tempore. The judge wouldn't have to give reasons, although if it was a more complex case, they would sometimes do so. The orders were generally unappealable. This is some-thing that would never go down in Australia (and I don't know if it still the position in South Africa). But really, in many cases it was remarkably effec-tive. In many cases it got people to settle on the day or, if they didn't settle, achieve a result that often wasn't that much different from what happens in these courts after huge volumes of material are filed, long judgements are delivered, appeals sometimes brought, etc. Now, I don't suggest that the South African Rule 43 model should even be considered in Australia, but I raise it to provoke consideration of a simpler, more robust system.

Very interesting. And that has been raised as well by some other inter-viewees, that interim hearings are clogging the Courts and need to be more streamlined.

Well, if the Judges were given more... what's the word? If one had greater faith in the Judges - instead of making sure that they have to tick every box, they were allowed to apply their experience and their knowledge as lawyers and as specialist Family Law lawyers. They shouldn't have to jump through the hoops that they're forced to jump through, which I think causes matters to be protracted and expensive, and is perhaps unnecessary.

You mentioned simplifying the legislation. Are you referring in particular to legislation with regards to parenting matters?

Well, that is what's in my mind to a great extent, when you look at the Section 60CC provisions in respect of the best interests of children, and the boxes that have to be ticked, and the pathways, and so forth. I just think that it's clear when you're looking at best interests of children that the courts are fully aware of the paramountcy principle and the principles to be applied.

Perhaps it would be a good idea to get away from reporting every single case that comes before the Court, which allows you to always find a case that says what you want it to say but which doesn't really assist the Court. Really what should be reported are only cases where new principles are set out. It would be better if one had a limited number of cases to look at each year.

> There should perhaps be an editorial board that decides which cases should be published, and one can then look at those cases instead of the masses of cases which usually are pointless reading...

because 90% of them go to setting out the particular facts of the particular case.

And something else that's been raised in some of the other interviews is - and it's perhaps already upon us in the form of the parent management hearings, which I understand are more inquisitorial in nature - do you have a view about adversarial versus inquisitorial?

I'm a bit old school there. I believe that the evidence should be put before the court in the proper way, and an experienced judicial officer should then weigh the evidence and make a decision.

I'm concerned about non-lawyers getting involved who may be influenced by things outside a proper analysis of the evidence. When I say a proper analysis of the evidence, I'm not necessarily talking about final hearing, but even when there has to be a determination on the papers, Judges know how to sift the evidence. They know how to weigh the probabilities, to look at what is confirmed by what's in other evidence or from the other side, etc. They know how to deal with matters on the papers, as well as in final hearings where the evidence is tested.

And your thoughts on judicial mediations (mediation with a Judge) being an option for parties, which is likely to begin from about 2019?

Well, my view is that if you come before a Judge, you run a trial before a Judge. That's what the Judge is meant to do and is qualified to do. If the parties do want to mediate – and obviously that's to be encouraged – then they should choose a mediator and do it in the traditional way.

Do you have any practical tips for, say, someone reading this book who's going through a separation? I know every matter's different, but is there anything to bear in mind if you are navigating the Family Law system, particularly as a litigant?

I think that litigants have got to remember that the Court is not in a position to trawl through everything that's happened in a 10-, 15-, 20 year marriage. I know clients get really frustrated when they're trying to tell their story and they are cut off by the lawyers, and in Court by barristers and Judges, with statements such as, 'Oh, we don't want to hear that; that's not relevant', when to these people it's very important.

Perhaps the solicitor, who's the first point of entry or first port of call for the client, should give the client a full opportunity to tell their story, and then carefully explain to them how the system works and what the court needs to know. It's not a question of not being sympathetic or empathetic or caring, but a question of just fashioning the evidence to fit in with what is required by the Court.

Particularly, if it's a property matter, to explain that if, for instance, there is a $3 million pool, it's not a $3 million case but maybe a $300,000 case being the range between possible outcomes.

They must also be made to understand that they're not being judged as people, that this is not really 'their day in court' where they're going to get justification for having suffered through 20 years of misery with their partner, but that it is really just a commercial exercise. They've got to focus on that. With children, of course, it's very different, but even there,

> they have to be made to understand what is important and what the court needs to hear in the interests of the children, rather than seeing the court as their private battleground.

Do you have any words of wisdom for solicitors in terms of how to prepare evidence? Things that you possibly see as a barrister and wish had been done differently by the time a brief hits your desk?

Well, perhaps if the solicitors would stop writing 10-page letters, which all get attached to the affidavits, and often do nothing but cause more argument, then things might be more manageable. Also, if they would think very carefully about exactly what they're trying to achieve, what the goal is, what the relief is they're seeking, and file evidence that is related only to that, rather than giving in to the client who wants to tell their whole life story.

Some of the interviewees suggested we should move to specialised lists, perhaps even specialised courts; for example, I was made aware that there's been an Indigenous list running in the Sydney registry for only Indigenous Australian parties. Do you have any thoughts about that?

Yes, I just think that there's more than enough specialisation, and to specialise further within specialised areas – to me, that is just going to make things more complex, more confusing, create more law, more argument. People who are properly trained, who have proper experience in the area of Family Law, should be able to deal with all these issues.

Perhaps that's part of being a first-world country – Australia really tries its level best to give everybody a fair go – and they've tried through legislation and various new ideas to give everybody the best chance possible of getting a proper outcome. But I think sometimes one can overdo that, and I think that this kind of idea is overdoing it. I believe in simplifying things.

I believe in getting the proper people as decision makers who have experience and knowledge across the board, and having a little bit more faith in them.

You have raised that Judges should be able to make decisions without having to jump through so many hoops, and we should have confidence in the judiciary to enable them to do this. Your ideas about reform are predicated on the quality of the Judiciary. Do you think that we have sufficient depth and breadth in the legal profession now for more quality Judges to be appointed?

Well, appointing the right people is obviously vital, particularly with regard to what I was saying, that they should have adequate power, really, without having to be so concerned about ticking all the boxes.

Judges should perhaps be chosen a different way, perhaps by having something like a judicial services commission, where candidates may be interviewed and chosen on a non-political basis as to who's best for the job.

I know a lot of people think that in Family Law you should only appoint people who are experienced family lawyers. I don't necessarily agree with that. I think that the Judges who have come from the commercial courts have often been excellent. They really seem to know how to listen to cases in an appropriate way, and to apply the evidence and their knowledge to determine the veracity of what people are saying, and what weight should be attached to what people are saying. Also, they have been generally very good in giving counsel and solicitors a proper opportunity to contribute. It is my view that the focus should be on appointing Judges who are highly qualified and experienced lawyers, even if they sometimes might not be Family Law specialists.

Or barristers?

Well, I think barristers are good people to be selected as Judges because of their trial experience. But I don't know if having more Judges is going to help. I don't think you would need more Judges if you simplified the system, and if you didn't have these masses of interim cases that are before the Court. I think it's these interims that go on and on and on that are really causing the courts to be so jammed.

And the huge volumes of material that need to be filed. And, as you said, there seem to be more restrictions on how much material can be filed in South Africa.

What in fact happened with the Rule 43 system in interlocutory matters was that the lawyers had a cap on what they could charge, and it was very low, which encouraged them to actually use the opportunity when they came to court to settle the matter. This was good for the lawyers, because they could charge for their time in settling the matter, and it was good for the parties, because they were able to reach settlement at an early stage and avoid the cost of going to trial.

However, I must point out that, in my days in South Africa, if the matter did not proceed to final hearing, then the trial was long and arduous, with no affidavit evidence and often with a plethora of adversarial expert witnesses.

Coming back to interim matters, I do not suggest that a 'Rule 43 approach' could ever work in Australia. Australians are not going to be rolled back to where they are not given a full opportunity of being heard and of not having somebody else look at a judgement if they are not happy with it. The Rule 43 system is a very robust approach, and I would imagine that there have been some changes to it in South Africa. Nevertheless, it may be that some of its elements could be usefully introduced into family law in Australia in order to streamline the process in respect of interim matters.

I mean, overall as I said earlier, I think

> Australia really tries its best. It's a Rolls Royce system, but I think it's got out of hand.

I think it should be simplified. I think the judges should be able to apply their experience and their knowledge without having to focus so much on form rather than substance. It is unfortunate, I think, that one has to go to so many different sections, and subsections, and subsections of subsections of the *Family Law Act* to work one's way to an outcome. That is something that I think should be looked at.

Tom Hutchings

Barrister

It takes a village to raise a child

Tom Hutchings was called to the Bar over a decade ago in 2007 and practices at Owen Dixon Chambers East, in Melbourne. He specialises in Family Law, but cut his teeth across various jurisdictions. Prior to being called to the bar he was deputy Associate to (the then) Federal Magistrate Riethmuller, and did his articles with Caroline Counsel. Tom has a particular interest in appellate work and more complex property and parenting matters.

In this interview he talks frankly about how much barristers charge, why it is that he believes delay and under-resourcing is at the crux of the problems in Family Law, why some clients actually do not want to resolve matters quickly, and why it is, overall, he believes, we should retain the current adversarial system in Family Law matters.

Tom also raises interesting questions about culture in Family Law and asks if there are hidden white cultural paradigms that exist in the Family Law system. Personally, I do think that although law appears as the truth, as the universal, the unconscious thinking in Family Law is Anglo centric. In particular, he and I discussed the issue, often in Chinese families, where grandparents have an extensive role in parenting children, following the old adage 'It takes a village to raise a child', and how, structurally, the current Family Law system is not set up to understand or respond to this situation.

What is your background and how did you come to be a Family Law barrister?

I completed my law degree straight after school. At the time I had multiple interests and my law degree was a bit of a fall-back in my mind. I was involved in the arts and running some businesses. I worked in forms of retail and did many other things.

What happened to me was that, when 9/11 happened, that caused a schism in the money coming in from another career I was pursuing. So I said, well, I'm in my late twenties, and I have this law degree, and the other career path is looking uncertain, so I started looking for articles. Having been some years out of university and done other things, it wasn't the same walk-up start as it might have otherwise been.

I started reaching out to various contacts, and as it worked out, a barrister friend of an uncle took me under his wing and assisted me in obtaining some work initially with a Judge in the then Federal Magistrates Court as an associate and then articles in Family Law.

So, it found me. It wasn't me finding it. As it turns out, it suits me. It's amazing how the universe can work. What I find about Family Law is it's a wonderful intersection of many areas of law.

I like how you said it found you. I think that, often, life does work that way. So you enjoy it then?

Yes. Family law can be practiced at a huge variance of levels. There are simplistic aspects (or those that could appear simplistic). But a lot of work I do is technical and legalistic. A lot of people don't appreciate that family lawyers deal with trusts and the *Corporations Act* and equity. I do some appellate work, which I really enjoy. I like the hard law and the personal contact too that I have with my clients.

What are your key tips for someone who has separated and is navigating the Family Law process?

It depends if they are at litigation phase or are recently separated.

If someone has just separated it does pay to find a lawyer and have a discussion and have them give you a roadmap. I also think seeking assistance from a psychologist is a good idea. I think people hope that their lawyer is going to be the one to help them get through all of this; however, as good as many lawyers and barristers are, that is not what they are trained to do.

Once you have a solicitor and if you have not been able to negotiate successfully with your ex-, make sure you listen and prepare things as efficiently as possible for your lawyer. For example, if your lawyer wants documents, make sure you provide them swiftly and efficiently.

> Consider advice carefully and take it on board,
> even if you don't wholly accept it.

Minimise your telephone contact and correspondence with your lawyer if you can. If you have someone objective supporting you, perhaps speak to them before you speak to your lawyer, as it's amazing how quickly expenses can run up for things that probably weren't necessary to deal with from a legal perspective.

Another thing everyone is thinking about, given the AG's review, is reform. It seems everyone has different ideas, so there's no right or wrong answer here. What are your thoughts on reform?

I noticed, in relation to the trial being rolled out in Parramatta, there was a submission by the Law Council that in fact it was a silly way to spend the money [$12.7 million] and I completely agree.

I think the way forward to improve the service and operation of Family Law is obvious. We are short on Judges and registrars, and other resources being contact centres, psychologists, counsellors, and courses to assist people.

There is no doubt in my mind one of the things that causes many problems for families are the delays in the system. It requires further interim hearings inevitably, costs go up, stress goes up - that's not healthy for anybody, in particular children. There is a form of limbo for everybody.

Often, finality is more important from the children's point of view than the result the parents might otherwise be after.

With regards to property, the vast majority of cases have a fairly obvious range of outcomes and it is about the litigants getting to that point of being able to argue it or settle it as soon as possible. Sometimes that requires the pressure of knowing the end is near, because I think people struggle with the idea of settling, unless they really have to, if they are not the type of person who has been able to do it earlier.

What is also obvious is the streamlining of protection orders (whether they be intervention orders in Victoria or whatever they are called in various other states). I can see child protection could come within the same umbrella. We have a push-and-pull-me going on between the jurisdictions, and often the first point of call is one of the parents going off and obtaining an intervention order. Then a magistrate will make orders, including for the children, meaning a father (and it is often the father), can't see the children for a period of time. It is often unnecessary that such an exclusion be made. It is often a long time before the matter comes to the Federal Circuit Court for hearing. It may then be that there is an inordinate wait for a (supervised) contact centre place to become available (often more than six months).

By the time individuals get around to getting lawyers and filing, many months have passed, and in my experience, the no time lack of contact that has occurred has been damaging for children. That's not to say there wasn't a good reason for regulating the time – for example, supervision – but I think it does great damage to the children in many cases when that happens.

That's one example of where I think streamlining of jurisdictions will be of great assistance. But it's a question of money. These are big questions and problems when it comes to state and federal funding, and I appreciate that.

These things are not impossible, however, and again there is little doubt in my mind that those things –

additional funding, more Judges, and a better streamlining of the jurisdictions – are the things that will assist people the most.

Something that has been raised in other interviews is whether we should move to an inquisitorial system instead of an adversarial system. Do you have any thoughts about that?

The reality is that many Judges at the coalface, and in particular in the Federal Circuit Court, operate in a quasi-inquisitorial fashion in any event. The *Rules* and the *Act* allow for a fair bit of that. I do appreciate the differences and I can see how the inquisitorial system could be more advantageous, particularly in parenting matters However,

> there are checks and balances that are built in our current adversarial system which I think are preferable on balance to an out-and-out inquisitorial system.

The fact that you have advocates there creates a check and balance on the process, and heading towards an appellate level, when you start talking about the Judge exercising inquisitorial powers beyond that which they already do, I wonder about the benefits at the end of the day. I suppose I am sitting on the fence.

I see pros and cons, but at the coalface, Judges who want answers to questions ask them, and they obtain the answers to those questions, and they have wide-ranging powers to perform in an inquisitorial fashion, in a sense.

I suppose what you are saying is that even though, technically, Australia (and England, which we inherited our legal system from) is adversarial, not inquisitorial, in its legal system, there are some inquisitorial flavours, for want of a better word, to our current system?

There absolutely are. Some Judges operate in a very inquisitorial fashion, and the rules allow for many things that you wouldn't see going on in a criminal trial in the Supreme Court. And they are commonplace in the Federal Circuit Court and, to a lesser degree, in the Family Court.

Where are the delays at in Melbourne?

It's in flux. My standard advice is to allow 18 months.

Well, that's pretty good, compared to Sydney.

I think we settle more in Melbourne.

Yes, well, why is that? You have appeared in the Sydney and Melbourne registries. Do you notice a difference?

Yes. Well, I have dealt with barristers in Sydney who try to get to the heart of the real issues and solve the problems for their clients, which I feel that most of us do. But I find, in Sydney, I am more likely to encounter barristers that are well, let's put it this way: For example, I turned up one day and sourced the barrister on the other side and said, 'Shall we have a chat?' which is a common place to start in Melbourne. Often, you stand the matter down and, as barristers, see if you can bring a fresh perspective to things. Of course, more lateral solutions can come from negotiations than more black-and-white outcomes from a Court.

This barrister said, 'Well, if you've got a proposal for me, give it to me'. I tried to ascertain whether we had any mutual ground, or a way to achieve what each of our clients wanted, but my opponent seemed hell-bent on simply running the matter. And I thought, ok, well, if you want to play that game, I suppose the boxing gloves are going on and that's the only way we can move forward! You rarely get that response from an opponent in Melbourne, particularly from someone you are used to dealing with. That matter took up Court time when it didn't need to.

It can be obstructive to reaching an outcome that would work for all parties?

Yes. Barristers bring a few things to the table. I think, from my experience, though, solicitors in Sydney maybe seem to have done more work earlier to try to resolve the matter. Perhaps we do less of that in Melbourne.

Barristers give a new perspective and have different duties to the Court and coalface experiences mean sometimes our analysis differs slightly. Even if it doesn't, sometimes this strange thing happens to litigants when they are faced with a barrister and Court, which means for some reason resolution can often be achieved when it wasn't looking likely.

Having said that, I am not saying that in Sydney versus Melbourne, one is better. Many Judges who come to sit in Melbourne from other registries, when barristers want to stand matters down, say, 'Why are you doing this now? Why didn't you have these discussions earlier? And waste the day you have been given in Court particularly when negotiations fall over?' So, there is something to be said for allowing barristers to have such discussions earlier, but that's a funding problem from the client's perspective. There are tensions and advantages and disadvantages in different ways.

Speaking of such funding issues, what's the range of how much someone might charge in Melbourne, depending on their experience, from a junior to more senior barrister, just for the reader?

Good question! I think that if you used the services of a first- or second-year barrister, you are looking at the low thousand. I am going to guess around $1320; perhaps some are even lower, say, $990. I don't know – this is just a guess – but a baby barrister for a first return date might be that much. Right up the other end, I don't know if anyone charges more than $10,000 for a first return date, but it is probably creeping up to that. There might be some silks who simply have a daily fee and it doesn't matter what they are doing.

For trial fees, we stagger them. Everyone is different. Some people charge full or half days. For a final hearing/trial, I would be surprised if there were many barristers who were much less than $2,000 a day at the low end and then right up to silks that would be around $10,000 a day.

I think your average 10-year barrister is between $3,000 to $4,500 a day for trials and between $2,000 and $3,500 for interim-type hearings. That is often the type of market most clients will be briefing in, cutting out the bottom and the top end, for around a 10-year-plus or an eight- to 15-year barrister.

I think Sydney barristers charge cancellation, or 'disappointment' fees as we say. Their fees are usually higher than Melbourne, and as a general rule, they charge more for preparation. In Melbourne we very rarely charge disappointment fees. For instance, I am able to do this interview as a trial was cancelled very late. In Sydney, I would probably have been sending a bill. So, not only are our fees lower but we don't get a disappointment fee. I think there's a marked difference between the way we charge in the two states.

Something else I wanted to discuss, having worked at Legal Aid. On the one hand, you have clients who are unemployed or on a very small income, and then you have people who have a high income and can afford solicitors and barristers. Then there is a whole group of people in the middle that might be on an income such that they aren't eligible for legal aid, yet they can't really properly pay a barrister or a solicitor.

Yeah, I recognise it as being a significant problem, and it is not unusual to for me to say to a client, 'I couldn't afford me.' I do appreciate it from a client's perspective how much big money it is. They might think they are an ok earner making $2,000 a week, a six-figure income, but when they are looking at a barrister who's turning up for two, three, or four thousand dollars a day, that's crippling.

But cases don't have to be as expensive as they end up being, (although there are exceptions). A lot of that boils down to one or other of the parties. Normally, legal fees get out of control when the client requires over-servicing, or when one or the other of the parties continually makes unreasonable demands. There are ways of controlling that.

The system as it stands doesn't need to run to enormous money in the way it sometimes does. A lot of that boils down to how clever the litigant is. I return to my first answer that ...

if people are organised in how they work with their solicitor, and they listen and make necessary compromises along the way, and see the wood for the trees, one's legal fees will not be crippling.

And you are almost certainly better off having adequate legal representation throughout the system, because it's too easy to make an idiot of yourself in front of the Judge, and things can go pear-shaped pretty quickly.

You mean if you are a self-represented litigant it's incredibly difficult?

Yes.

On another issue, regarding arbitration, is that something that has been picked up on in Melbourne?

No. I actually think there's some Judicial reticence to support arbitration.

I personally think it's a really good thing. But it will only suit so many people. The personalities of those who go through Family Law – obviously there's an enormous range. On one end, there's the couple who separate who do the deal between them and barely need a lawyer, maybe just to make formal their agreement.

Then, you have, at the other end, the two who perhaps have personality difficulties, or there are abuse situations, and those matters aren't suitable for arbitration.

Then you have the middle. Why do those people still fail at mediation and still get to the door of Court prior to settling or in the lead-up to trial? I actually think it's the emotions involved that all but completely obliterate their ability to see the wood from the trees and listen. They are driving an agenda that isn't one the Court is going to be overly concerned about, and they find it very difficult to let that go.

Those are the people whom an arbitration model would be best aimed at. They can't settle it at mediation or by a few letters between lawyers; instead of going to Court, we would get someone to make a decision. Now, obviously, they would need to spend money on the arbitration, but it would save money by having the matter resolved sooner.

But, deep down, do they actually want to use arbitration, to send in paperwork and have someone make a decision? No, they don't. They do on one level, but they don't. It doesn't help them because, on another level, they still hope to prove that they are right and to get 'justice' or to score a point.

You can go for a full-blown arbitration trial model, but then all you're doing is getting an earlier decision that is more easily appealed and set aside than a traditional one, so you have just saved time; you haven't saved money.

On one level it makes sense, but I actually don't think there are many people who, deep down, want it or would sign up for it.

I just don't think it suits the personalities or the stage of life they are at. I mean, it's a magic bullet for us when we look at that matter – why don't they just send it to arbitration, get an answer, and get on with their lives? But in reality, most people don't actually want it.

Interesting, because I used to work in trade and transport and shipping law where, obviously, there is a lot of use of arbitration, but it is quite a different situation, a different area of law. It's not about someone's relationship breakdown, so there are different agendas and motivations.

Commercially, it makes sense. I mean, it is almost inarguable. Are we going to wait 18 months for a trial or get a decision in four weeks? It's a no-brainer.

But the thing is, as you say, they aren't emotionally ready.

They're not emotionally ready as a general rule, and if the wife is in the house with the kids, she's still clinging to the idea of retaining the house. And if you're her lawyer and it's going to buy her an extra 18 months of staying in the house, and if the husband's paying the mortgage, is it really advantageous for her to settle sooner? Or is she better staying in the house and then also the kids aren't moving or facing a sell-off of the house? In a way, she is better staying as long as possible in the house and receiving rent-free accommodation while her husband continues to support the family financially. And we know plenty of lawyers who manipulate that situation to their client's advantage (sometimes completely unfairly). Why would she want an earlier outcome?

As you say, the delay, while it frustrates most clients, in some cases it serves at least one party, if not the other.

Yes, exactly.

Moving onto something totally different: I am reminded of a matter we worked on involving clients with a Chinese background and some issues there in that matter. Do you think our system works well more generally with a multicultural society?

Something I am interested in is what psychologists tell us about attachment theory. For example, with a lot of Chinese families, they have children raised by grandparents.

Our model and assumption that underpin the way a lot things are decided, and, to a degree, the presumptions in the *Family Law Act* and the like, may not fit particularly well with cultures that have that type of approach. I really do wonder what analysis psychologists would do, because we don't have an entire country of kids that are completely messed up due to their attachment being disjointed. Now, does it mean the attachment theory is flawed? Does it mean that these children form a primary attachment to a grandparent?

I don't think our system works very well with those cultures. At the first return early stage what I commonly see is one parent comes along – let's say it's Dad – and says, 'You know, it's actually my parents, the children's grandparents, who have been raising those children. They have been basically living with my parents since they were very young. And my wife, well, she parties, or she's been off at work.'

Then the wife turns up and says, 'Oh no, no, no, no. The grandparents didn't really do that much and in fact it's me who's been caring for the children.' And the Courts, because of the way that they work, as a general rule, say, well, of course it was the mother. We won't cut out the grandparents but will make Orders for the children to live with Mum and spend time with Dad, and maybe there's a bit more time for Dad/the grandparents to allow for the argument. But the starting point is actually completely contrary to how I understand it is, more likely than not what, in reality, probably was going on.

So, the way families are structured in other cultures is perhaps not really understood or appreciated. It is sort of like trying to fit that structure into a different, Western paradigm.

Yes, it is. We have all sorts of cultural paradigms that underpin the written and unwritten presumptions or assumptions or leanings that Judges, as human beings, and the system have.

As we have greater subsets of other cultures living with us, and requiring the help of the Family Law system to deal with their particular situation, I wonder: Is our model fully equipped, with all its written and unwritten assumptions?

And often hidden assumptions – because people don't even realise they are applying those assumptions, you know what I mean?

That's right. I have a case where just this is happening at the moment and we are engaging a psychologist who specialises in attachment theory to do an analysis of the attachment. I am fascinated to see where that lands, and that is in an effort to allow for the cultural differences and analyse them to assist in reaching an end point which is in fact in the child's best interests.

I still wonder about how the attachment theory model applies to other cultures, in particular, but without meaning to single out the Chinese, in matters with Chinese clients.

I would agree with that. I am of an Asian background and I don't think it is racist to say you notice certain trends and the different ways that families do things in different cultures.

I don't think it is either. I just want to be sensitive in the way I have given examples. I have seen it in plenty of other matters in other cultures, but it seems so much a common theme in cases involving Chinese clients.

I agree with that too, in several matters I have had, and I have found that, often, clients in this situation feel a bit ill at ease, or perhaps fear the Court doesn't understand their situation.

It doesn't.

> The Court is not built to understand their
> [Chinese families] situation.

And, indeed, the *Family Law Act* prescribes that mothers and fathers are, in essence, to be recognised above all others. I mean other parties can join and seek orders – it is open to them. But the same considerations do not necessarily apply to grandparents, and the underlying assumption of ensuring children have a meaningful relationship with each of their parents is important. But does it apply in the same way to, say, how the Chinese raise their children? And how does it overlap with attachment theory? Who are these children primarily attached to? How do you work it out? When will that be able to be known? Is, indeed, there such a thing as an out-and-out primary and secondary attachment? Does a child actually require one primary attachment, or can they have very good attachments – solid, good attachments – from a selection of reliable adults in which they can learn to explore their world? I think of the old adage, 'It takes a village to raise a child'.

I am not a psychologist; I don't have the answers, but am simply raising the questions. There might be papers out there which I am not aware of, but it is just something that has recently created an intellectual interest for me. It is interesting to question how we do things in a world in which, increasingly, culture is being mixed and the law is required to deal with different paradigms and cultures.

Sandrine Alexandre-Hughes

Barrister

A potential loophole

Sandrine was admitted as a solicitor in 2010 and was called to the NSW Bar in 2011. She has a general practice with a strong focus on international law.

Sandrine regularly appears in the Supreme Court of NSW and Family Court of Australia in international succession and family law matters respectively. She also advises and appears in international commercial matters, as well as in migration cases. Sandrine holds a keen interest in human rights, which she studied in both Australia and France.

Prior to moving to Australia, Sandrine worked in the banking industry in Paris, and as a Legal Officer with the Permanent Bureau of the Hague Conference on Private International Law, where she was involved in the negotiation and was a Member of the drafting committee for what is now the 2007 Hague Convention on the International Recovery of Child Support and Spousal Maintenance. Sandrine holds Bachelor's and Master's degrees in law, both in Common Law and Civil Law systems.

In this interview, Sandrine speaks about international issues in Family Law; in particular, international parental abduction, enforcement of foreign court orders and foreign binding financial agreements, and why more predictability is needed in these areas to prevent Australia becoming an international loophole.

How did you come to work as a Family Law barrister? And what is your background and experience?

I did a Master's by research in Family Law in France, which involved comparative and international Family Law components, I also studied Family Law as part of my LL.B. in England, and worked for two years as a legal officer at the Hague Conference on Private International Law, in the Family Law team. When I came to the New South Wales Bar in 2011, practising in Family Law was a natural path to follow. Family law represents approximately 50% of my practice.

Describe what it is you do.

I meet in conference with clients and instructing solicitors. I advise on the strategy of the case, on the evidence to adduce, and the law applicable. I settle the evidence and prepare my cross-examinations and submissions.

When I appear in Court, I cross-examine the other side's witnesses and make submissions. In addition, during the course of the proceedings, I manage the client's expectations and ensure that the client understands the pros and cons which come with alternative dispute resolution mechanisms, as well as with settling the proceedings.

What should solicitors and clients look for when choosing a barrister?

They should look for someone with specialist knowledge. Beyond specialist knowledge...

clients and solicitors should brief someone who also has a capacity to react and adapt quickly to the particular challenges of their case, a barrister who is able to understand the client's objectives and perspective, whilst ensuring the client understands the realities and risks of litigation.

How would you describe the approach in Sydney Family Law litigation?

Besides the costs associated with lengthy proceedings, the aggressive tone in the correspondence drafted by some family practitioners can be a further source of frustration and difficulty for the clients.

Clients who have been involved in proceedings in other areas of law are astonished by the aggressiveness which can come with Family Law litigation. It is my job to encourage my clients to retain their cool and not to engage, as an aggressive tone does not achieve any positive outcome for anyone. The use of a bitter tone can only escalate the disagreements (and the proceedings) in a context where the parties often have difficulties focusing on their case and overcoming their pre-existing personal tensions. Aggressiveness in the correspondences is said to be part of the culture, 'part of the game', yet I do not see any benefit to it. I cannot speak on their behalf, but I cannot imagine that judicial officers are impressed when they come across aggressive correspondence which could have politely conveyed the same legal principles and relevant facts.

> One does not need to be unduly aggressive to efficiently advance one's client's interests and obtain a favourable outcome.

What kind of matters do you assist parties with?

I represent clients in property and parenting matters. In the last few years, I have predominantly been briefed in property matters. Most of my matters involve an international element or conflict of laws.

So, you specialise in international matters?

Yes. In relation to international matters involving children, the issues which come up are not only technical in nature but also challenging from a practical perspective. Making submissions as to with what parent a child should live often means addressing in what country the child will live. Making submissions relating to how and when the child will spend time with the other parent means addressing travel safety and financial questions.

The issue of international parental child abduction is relevant, too, in an international family context where the relationship and trust between the parents has broken down. Although international parental abduction (or wrongful child retention) is a danger which most parents would be aware of, I do find that clients, and the general public, would benefit from further information and education on the topic.

What are some of the problems you see with regards to how international matters are dealt with? Do you think any reforms are necessary concerning how international matters are dealt with in Family Law?

In my practice, I see two recurrent issues relevant to international family matters which call for a reform creating a comprehensive regime of substantive and procedural rules.

First: the recognition and enforcement of foreign court orders relating to the division of matrimonial property. Second: the recognition and enforcement of foreign financial binding agreements (also called pre-nuptial agreements or marriage contracts, in other jurisdictions).

These issues arise in a context where, further to the dramatic increase in international family litigation over the last few decades, a number of important multilateral instruments have been agreed to facilitate the recognition and enforcement of foreign judgements relating to family disputes such as the recovery of maintenance and child support, international parental abduction, and other parenting issues. However, the recognition and enforcement of foreign binding financial agreements and of foreign decisions determining the division of property do not benefit from a multilateral treaty, or from any specific provisions in the Australian domestic legislation.

Whilst Australian Judges may recognise and give appropriate weight to the orders made by a competent foreign jurisdiction in relation to matrimonial property, the foreign orders are not enforceable per se.

In such context, it is often difficult to assess the extent of the weight that the Court will give to the foreign decision - it can range anywhere from mere acknowledgement in Judicial reasons to the making of orders mirroring the foreign orders.

Similarly, in Australia, the Court may, through its discretionary power, give appropriate weight to a foreign binding financial agreement, but the foreign agreement is not recognised and enforceable per se. As I mentioned before, assessing the extent of the weight that the Court will give to the foreign binding financial agreement is a difficult exercise.

A number of technical and practical difficulties flow from the absence of specific principles that allow for more predictability in this area. In relation to foreign decisions, from a technical perspective,

> any application seeking the recognition of a foreign decision and a mirroring Australian order is likely to face a number of defences.

From a practical point of view, the current situation leads to lengthy proceedings, to costs associated with the number of defences raised, and with the expert evidence required to explain and contextualise the foreign decision at the centre of the proceedings.

In general (not just matters with an international element), most clients are frustrated by the length of the proceedings and the resulting costs. This is especially the case with clients who are in a position to compare these two factors with those of another country's legal system but are caught up in this jurisdiction.

In relation to foreign binding financial agreements, the lack of predictability in relation to the weight which they will be given is also reflected in the length and costs of the proceedings. Therefore, the current state of Australian law is a potential loophole to avoid an agreement which is binding in another jurisdiction. The possibility for forum shopping and filing proceedings in Australia is made relatively easy by the breadth of the jurisdictional grounds set out in the Family Law Act.

David Blackah

Barrister

Work with the system, not against it

David Blackah has been a lawyer since 1980 and has been a barrister since 2007. David has broad experience in property law, deceased estates, commercial and building litigation, insurance law, and for the past 14 years, principally Family Law.

Currently, he appears in the Federal Circuit Court of Australia and the Family Court, including the Full Court, predominantly in the Sydney and Parramatta Registries. From time to time David represents people in regional and interstate cases. David also continues to appear in Supreme Court cases in contested wills matters.

David is a member of Trust Chambers, which is conveniently located close to the Sydney Registry of the Family Law Courts.

David is the author of 'Child Protection Law', a chapter in *Lawyers Practice Manual New South Wales* (ThomsonReuters) He has also written papers, including 'The Importance of Financial Disclosure in Family Law Matters' for The College of Law.

In this interview David talks frankly about barristers' preparation for Court, how he charges fees, and shares his insights about how to best prepare evidence for family lawyers. He also talks about potential reform, and ways in which communication between lawyers could be improved.

How did you come to work as a Family Law barrister? And what is your background and experience?

I got into Family Law more or less by accident. The law firm I was working for at the time, doing insurance work, approached me when their senior family lawyer left and asked if I was interested in taking the position. As it happens I was. I later went to the Bar.

I predominantly advise and appear in court in Family Law proceedings concerning children and property settlement. I also do some cases in which people are contesting a will, and sundry other bits and pieces of court work.

Describe what you do when you receive a brief for a new matter.

The first thing I do when I get a new case is try to work out what it is about. That is not always the same thing as what I have been told it is about.

I am paid to use my own intellect, knowledge, and experience. What I do is important, and carries a lot of responsibility. If I get it wrong, that has serious consequences for my client.

I try to gain my clients' confidence and convey that I do empathise with their predicament. That is just basic decency, in my opinion.

Then I have to read the court documents carefully – find the holes not only in the other party's case but also in my own. What further evidence or witnesses do we need? What subpoenas should issue? Do I really want, or need, to rely on that affidavit? Who is the Judge who will hear the case? Who is my opponent? Some people are sensible and reasonable; others aren't. What settlement offers have been made? If none, should an offer be made? If the case has to proceed to trial, what is my thesis? Is it ready? If not, should the Court be told that and later hearing dates sought? How long will it take? Have enough days been allocated?

Then there is the preparation work. That takes days, often on week-ends. As I develop my case theory, I work up my cross-examination notes. I type them all because that helps me to question witnesses in a logical and efficient manner, as well as giving me a reference point if I am interrupted by an objection or a question from the judge. I often depart from the script though, according to the way the case develops and the answers the witnesses give.

What should solicitors and clients look for when choosing a barrister?

It is important to choose a barrister whose style and personality matches that of the solicitor, and especially the client.

> Court cases involve teamwork, and personality clashes can undermine the whole enterprise.

The barrister also needs to know their onions and have a good reputation with the court and their peers.

How do you charge for your services?

It varies according to what I think is reasonable and affordable. I have done cases for nothing and I still do some legal aid work. As a general proposition, I charge by the day for court appearance work, and by the hour for advice work. When I say 'hour' I mean whole hour, not that I charge for one hour even if I only take a five-minute phone call. I am very conscious of the fact that many of my clients struggle to pay their legal fees and I want to give them value for their money. Frequently, I don't charge at all for short phone calls or email exchanges.

What would you suggest to a litigant with limited funds to pay for legal fees?

My suggestion is to engage a lawyer on a limited basis; for example, to prepare the trial affidavit and appear at the final hearing only.

Do you believe that *Thorne v. Kennedy* is the 'death knell' for 'prenups' – or, rather, binding financial agreements – as reported in the media?

No. Hopefully it will lead to more ethical behaviour on the part of people who want to stitch up their partners. I cheered when I read the judgement.

What are the biggest challenges as a family lawyer working within the current system?

Delay in dealing with cases, which in turn is a consequence of under-resourcing of the courts; in particular, the failure to appoint more Judges.

Given the current delays in Court, has this changed how you run Family Law matters?

Yes. I have to make a value judgement about whether to run an interim hearing, which will delay the allocation of final hearing dates, or leave all issues for determination at the final hearing.

Do you make use of any alternative dispute resolution (ADR), such as mediation, collaborative law, or arbitration?

Yes, ADR can be a very effective way of resolving a dispute. It only works in cases where both parties and their lawyers are sensible and reasonable. Sadly, that is not always the case.

What are the most significant frustrations or difficulties your clients have with regards to the Family Law system?

Delay, cost, and obstructive behaviour by the opposing party and/or their lawyers.

What is the one thing that you would say to someone about to go through the Family Law system?

Work with the system, not against it.

What other areas of law sometimes become relevant in Family Law matters?

Property law, equity and trusts, company law, bankruptcy, personal injury, and taxation.

What changes do you see in how social media and/or technology is being used in Family Law matters?

Yes, this is an interesting one. It is common now to see text messages and Facebook material in people's affidavits. Often lots of it, not all of which has the slightest relevance to the issues for determination in the case.

What do you think are the Family Law implications of the recognition of same-sex marriage?

Not much, from my perspective. Divorce is comparatively simple in the vast majority of cases, and it is rare for barristers to become involved. I suppose that the two-year minimum relationship length requirement for de facto property cases would not apply to same-sex marriages, and that may have a small impact on the volume of litigation.

In an increasingly global world, what issues are you seeing for international couples that separate?

The biggest would be the Hague Convention, which stipulates that, except in very limited circumstances, children be repatriated to their country of habitual residence if they are removed from one member country to another without the consent of the parent left behind.

I have also encountered difficulty in identifying and valuing overseas property.

Enforcing orders can also be an issue because Australia will only enforce judgements of a foreign country if they enforce our court orders, and even then only in relation to judgements for the payment of money. An order for the transfer of title to a property is not such a judgement.

Do you have any views about whether there is a particularly aggressive manner in which Family Law is practised by Sydney family lawyers, as referred to in Justice Benjamin's 2017 judgement?

I suspect that His Honour may have a point. I have encountered the approach that he describes from some lawyers in Sydney. I would like to think that they are in the minority, and that the publicity that has attended the judgement will have a moderating influence.

Do you believe there are any systemic biases against women or men in the Family Law system?

Judges are people, and some have a tendency to favour one sex over the other. I do not think that the system as a whole could be said to be loaded in favour of either sex.

What are your views with regards to the way family violence is understood in Family Law matters?

Family violence is easy to allege, and can be used for tactical reasons. In cases where it is real, it is taken very seriously, as it should be.
   I would also add that...

> there should be support and protection mechanisms for people who are falsely accused of perpetrating family violence, because that happens too.

Are there any reforms that you believe should be implemented to the Family Law system?

Appointing more Judges would be a good start.
   I also think that greater discipline should be imposed on the length of trials.

> A compulsory phone conference between the lawyers in the days leading up to court events to see what can be agreed, what procedural orders should be made, and what should happen next would save a lot of time on the appointed court date.

Judges also have a role to play, by starting on time, taking shorter breaks, and shutting down people who make lengthy speeches, for example.

Any words of wisdom for solicitors with regards to preparation of evidence for trial?

Focus on what your client hopes to achieve and what you are trying to prove.

Read the Family Law Act. For example, it tells courts how they may inform themselves about the wishes of children (in Section 60CD). What parents say in their affidavits is not one of them, and yet I routinely see vast amounts of material devoted to that topic in parents' affidavits.

If it is a property case, the rules of evidence apply; thus, hearsay and unqualified opinion evidence is inadmissible. In parenting cases the rules of evidence don't apply, as a general proposition.

Mark Holden

Barrister

When women tell men things

Mark Holden was first called to the Bar in 2009. He primarily practices in Melbourne and in addition to his work in the Family Violence court, Mark has also specialised in IVO and Stalking matters. He has undertaken cultural awareness training provided by Kellawan Indigenous Consultants.

Prior to being a barrister, Mark Holden was a well-known artist and entrepreneur in the entertainment industry in Australia and the United States of America for over 25 years. He also has extensive experience in contract, copyright and licensing in the Australian and international publishing, touring, merchandising, personal services, artist management and recording arenas.

In this interview Mark discusses the issues he sees on a daily basis in the specialised Family Violence courts, including addressing the perception that personal protection orders (AVO's in NSW) are taken out strategically with hidden agendas. For Mark the issue of family violence is highly gendered. He has observed that in the court system there continues to be a predisposition to not believing women. Referring back to Michael's experience about men as victims of family violence being disbelieved, if this view is accepted it seems it is not only men, but women too, who we resist believing. In Mark's view the system would benefit from positive discrimination so that a minimum of half the magistrates and prosecutors were women. Mark also provides practical tips about gathering evidence and filing an application for anyone who has been subjected to violence.

Mark, I understand you regularly appear in the Family Violence Court in Melbourne. What types of matters are listed in that court?

All kinds of matters go through that Court that are involved with personal safety. It might be two men having a fight or someone intimidating or stalking another. It doesn't have to be the traditional husband and wife. There are all kinds of different family violence and personal safety matters, but the majority of matters involve those who have been or are in a personal relationship.

What are some of the challenges in that Court at the moment?

What I've found is that the women magistrates do seem to have a very good hold on family violence. They're often tough, but they do understand what family violence is. What I have found though, at the risk of generalisation, is some males still even in that court specifically designed for family violence, just don't really have an understanding of what family violence is. It astounds me. After all the reports, awareness within the profession, the Rosie Batty story. Everything. Despite all of it, there still seems to be some gatekeepers- and I have to say they are usually male – who don't have an understanding of family violence. But sometimes it has been a young man that's come in and been the positive force, so I need to be careful here about being overly general.

What do you mean when you say they lack understanding of family violence?

There is still this old attitude of blaming the woman. The first position is to disbelieve the woman.

> There's still an issue of suspicion and how can we believe when women tell men things?

Some men just find it hard to believe women. I mean at least that's my personal observation. Obviously, it's better than it was perhaps 20 years ago and also obviously many, many men in that world do have a good understanding, but I seem to have tripped over some that very clearly don't. And in the Family Violence courts of all places.

You have to be really forthright with them. Because I'm older, I'm not afraid to be forthright, but if the woman were unrepresented, she'd find it very difficult to deal with. There is a predisposition to thinking that actually the true agenda underlying this matter is not about family violence and an attitude as follows: This is really about access to children. Or this is really a property matter. This shouldn't even be in this court. These are the kind of attitudes victims of family violence come up against. Also in other courts, I've seen the court system being used as a form of perpetrating family violence to punish the woman, and to cause distress.

I've seen that and when it's raised, the magistrates don't seem to understand that. Even though there have been parliamentary recommendations about using the court system improperly and exhausting somebody or just causing them anguish and cost with improper cases as a form of family violence. That still hasn't sunk in yet.

Also forcing a woman into a mediation when there has been family violence can be ridiculous, because again, my experience is that the mediation ends up being opportunity for the men to have another eight hours of attack.

I think we have a long way to go particularly with the male magistrates. I'm happy there are more women becoming magistrates in the area because in my experience having done this for nine years, the women are tough, but they at least have an understanding of what family violence is.

How do you see this ongoing bias against women improving? What can we do to make things better? Is it education?

I think there's been education. I would urge the government to have more women involved in that area.

> There should be female magistrates
> at the level of 50% or greater.

I think that's a pretty simple equation.

Now that is interesting. You are the only interviewee who has mentioned positive discrimination in their discussions.

Also in terms of the prosecutors as well, a minimum 50% of them should be women. I mean right across the board, prosecutors, magistrates. A minimum of 50% women.

Is resourcing sufficient at the Family Violence court?

In terms of resources, just like all the other courts, the Family Violence court is just barely coping. There's no area really that has enough resources. Particularly with the ice crisis, and how that affects family violence, it's unbelievable. There's just not enough resources. The Salvation Army can only do so much. The ice use is so pervasive.

Can you tell me more about the use of ice use in Family Violence court matters?

When younger people are involved, for a good proportion of them, ice is a factor. Many services for rehabilitation are full. You can't get into them, and the ones that you can get into are exceptionally expensive. So somebody in the family's going to dip into their pocket and come up with anywhere from $30,000 to $200,000. There's just simply not enough resources for the explosion of ice problems. Also it's getting worse, and worse, and worse.

Okay. I would like to touch on something else you raised. How there is a suspicion that family violence orders are really about something else, namely for example about blocking access to children or about property. I have to say, there is a perception among some family lawyers that protection orders, we call them AVO's in NSW, are sometimes used strategically in family law matters. Do you have any thoughts on this?

Well, I've seen strategies to fight personal protection orders. But matters that I've been involved with, mainly from women, have had a very real basis.

If there are strategies, they are only the strategies of the blokes trying to avoid them.

What about on the other side? Do you often see men being victims of family violence?

I've seen that, and one of my very first cases was a man that the woman's family was abusing, was bashing, but that's the exception. It's mostly either a same sex couple men and men. Or heterosexual, men and women.

I know in other countries, other jurisdictions overseas, there's one court that deals with all issues pertaining to a family. So the same court would hear personal protection orders, family violence, property, parenting, children. Or do you think it's better that there's this specialised Family Violence court?

I think it's a specialised thing. It can't go through the regular process. There's no rules of evidence. I think that's good. I think it's a specific discrete area that has to err on the side of speed and the side of the person who is the subject of the family violence, which can include children. Or at least children witnessing it, but generally speaking it's a woman. So urgency is important, and not having to apply the same rules as is required in a regular family law matter.

If someone is reading this, and they are going through a situation where they're being subjected to family violence. What would you say? What should they do?

They need to gather the evidence and they should film it.

They should get their phone out and film it. That's great evidence. When it's happening, that's one of the best weapons that you have. You should gather everything you can when the police are called, and the perpetrator is out of the house and put it in a safe place.

All your emails, all your texts, you need to gather. Then you need to come to court with evidence.

> You need to show the police and the court that this is a dangerous situation for you.

As I said, unfortunately sometimes it is hard to get others to believe you, so you need evidence to show them what you are saying actually happened. Also people who'll back it up, witnesses.

In terms of what you actually do in court, just go down to the court, and make an application. At every place there will be a family violence desk. In the Family Violence Court there is a separate floor to get counselling and some advice from the help desk. I must say, I've found the court system in that sense is very good. You can just head on down to your local magistrate's court.

> Just Google the local magistrate's court and once you are there find the dedicated family violence desk.

Also most courts will have a women's legal service. Certainly the Melbourne Magistrate's Court does. It also has a duty barrister. In the suburbs, it's generally speaking a duty solicitor, and quite often it is a community-based law person there.

After, when you actually turn up for the first return for them to get the interim order, there will be somebody there who can help you. You don't have to do it on your own. There will be somebody in the court who can help you whether it's women's legal, the duty barrister, the duty solicitor, or it's just the local community-based legal service. You might have to stand in line and wait, but generally speaking, there will always be somebody there for you. Unfortunately on some rare occasions there may be some days there may not be someone. But the vast majority of the time, there will be somebody there who will help you.

Greg Kenny

Barrister

The persuasive impact of a concession

Greg Kenny has worked in Family Law since he became a solicitor in 1986 and has been a barrister since 1996. He frequently appears in the Sydney Registry and in particular in the Parramatta Registry. In 1994 he achieved Specialist Accreditation in Family Law. Since 2009 Greg has been a qualified mediator, and since 2012 a Family Dispute Resolution Practitioner.

Greg is known for his ability to deal with the complex legal issues and appreciation of the other human issues that arise in family law matters, as well as his personable style. With over 30 years' experience in the field, in this interview Greg talks about how to choose a barrister and how to manage delay in matters, and shares his key tips and insights for clients and lawyers on preparing Family Law matters.

⁞⁞⁞⁞⁞

Tell me about your career path.

After completing my studies, I worked in a medium-sized solicitor's firm, in Western Sydney, in a number of different departments.

I was attracted to Family Law because it was people-oriented and it gave me an opportunity to get out of the office and go to court.

I knew from the start that I wished to be a barrister, and I did so as soon as I thought I could make a go of it. It was **22** years ago that I went to the Bar, and in that time I have mostly practised in Family Law.

What kind of matters do you assist parties with?

Financial and parenting disputes in court, advice, and conducting and representing people in mediation. I particularly enjoy cases involving expert evidence from psychiatrists/psychologists/Family Consultants in child disputes.

Knowledge and experience are important.

What should solicitors and clients look for when choosing a barrister?

A barrister should have some empathy for the client.

> A young, capable, and hungry barrister is
> often great value for money.

How do you charge for your services?

A daily rate for court and mediations and an hourly rate for all other work.

Given the current delays in Court, has this changed how you run Family Law matters?

A likely delay in having a case decided has to be factored into all advice given to clients. Strategy is often developed in cases to respond to the disadvantage of a delay, or, in some cases, a delay operates in your client's favour.

What are the misconceptions clients can have about Family Law?

That having your day in court will result in complete vindication. That all lawyers are unscrupulous.

What areas of law become relevant to Family Law?

Equity and criminal law would be the two most encountered by myself.

A lot of my interviewees talk about Sydney as a difficult place to practise Family Law.

Sydney Family Law is a bit like the city itself: ostentatious, brash, aggressive, and obsessed with real estate.

What do you think about the way we represent children in the Family Courts?

It's not perfect. Provided the ICL is capable and committed, it works pretty well.

What about cultural issues? Are these understood well?

No. Judges and lawyers should do some training in this area.

What are your thoughts on how violence in families is handled?

Usually, allegations of family violence are vitally relevant in children's matters and important in financial matters. The allegations must be scrutinised, and in a child's case,

the impact of family violence on the future welfare of the victim and the children should be the focus. Family Court cases should not turn into criminal trials.

Do you have any thoughts about reform?

I think it would be helpful if Federal Circuit Court Judges were allowed to deliver short-form summary-type decisions without the need for polished reasons, unless a party requests them. This could seriously reduce delays.

And words of wisdom for lawyers?

Affidavits need to be readable. Chronological order, generously spaced, short paragraphs, and the overall document should be as concise as possible without leaving important matters out. Content should be honest. A lawyer should reality-test their client's story. Understand the persuasive impact of a concession. Do not leave it to your paralegal or clerk. It is a lawyer's job to draft and settle evidence.

And for clients?

If you trust your lawyer, take their advice. Insist on trying to resolve your dispute without spending a fortune. Settle, if at all possible.

Court should be the last resort in most cases.

Bridie Nolan

Barrister

Don't die on every hill

Bridie Nolan is an experienced barrister, having been called to the Bar in 2006. Also an arbitrator Bridie has a broad practice traversing all areas of law, including Family Law. She has extensive trial and appellate experience in a wide range of matters. She appears regularly in complex Family Law matters involving issues of complex commercial interests, equity and trusts, third party interests, insolvency, and jurisdictional questions.

Bridie was the associate to The Honourable Justice James L. B. Allsop, then a Justice of the Federal Court, subsequently the President of the Court of Appeal of New South Wales, and now the Chief Justice of the Federal Court of Australia.

Bridie began her legal journey as a barrister's research assistant and solicitor at Freehills, practising in Litigation and Intellectual Property. She was subsequently a lecturer at the Faculty of Law, University of Sydney, lecturing in Litigation and Evidence and Administrative Law. Bridie is passionately dedicated to education and currently lectures in Advocacy, Planning Law, and Administrative Law at the Australian College of Law, and in Legal Professional Responsibility at the University of Sydney.

In this interview Bridie talks about why it is you can never 'win' a Family Law matter and what needs to change in the culture of the way Family Law is practised, in particular with practitioners' aggressive and obstructive approach. Instead, Bridie calls for a more measured approach, where concessions are made where appropriate, as opposed to dying 'on every hill'.

:::::

How did you come to work as a Family Law barrister? And what is your background and experience?

I am a commercial and public law barrister who became involved in Family Law through my work on various insolvency matters and matters involving statutory construction. Since commencing practice in the area of Family Law in about 2010, I have been involved in a variety of matters ranging from the commercially complex to the very straightforward. I also have also had my own personal experiences in Family Law, which inform my empathetic and considered approach to Family Law dispute resolution, especially those matters involving children. I am fortunate to have an excellent relationship with my ex-spouse, the insights from which relationship I endeavour to bring to my practice.

What kind of matters do you assist parties with?

In family law, no two matters are the same. The issues are idiosyncratic to the relationship from which they derive.

I have a very diverse practice, which allows me to manage all aspects of Family Law cases, from the simplest to the most acutely complex financial matters. I am a lateral thinker who is able to challenge preconceptions commonly held on issues and helpfully suggest alternatives.

What should solicitors and clients look for when choosing a barrister?

Modern litigation requires one to be across all areas of law. Specialisation leads to a very narrow focus on the issues, particularly in Family Law matters. Solicitors and clients should look for a barrister who is experienced in all areas of law, not just Family Law.

You want a problem solver, who can think outside the box. You also want someone who is an experienced litigator, so they know how to keep you out of court when needed and assist you ably if your matter does go to court.

What are your thoughts about BFAs?

Binding financial agreements have always been and remain problematic. *Thorne v. Kennedy* said nothing new about contracts that had not been said before. One area of practice I am very involved in is reviewing prenups, or BFAs, to ensure that they are binding, as a matter of jurisdiction, procedure, and equity and/or fairness.

Given the current delays in court, has this changed how you run Family Law matters?

My approach is unchanged. I have always tried to resolve Family Law matters amicably through keen strategy and negotiation, and otherwise through alternative dispute mechanisms such as arbitration and mediation, which I prefer to the court system.

What are the common misconceptions about Family Law?

The most common misconception in Family Law is that you can 'win' a Family Lawsuit.

A divorce, let alone divorce proceedings, especially those involving children, is an experience that I would not wish on my worst enemy, least of all my children.

In Family Law there are no winners; everybody loses.

I urge all my clients to take a sensible approach to the resolution of their dispute so that they can begin the process of healing with as much expedition and as little collateral damage as possible.

How would you describe the culture of collegiality in Family Law?

I am seriously unimpressed with the belligerent and unintelligent approach taken by so many of my Sydney colleagues to the practise of Family Law. This is particularly my experience with the larger Family Law firms which pride themselves on having a reputation for 'taking no prisoners'.

Too many lawyers conduct their practice as a post box, simply forwarding on the views of their clients and making every decision in the dispute on instructions.

There are certain decisions in Family Law, as with all litigation, which do not require the instructions of clients, and there are decisions which should be made further to the advice of lawyers, which has shaped a client's instructions.

> Lawyers need to be a sound, steady, and empathetic hand guiding parties through the process, rather than a mere conduit for the ruthless execution of vendettas.

A more commercial approach needs to be taken to the practice of Family Law and its litigation, rather than the current currency, which is something akin to a Year 10 locker room, where untrammelled puerile nastiness is commonplace.

Are there any reforms that you believe should be implemented to the Family Law system?

Where does one start? All the experts agree the area is ripe for serious reform.

I agree with former Family Court Chief Justice Diana Bryant that the *Family Law Act* is too complex and needs to be rewritten.

I also think that the Family Court should be abolished and a new Family Law division of the Federal Court created so that federal spending can be better managed and allocated, and the backlog of cases cleared by commercially experienced justices.[2]

---

2   This interview was conducted just before the announcement by the Attorney-General that the Family Court would merge with the Federal Circuit Court.

This is especially so when the back-office functions of the Federal and Family Courts are already combined, saving on administration costs. Merging the justices of the two Courts would bring a much-needed commerciality to the practice of Family Law.

If a more commercial approach were taken to the practice of Family Law, only the really important rabbits would be chased down their respective warrens. At present, the Family Law culture permits parties to air all their grievances, even down to little Jimmy returning home to Mum from a weekend with Dad with dirty socks in his bag. The cases are replete with matters where two days of court hearing time, not to mention the countless hours of preparation for those days in court, have been allocated to determining who receives 5% of $140,000. Inept counsel are permitted to cross-examine self-represented litigants for a day, costing their client that entire 5%! This sort of approach to practice would not be condoned in a commercial court.

The savings of combining the two courts could fund extra services, such as mediations and conciliations, aimed at settling disputes once they are in the court system, but before they reach trial.

I also believe there should be 'Counsel Assisting' introduced to the court, particularly those matters with self-represented litigants, and where family violence allegations or other safety concerns for children are involved. This would be more effective than the allocation of Independent Children's Lawyers to children, particularly where Mum and Dad are not represented.

What are the key tips you would like to share with readers?

A relationship breakdown is a time of enormous stress for families, especially those with children. Do everything you can to minimise that stress.

Don't die on every hill. Make concessions where appropriate. Be fair. And never use your children as a tool by which to execute revenge on your estranged partner.

Do everything in your power to work towards a businesslike co-parenting relationship with your children's other parent. Don't spend a fortune to make a point.

Save your money and get on with your life as quickly
and as cleanly as possible.

Lawyers

Maurice Edwards

Family lawyer

Justice delayed is justice denied

Maurice Edwards is an Accredited Family Law Specialist, Family Dispute Resolution Practitioner (FDRP), Accredited Mediator and Arbitrator. He is a collaborative family lawyer and is currently President of the Greater Sydney Collaborative Family Law Group.

He has over 35 years legal experience. Maurice's experience across a variety of legal areas has assisted in his understanding of many problems confronting clients involved in family law issues.

Maurice encourages people to consider alternate dispute resolution options as a way of settling disputes, and uses his knowledge and experience to negotiate beneficial outcomes for clients.

In this interview Maurice discusses how family law has changed as societal roles for men and women have changed. Although the first wholesale review of the family law system is currently taking place and there is much criticism, Maurice explains how family law has, to some extent, responded in its practical application as gender roles have changed. He also speaks about delay, and how collaboration, mediation and arbitration are viable alternatives for parties wanting to have their matter resolved more swiftly and effectively. He also discusses his journey in family law and the specific areas that have captured his interest.

Lastly, Maurice gives readers crucial tips including how they can save legal fees by helping their lawyer collate and prepare documents. I think this is particularly important as one of the first things I explain to my clients is, in legal services, time is money, because the vast majority of lawyers charge for their work in time intervals.

⣿

How did you come to work as a family lawyer?

Zoë, there was no grand plan to be a family lawyer. In 1982 I was grateful just to secure a position as a solicitor. I recall there were 30 applicants for the lawyer's position in a firm in Orange in the Central West of NSW. I was in fact the second choice.

As a newly admitted solicitor, I did whatever legal work was asked of me, which was generally everything the partners did not want to touch. So it was, that I practiced in the areas of family, civil, criminal law and debt recovery. However this provided a solid foundation for a future more specialist legal career although I was not aware of it at the time. Country practice provided variety and diversity and an opportunity to gain legal skills and experience at an early stage.

My initial family law experience occurred in the first three months of practice. I had been asked by the partner to travel from Orange to Dubbo to instruct a barrister in a bitter custody dispute between the mother of a child and her mother, the paternal grandmother. Unfortunately, the barrister that had been engaged missed his flight from Sydney to Dubbo, however, the judge and opposing counsel did not. The judge was his Honour Justice Watson and he had a formidable reputation. I still recall how hard my heart pounded as I mentioned the matter before his Honour and his Honour indicated that I would need to run the case on my own. Fortunately for me his Honour flagged a suggested outcome in the proceedings and ultimately gave us some time to resolve the matter. I was and have remained grateful for the collaborative approach and attitude taken by the opposing counsel, who is now a Family Court judge.

My next experience in family law was just as stressful. I travelled to Parramatta from Orange with a client to what was then called a Regulation 96 Conference (settlement conference with a Registrar of the Court). I advocated my client's position in the conference before Registrar Halligan as he then was. Registrar Halligan's reputation was also quite formidable, however, at the time in my youthful ignorance, I was blissfully unaware of it. The Registrar was not backward in indicating that my client's position in so far as a property adjustment was somewhat misguided. The Registrar did not hold back. The trip home with my client was very quiet and rather subdued.

I learnt two very important lessons from those experiences. Firstly, always be prepared for the unexpected. Secondly, never travel to or from a court event with your client.

Notwithstanding those first two experiences, family law remained a significant part of my legal practice for the next 35 years.

In 1988 when my wife and I decided to return to Sydney from the country, I established the Parramatta branch of the Orange firm. The reason Parramatta was chosen was that it was the location of the Registry of the Family Court that serviced the Central West of New South Wales. Notwithstanding that for the next 20 years or so the majority of my own legal practice involved acting for banks and financial institutions in preparing documents and securities for residential and business loans and acting for the State Rail Authority of NSW in litigated workers compensation claims, family law still remained a significant part of my practice. I was always drawn to it. Providing advice to people dealing with family law issues, assisting them through their darkest time and helping to put them on a path to a brighter future always held a special reward for me.

So 30 years after having moved from Orange to Parramatta, and now as Special Counsel for Watts McCray Lawyers, family law has become my professional focus. Zoe this is a long answer to the question but for me, the path to becoming a specialist family lawyer has been a long and winding journey rather than a direct route.

How do you attempt to resolve family law problems?

As quickly and as amicably as the circumstances allow. I do encourage and assist parties to attempt to resolve their family law problems at an early stage if this is practicable. Not all of these problems, however, can be resolved in this way. The first task is to build a good rapport with the client to ascertain what it is that they want to achieve. Then the task is to strategise a plan to achieve that outcome. Some clients want to move on quickly from the end of a relationship or marriage without always considering what might be in their best interest and/or the best interest of the children if there are children involved. Other clients want to drag out the process as long as possible, some because they are unable to face or deal with the consequences of a break down of a relationship and are indeed "paralysed" by the circumstances, others may have more sinister motives.

If the breakdown in a relationship is amicable and there are no hotly contested issues and there is a reasonably approachable lawyer acting for the other party then a collaborative approach may be appropriate. A round-table conference with the parties and the other lawyers can be arranged to discuss and attempt to resolve parenting, property or other issues. In matters where the issues are more complex but there is still some good will, an experienced mediator may be able to assist the parties and their lawyers reaching a resolution. My experience has been that most matters can be successfully mediated, even if there are significant issues in dispute whether by traditional mediation where both parties come together with their lawyers and a mediator in one room or whether by shuttle mediation where the parties remain in separate rooms and the mediator shuttles between the parties and their lawyers.

In some situations the parties are at 'loggerheads' and the relationship breakdown is toxic. Parties may not be thinking rationally. There may be manipulative or threatening behaviour. Someone in the relationship may seek revenge for past misdeeds. The lawyer representing one or both of the parties may have a combative style. A collaborative or mediated approach is then generally unsuitable. These cases are a little more difficult to strategise and resolve and can be rather challenging in a court system where delays for interim matters can take up to 6 months to be heard and delays for final hearings 3 years and longer is not uncommon. Of course usually a long delay provides great advantage for one party at the expense of the other. Someone who has the children living with them will be advantaged by delay in a parenting dispute. A party living in the former matrimonial home will often be advantaged by the Court delays in a property matter. We are starting to see the Court refer matters to both mediation and arbitration to attempt to combat delays.

When resolving or attempting to resolve family law matters I almost always use 'the carrot before the stick' in an attempt to resolve matters on an amicable basis prior to heading to court where the result can be unpredictable. Joseph Grynbaum once said, 'an ounce of mediation is worth a pound of arbitration a ton of litigation'. I say, *a sign of collaboration is worth a taste of mediation, a sample of arbitration and a smorgasbord of litigation.*

> In my view it is important to provide clients with a wide range of options to resolve their family law problems and try to match the appropriate strategy to the circumstances.

Do you have any special areas of expertise or interest in family law?

Zoë, I have developed three particular areas of interest.

- Binding Financial Agreements;
- Childhood Gender Dysphoria; and
- National and International Relocations.

I have always been interested in Binding Financial Agreements (BFA's). It seemed a little odd to me when in 2000 the Australia Parliament legislated the Agreements, the effect of which was that parties could opt out of our family law system. At the time Australia's 'no-fault' family law system had been in place for 25 years and was regarded as one of the fairest family law systems in the world. It intrigued me as to why parties were allowed to opt out, thereby potentially putting one vulnerable party at great disadvantage. There were of course protections provided where that each party was required to have independent legal advice and further that these Agreements could be set aside in various situations including fraud, unenforceability, impracticability, or if there was a specified material change in circumstances. I have been particularly interested in the way that the Family Court and the Full Court of the Family Court have struggled to interpret the law surrounding Binding Financial Agreements. On the one hand many judges have attempted to give effect to the rights of the parties to opt out of the family law system. On the other hand others have attempted to protect the disadvantaged party and set aside unfair Agreements.

My interest in this area started when I was involved in one of the first reported cases interpreting Binding Financial Agreements. I had refused to provide the independent legal advice requested of me as I thought the provisions of the Agreement were quite unfair. That Binding Financial Agreement was subsequently set aside by the Court. My interest in this area has continued up to the recent High Court decision of *Thorne and Kennedy* which was the first time the High Court of Australia had considered Binding Financial Agreements in the family law context. I was not surprised, and indeed quite heartened that the High Court set aside, what in my view was an unfair Binding Financial Agreement despite the fact that each party had received proper and independent legal advice. I have presented a number of papers on this topic including "A Voyage Through the Troubled Waters of Binding Financial Agreements".

Secondly, I have held an interest in legal developments in Childhood Gender Dysphoria (where a child does not identify with their biological sex) and the necessity of the Family Court to be involved in decisions for the treatment of children even when there is an agreement. I became interested when I was called upon at short notice to provide comment on an SBS Insight program in 2013 regarding these issues. I found it interesting to follow developments of the Family Court which gradually has withdrawn from its involvement in the stages of treatment for Gender Dysphoria. This prompted me to present a paper earlier in the year to the college of Law titled, 'Children with Gender Dysphoria - the Journey from Marion to Matthew'.

Lastly, I have a special interest in relocation matters including international child abduction cases.

Many years ago I acted for a mother who had brought her two year old child from Norway to Australia to escape a violent relationship. We were able to successfully argue one of the 'Hague defences' to an abduction that there was a grave risk to the child, or that an intolerable situation that would arise if the child was returned to Norway to live with the father. Further we were able to successfully defend that decision in the Full Court of the Family Court, and also in the High Court of Australia. The government in Norway had assisted the father financially to attempt to have the child returned including financing one of the leading special counsel in the country to present the argument in the High Court. This was my first involvement in a Hague Child Abduction case. As a result, I became interested in child abduction and relocation matters generally, and have over the years appeared for many parents seeking to relocate and others seeking to resist relocation.

I was honoured to participate in a delegation of Australian lawyers, mediators and social scientists in 2015, led by his Honour Justice Benjamin training in the international mediation of child abduction matters between Japan and Australia, shortly after Japan became a party to the Hague 'Child Abduction' Convention. It was a fabulous experience and I have had a number of opportunities to present papers on this topic since.

You mention in some detail the alternative dispute resolution processes available, such as mediation and arbitration, and also that some lawyers are more combative than others. You would be aware Justice Benjamin recently referred two Sydney lawyers to the office of the Legal Services Commissioner, and also more generally commented, 'there seems to be a culture of bitter adversarial and highly aggressive Family Law litigation'.

Zoë, yes many lawyers have been trained in or have developed an adversarial or combative approach to family law.

My recollection was that initially when the Family Court of Australia was first established, it was to be 'the friendly Court'. Many lawyers and some parties, though, have difficulty adopting a friendly or less adversarial approach and want to win at all cost, irrespective of the consequences to the parties or indeed the children.

I think His Honour's observation and criticism of some lawyers in Sydney is valid. I have had to deal with some of those lawyers. There will always of course be those cases where litigants are hell-bent on having their day in Court and venting their frustration, their anger and attempting to exact their revenge. There will always be lawyers ready to serve that purpose. Family law after all is a highly emotive area. The challenge is to convince those litigants and lawyers who want to go down every burrow and who concede little or nothing at all, that this is not always the best way to achieve a desired outcome. I suspect that for some litigants and even some lawyers that is a hard sell. In my view you need to help litigants choose their battles.

Do you believe there are any innate or systemic biases against women or men in the family law system?

I don't believe there is an innate gender bias in our family law system in Australia. Despite much criticism, fundamentally our family law system provides outcomes that are in the children's best interest in parenting matters and a just and fair result in property matters irrespective of gender. Let's face it England is still grappling with the concept of no fault divorce, 40 years after we in the Antipodes adapted the concept. There have indeed been changes in Court outcomes over the years but I think that change has reflected the changes in our society.

When I started to practice family law in the early to mid-1980s family life looked a little different. Often the father worked full time and the mother either did not work, or if so, worked part-time. In parenting matters the Court Orders reflected what was then regarded to be in the best interest of the children, for example, that children live with their primary carer (mostly the mother) and spend time with the other parent (mostly the father) say each second weekend and half of the school holidays. Now we often see Shared Parenting Court Orders, for example, one of the parents spending 8 or 9 nights per fortnight with the children and the other parent spending 6 or 5 nights per fortnight. This change really just reflects the changes in our modern family whereby in many instances both parents are working or able to care for the children, rather than any particular gender bias.

Similarly in property matters there is perhaps a greater focus on the financial and non-financial contribution of the parties to the relationship and less of a focus on the future needs of the parties. I think again it reflects the modern family reality these days with both parents are often working and in many situations there is a more equal earning capacity of the parties than there was in times gone by. Interestingly I have found that it is often the female judges that are often less generous in the adjustment of future needs in property matters. This may reflect their own experiences in juggling demands of work and family and the change in our modern society.

As you see it, what reforms should be implemented in the Family Law system?

The proposal by the Attorney General to merge the Family Court and the Federal Circuit Court so that there is one point of entry for litigants is a good and overdue proposal.

I know that there has been spirited arguments about how the appeals against trial judges decisions are dealt with. Whether these appeals should be heard by a judge with specialist family law knowledge or before a judge with more general legal knowledge. From my perspective I think limiting simple appeals to a single judge with specialist knowledge and freeing up other judges for trial work has merit. The more important or significant appeals can be dealt with by the judges with both specialist and general legal experience.

The biggest problem, however, with our Family Law Court system is delay, particularly in the Federal Circuit Court. As set out above delays of up to 6 months for an interim hearing and 3 years plus for a final hearing are typical and are not acceptable.

The changes that have been made in the last 10 or so years, in relation to parenting matters, that require mediation of the issues (other than in exceptional circumstances), prior to the parties being allowed to file a Parenting Application in Court was a good move in my view and alleviated delays for some time. However the delays have returned.

Perhaps there should be a similar requirement for the parties to attend upon a mediator prior to being allowed to file a Property Application in Court. I suspect this would significantly reduce the delays in the short term.

Some judges are now actively referring parenting and property matters out for private mediation. We are now seeing successful resolution of such matters. In my view judges should be encouraged to do this. In the Parramatta Registry a couple of the Federal Circuit Court judges are actively now encouraging lawyers and litigants to have property matters privately arbitrated. If other judges in the other registries around Australia were of a similar mind, I believe the delays in the family law system would be significantly reduced. Perhaps if the rules were changed so that arbitrators were able to determine simple parenting matters and not just property matters (as is the current situation) there would be even less delay.

The encouragement of judges in both the Family Court and the Federal Circuit Court for parties to use alternate dispute resolution options, in my view will provide a better outcome for those parties that are seeking to resolve their family law disputes in a timely fashion. After all "Justice delayed is justice denied".

What are the key tips or pieces of wisdom you would give readers regarding how to best navigate the system?

My first tip for anyone going through the family law process is to become informed. It is much easier to do now than it was a generation ago. With the internet and access to the Courts' websites www.federalcircuitcourt.gov.au and www.familycourt.gov.au and articles and papers on decisions, it is relatively easy to stay informed. Valuable information is also available through bodies such as Relationships Australia, Anglicare, Catholicare, and Unifam to name a few.

My second tip for people is that when choosing a lawyer to assist in family law issues, choose one with particular family law knowledge and one who is aware of all the options available, collaboration, mediation, arbitration in addition to litigation. This will provide the opportunity to achieve the best outcome emotionally and financially.

> My third tip is that people would be wise to prepare an accurate
> chronological story of their relationship.

... That is, to detail all the major events such as date of cohabitation, where cohabitation took place, the assets each of the parties had at the cohabitation, date of marriage (if applicable), date and details of any property purchases (if applicable), dates of birth of children and details as to the care of the children (who did what at home). It is of great assistance to a lawyer if he/she is armed with accurate information it makes the lawyers task easier and often saves a great deal of time and expense for all parties involved. It also assists strategising a matter and enables the lawyer to focus on the favourable aspects of their client's case and whether alternate dispute resolution is appropriate.

My final tip is for parties to take a step back and think about what they say or said (either by text, email or on social media). It is safe to assume that what is said or sent or posted may appear in an Affidavit down the track. A post uploaded or text sent in the heat of the moment, can often lead to unfortunate outcomes for parties at the end of the day. Such outcomes may have been different had parties stepped back and taken a breath to consider, 'what would a judge think about this message I propose to send or post?'

> The delete button on the keyboard is perhaps one
> of the least used, but perhaps is one of the most important keys.
> It is there for a reason.

Cristina Huesch

Family lawyer

The way to get there

Cristina Huesch is a founding partner of Alliance Legal Services in Canberra and has a particular interest in offering out-of-court solutions to Family Law problems. She encourages our clients to think of court as a last resort, only to be pursued once all other settlement avenues have been explored and failed to lead to a fair outcome.

Cristina has a Master's degree in Applied Law (Family Law Practice), is an accredited specialist in Family Law (Law Society Accredited Specialist Scheme), and holds a Graduate Diploma in Legal Practice, a Diploma in Law, and Bachelor of Arts. Cristina is qualified to practice collaborative matters and is a qualified Independent Children's Lawyer.

Cristina is a member of the Law Council of Australia (Family Law Section) member, ACT Law Society member, Canberra Collaborative Practice Group (specialising in non-court solutions), Legal Aid panel member to accept grants of Legal Aid (NSA and ACT), and Volunteer Solicitor at Women's Legal Centre (ACT and Region). Cristina is fluent in German.

In this interview Cristina spoke candidly with me about her winding path to becoming a family lawyer, and detailed the nuts and bolts of the pathway a Family Law matter might take through the family system (For anyone about to embark on the process, this is a must-read!) She also discusses her work as a collaborative lawyer and the limits a Court has in being able to change a person. Importantly, Cristina spoke about how although often in alternative dispute resolution, such as collaborative law, the outcome is often similar to what could be achieved in, say, Court, but 'the way to get there is different (and usually better).' In my view it is not merely the outcome but the method of achieving it – the way – that is important when you are dealing with families because there can often be an unintended therapeutic or on the flip side damaging affect to a Family Law process. In this sense the way of reaching resolution itself has real consequences for a family.

How did you come to work as a family lawyer? And what is your background and experience?

I sort of fell into it, like most family lawyers. I had studied law subjects within an Arts degree, then decided to try different things, including travelling, working as a stage manager at the Sydney Opera House, working in music management in Munich, working in a patent attorney's office, waitressing, nannying, working as business affairs co-ordinator in a Government film investment body, working as a legal secretary for a TV production company – just anything other than straight law.

When in my thirties I decided to get my act together, I thought what can I do that's a bit more people-orientated, and ended up going back to uni, focusing on Family Law, getting qualified, and just starting work in a small law firm. Everyone else hated Family Law so, happily, I got given all the files! My previous work background involved dealing with a wide range of people, of all sorts of ethnicities, sexual orientations, ages, levels of education, abilities to express themselves, and so forth, all of which, I think, has helped me develop good listening skills in my Family Law work, which I find has really helped me.

What kind of matters do you assist parties with?

Prenups, divorces, children's matters, financial settlements, appeals. I've done an annulment application in a divorce, I've stopped people leaving the country with a child at short notice, I've got international matters, and I also do collaborative law. We also sometimes get interim spouse main-tenance applications, and orders that one spouse gets sole use of a house until further order. We also deal with cases of family violence (both in the Family Law Courts and the Magistrates Courts, which are State-based). We are also just starting to do a bit of Children's Court work. Oh, and we also represent grandparents who wish to spend time with their grandchildren. Just anything and everything to do with people getting together, splitting up, and everything in between.

Do you still do BFAs?

We do BFAs, yes, but we do charge for them, and often draft extremely long advices! I also won't take on clients if they are going to argue with me and try to push me around, or try to get me to give them only the advice they want to hear. I'll refer those on. I think some of the cases where BFAs have been set aside are a wake-up call though, in terms of the nature of the advice you give, and also the timing of the advice, to give people time to reflect.

Describe what it is you do. If you could, describe the kind of pathway a Family Law matter in both parenting and property could take. Just the basic real details would be great.

People come to see me either before, during, or after their separation. Sometimes they want to know where they might stand if they separate (for example, how much money they'll basically walk away with, or would they have sole custody of their kids, and so on).

Other times, they have just separated and will ask me to give legal advice, or sometimes immediately prepare court documents so they can start their court case straight away. At other times, they are confused, or blindsided, and don't even know where to look, and need referrals to media-tors, counsellors, child experts. I'll usually discuss collaborative practice with clients and see if they are open to sitting around a room with me, their ex-, and their lawyer, and talking through a solution in an interest-based way, rather than looking at it as a traditional adversarial and positional way to resolve conflict.

So, we initially talk through where they're at and what they need. Sometimes that's all they want, to talk things through.

For some couples, that's it - I might never hear from them again. Sometimes I hear later they've reconciled, or decided to stick it out and get counselling.

For most clients, particularly in financial matters, we'll then start work looking at their assets, debts, income, getting valuations, looking at trusts or family businesses, and superannuation. We'll always give them some advice of what they could expect from a Judge. Sometimes they want to go home and try and do a deal with their partner. If they are not ready to talk with their partner directly, we'll take over and write to the spouse or their lawyer. We do this regardless of which pathway they choose.

There's an information-gathering stage, then an advice stage, and then we get to the pointy end and help them get to a realistic deal. When it's all sorted, we'll make it all legally binding, drafting up the documents and filing them in court.

With children's matters, because there's a requirement that the parties do mediation before starting a court case, we send them off to Relationships Australia or an equivalent. Sometimes that's the last we hear of it, and they either do an informal deal at RA, sign a parenting plan, or come back to me with bullet points of a deal, and I draft the consent orders.

At other times, when mediation fails, they come back to me with a certificate showing mediation has failed. We then prepare court paperwork (usually an Affidavit, Initiating Application, and Notice of Risk) and assist them through the court process. We turn up to court and tell the Judge where the matter is at and what the issues are. Sometimes we run an interim hearing and, later, a final hearing.

Most matters do settle. I've only had about 10 matters run to final hearing (with witnesses being cross-examined, etc.) in about 15 years of working in the field, so it really is rare.

We put a lot of effort into helping people settle parenting matters early, because the court delays mean it can take two or more years to a final hearing.

We'll suggest using child experts, mediators, or having a roundtable discussion. We will keep advising them about the rising costs and the reality that no court may give them the sense of vindication they seek, or 'punish' the other parent. We'll try to help them see that making compromises and having finality of proceedings can be the best thing for the children. It isn't always true for Family Law matters, but where appropriate, we will help people navigate their way through the system and out the other side with the least cost, time, and hurt feelings.

There's a lot of listening, negotiating with the other side (verbally or in writing), and drafting. The court stuff that people think happens is actually the least of what we do.

Thanks. I really appreciate that practical description of how a matter might run from start to finish. Do you have any special areas of interest or expertise within family law?

My special interest is collaborative practice. It is based on trying to resolve disputes in a win-win way.

The easiest way to describe it is to look at dividing an orange. Rather than fight over how much of the orange each person gets, we ask them what they want to do with the orange. One person might say, 'I want to make a glass of juice', the other, 'I need the peel for a cake'. Everyone gets what they need, and the orange does end up getting divided, just in a different way. It's a good way to step back and try and look at outcomes creatively. Having said that, interestingly, most collaborative matters end up resolving on terms quite similar to traditional law, but the way to get there was a bit different (and usually better).

What would you say is your law firm's point of difference as compared with other firms?

We are really big on using all modern technology to minimise legal fees. We grant our clients, barristers, and other experts access to our portal – each has their own folder – to upload and download files, evidence, briefs, etc. It's a lot quicker to circulate information, and we can give them draft documents to work on and they can upload their edits to us.

We'll do Skype or FaceTime conferences to minimise travel for clients, or for mums with bubs who just can't get to our street address.

We also offer a free half-hour conference for them to meet us, get a feel for us, and decide whether or not to use us before they have to incur any fees. We think that choosing your lawyer is as important as choosing your family GP, or the architect who designs your home; and the clients need to feel comfortable that they are a good fit with us before they start spending any money.

We are also a women-only firm, which is unique!

What should a client look for when choosing a family lawyer? What should they look for in their initial conference with a lawyer?

They should choose someone who they feel in their gut they can trust.

> It's important that they feel they can tell the lawyer anything and everything, and not hold back something because they are intimidated by the lawyer, or worry the lawyer will think they are stupid.

The client might know some relevant fact that seems unimportant at the time to the client but the whole case might turn on that. So, if you have rapport, then it's a good start, because you'll work as a team. You may have this lawyer in your life for two years, so you have to have that basic foundation from the beginning.

> The client should expect the lawyer to be straight with them. This includes being honest about the client's prospects.

If you go to see an accredited specialist, or someone who has been doing Family Law a long time, trust them - they will know the law! If they give the client advice which is different to what the client wants to hear, it's usually spot on. The client ought to leave the initial meeting with a sense that their lawyer is prepared to give them honest advice. Ultimately this will save the client money.

Other than in rare cases - family violence, money about to disappear from joint accounts, houses about to be disposed of, children rushed out of the country, etc. ...

> clients should be wary of lawyers who start
> talking about court straight away.

There are many more productive and cost-effective ways to resolve matters before you consider court.

Speaking of costs, how do you charge for your services?

We charge a flat fee for divorces and an hourly rate for other work. We are looking at moving to fixed-fee work.

Fixed-fee work seems to be the way quite a few firms are heading. But what would you suggest to a litigant with limited funds to pay for legal fees?

Ask what you can do to minimise fees yourself - how much homework are you prepared to do? Are you ready to go to court alone, with just your lawyer in the background giving you some shadow help, without them being on the record and charging you for sitting around at court for four hours, when your matter might be on for 10 minutes only?

Try all the mediation services which aim to help you settle the matter, once you have got some basic legal advice about your entitlements. Know what is an acceptable bottom line from a lawyer, but then try to do the negotiating yourself. Unless there is a power imbalance, or violence, this can be a cost-effective way to resolve your matter.

Listen to legal advice and take it! If your lawyer is telling you that you can go to court for two years, spend $40,000, and end up with potentially only an extra night per fortnight with your kids, then ask yourself if that time and money is really worth it, or whether you'd rather move on, spend that money on your kids, and keep the relationship with your ex- as functional as possible.

Spend the money early to get realistic legal advice, as this is often money well spent. If you muddle along alone, then engage lawyers to fix a problem, it can cost more down the track than if you'd seen a lawyer at the beginning.

At the end of a matter, is there anything clients often tell you they now realise in hindsight that they wished they had known from the start?

They usually tell me they wish they'd known they could spend a lot of money and still not get a sense of vindication or 'justice' or 'fairness' after years in the system.

We try to tell them this in the beginning, but clients might feel very hurt or angry at the ex- and they don't always listen. Some believe that if they spend the money on the perfect affidavit about how terrible their ex- is, the Judge will 'punish' the ex- and really see things from the client's point of view.

Yes, I completely agree. People are waiting for that vindication and sense that the Court acknowledges they have been aggrieved by their ex.

Unfortunately, this just doesn't happen, and the court does not have the resources to do this; nor is that how the system works. We don't tell the clients to settle because we want to wrap up our files; it's because we often have years and years of experience and know that some of what the clients want is just unachievable. The Judge cannot turn their ex- from a narcissist into a better human being, for example. They may never get that satisfaction. We try to help them settle, because it really is in their best interests.

David Barry

Family lawyer

The benefit of an outcome, in and of itself

David Barry is an accredited specialist in Family Law practising in Sydney and is a Doyle's guide recommended solicitor. He is a graduate of the University of Sydney and a former Legal Associate to The Honourable Justice Lindenmayer. As a lawyer dual-qualified in Australia as well as England and Wales, David has a particular interest in Family Law matters with international aspects.

He works with people on all aspects of Family Law, including property settlement/asset division and parenting arrangements.

In this interview David talks about how to choose your family lawyer, how to manage legal fees, and, in particular, discusses his ideas for making Family Law more efficient by way of standardised orders and provides his key tips to anyone separating.

!!!!!

How did you come to work as a family lawyer? And what is your background and experience?

Family law mooting at university gave me a taste of this type of work, and I was well and truly hooked after a year as a legal associate in the Appeal Court of the Family Court. The Judge I worked for told me to do something other than Family Law when I was leaving the Court. So, I did a year of commercial litigation and hated going to work every day. I returned to Family Law and can honestly say I have never hated coming to work.

More generally, I am the child of Irish immigrants and was the first person in my family to go to university. Via my personal relationship, I have come to be part of an extended South African Jewish family.

I'd like to think I have an open mind, and not a lot shocks me.

I agree it is crucial to have an open mind in Family Law. Otherwise, I think people can just sense when they are being judged, even if you don't say anything. So, what kind of matters do you assist parties with?

The people I work with don't come in legal boxes and I can assist people with any Family Law legal issue that they require. I'm not a lawyer who is snobby about what I do or who I act for.

Those issues range from questions of expert evidence in complex disputes over children's care; international taxation consequences of offshore trusts; or helping people negotiate their way out of situations that they find impossible to solve.

As a family lawyer though, I think one's work is about 5% law and about 95% people management, the applicable people being clients, other lawyers, and Judges.

I agree with your 5/95 equation. Perhaps instead of saying what matters you do, I should have asked whether you have any special areas of interest or expertise within Family Law. If so, what are these?

Families that cross international borders and cultures particularly interest me.

The reason for this is that each time I look into a legal system outside of Australia, it reminds me how we create our own legal systems by the cultures and practices we take on. The real issue in this space is how applicable and relevant foreign laws are becoming to the Australian community.

In addition to international law issues and foreign laws, I think Family Law is an area where so many other areas of Australian law are relevant.

Indeed. All areas of law come up in Family Law. It is the last bastion of general practice in many respects. Often, the pre-existing general law issues (for example, tax liabilities or regarding real estate) can be magnified and more difficult than they ordinarily would be because of the breakdown in the personal relationship between the separating couple. In short, clean up your affairs before you get separated.

Returning to your interest in international law issues, what issues are you seeing for international couples that separate?

Many non-married international couples can obtain a rude shock about the breadth of Australian Family Law when their relationships break down here and they realise the rights and responsibilities are pretty much the same as if they had married.

By the same token, Australian de factos who live in foreign lands when their relationships break down also receive a rude shock when they realise the place that they live, despite having, say, same-sex marriage, offers them little or no protection as former de facto partners. The shock is compounded when they may not be able to rely on the Australian law concerning de facto partners due to our geographical requirements as to de facto couples. This is a big loophole in our Family Law that people often learn about in hindsight.

You mentioned same-sex marriage. What do you think are the Family Law implications of the recognition of same-sex marriage?

The implications are largely symbolic, but that said, there are important legal implications in various states. For example, same-sex married couples who moved to Western Australia and then whose relationship broke down could have been in a position of non-recourse under Australian de facto relationship law; however, that is no longer the case.

What should a client look for when choosing a family lawyer?

Someone who listens, not talks. People who consult a specialist family lawyer assume they have the technical know-how and, frankly, if the lawyer got to that position, then they know what they are doing. So, choose someone whom you feel comfortable talking to and that you like - without assuming they are your friend; they are not! You are entitled to technical competence and personal understanding of your situation, but also respect the fact that the lawyer does have your interests at heart, and don't blame them for what are, yes, your problems.

What is your unique style as a lawyer?

Objectively, you might not like what I tell you, but you may ultimately be glad to have heard it.

How do you charge for your services?

We have a suite of charging methods that range from flat fee (yes, some Family Law work is of a flat fee nature) to hourly rates (the majority of our work), and unbundled/premium (think Jetstar and Qantas).

You mentioned Jetstar versus Qantas; I like the analogy. But what should a litigant with limited funds to pay for legal fees do?

All litigants have limited funds to pay for legal services, so the first thing to realise is you are not alone or exceptional.

Be organised - some basic organisation of documents, information, and your briefing to your lawyer will save you real money. Make costs part of the dialogue you openly have with your lawyer, without trying to micro-manage everything the lawyer does. Think strategically about your legal spend and what value you are getting for it - talk your best friend's ear off about how awful your ex- is and restrict the lawyer's work to preparing documents that add value, because other people cannot prepare those documents as efficiently and accurately.

What do you find challenging as a family lawyer?

Managing human expectations in our digital age. People I work with often expect instant answers to complex issues, no doubt informed by their general engagement with technology. They do not understand how the legal system is a remnant of a mode of thinking that is very different to our current expectations.

Speaking of the digital age, what changes do you see in how social media and/or technology is being used in Family Law matters?

I'll keep this simple:

> Assume anything you put in black and white, anywhere, at any time, is capable of being accessed and shown to the person who may ultimately decide what it is best for your child.

Stop and think. Don't let the immediacy of the technological medium make you look like a fool.

Do you believe there continues to be gender bias issues in the Family Law system?

No, the Family Law system is not that consistent. Gender definitely plays a role, but it is only one factor in a complex suite of issues that varies enormously from decision maker to decision maker.

> The inconsistency of procedure, approaches, and outcomes is, perhaps, a greater issue than gender.

Are there any reforms that you believe should be implemented to the Family Law system?

Standardising and limiting the paperwork that is put before the Court. A lot of money is spent by a lot of the community on slightly different versions of, for example, a school holiday order for children. Clearly, there will always be situations that are unique, but for the vast majority of matters that come before the Court, if there were an accepted standard template that everyone could work from, I feel it would save litigants money and also reduce conflict and discussion.

Whilst the ability to present a legal case is part of natural justice that should not be taken away from people coming to the Court, there needs to be a realisation that the Court is a public resource which is being shared by many people in the community. If that means that the paperwork is limited, then it will spread the resource equitably.

At the end of a matter, is there anything clients often tell you that they have learned about the Family Law system that they wished they had known from the start?

Innumerable people that I have worked with often tell me how relieved they are that the Family Law issues are over. Sometimes I scratch a bit and ask them about a particular issue that seemed really important to them when I was negotiating with them, for example, how Christmas is arranged for a child. Invariably they don't even remember our discussions on the issue, despite it having played a big part in their legal case and bills.

> I guess the message is to evaluate the benefit
> of an outcome, in and of itself, against the
> perceived ideal outcome.

What are the key pieces of wisdom you would give readers regarding how best to navigate the Family Law system?

Write notes – everywhere, all the time. Your lawyer creates a file and writes notes – mimic this process in order to remember what the lawyer has said – if you ask twice, you pay twice – stay organised, and remain objective. Read the notes at different times to help you make your decisions.

Your problems are not your lawyer's problems. You cannot just hand them over and forget about them. Remain engaged.

Don't forget your common sense – if you have been married for a short time to a millionaire, you won't be getting 50% of the assets.

Too many cooks spoil the broth. Support from family and friends is essential at this time, but each legal situation is somewhat unique and just because your cousin's best friend got 60% of the assets, that does not necessarily mean you will get 60%. Keep a lid on 'helpful' advice if it starts to cost you emotionally and financially.

> Lastly, be realistic. Neither the Court nor your lawyer can solve every problem you have with your ex.

None of us have a magic wand. Be real about what the law can and cannot do.

Joanna Knight

Family lawyer

Sitting at an airport, waiting for your flight

Joanna is an Associate at Marsdens Law Group, working exclusively in Family Law. She has a Bachelor of Arts from the University of Sydney, with a Double Major in Chinese Studies. Her legal qualification is a Juris Doctorate from the University of New South Wales.

Previously, Joanna taught English as a foreign language and worked as an advisor for both the State and Commonwealth Governments, and has developed a wealth of experience in policy formation and service provision. Joanna sees her role as a solicitor as one of empowering people. She believes that solicitors solve problems, but they should also give people the tools to solve problems independently.

In this interview Joanna talks about the lack of resources in the Family Law system, how Facebook Messenger can be used in Family Court proceedings, why mediation is often the first step in her matters, how we need a referral system for matters from the criminal courts, and how Family Law matters involve lots and lots of waiting around.

Describe what it is you do, and your approach to matters.

When clients come to see me, they're often nervous, and grieving. I listen to their story and work out what legal issues I can help with.

Believe it or not, I spend a lot of time trying to keep people out of Court. Sometimes, it's necessary to take a case before a Judge, but it should be a last resort.

In most parenting matters, at the end of the day both parents will be involved in their children's lives and they'll need to work together. Spending one to three years in Court makes that harder to do. When it comes to property matters, I encourage clients to focus, in or out of Court, on a settlement that's value for money.

What are the biggest challenges as a family lawyer working within the current system?

A lack of resources. We need more Judges and family consultants (who write independent reports to help Judges make up their minds). Court can take a long time.

> Many clients think we will have one Court date and then it will all be over. Most of my Court cases take one to two years.

There might be many months between Court dates, but the stress of the ongoing case never really eases up on clients.

What should a client look for when choosing a family lawyer?

Look for someone who mainly does Family Law. It's a specialised area, and not one that all lawyers understand. You want someone you feel comfortable with, because they will ask you very personal questions and need you to make some tough choices.

Do you make use of any alternative dispute resolution?

Mediation is the first step in many of my matters. Clients think that coming to see a lawyer means things are going to get nasty. Quite the opposite. If we can work out something calmly and fairly, that's fantastic.

Mediation is a great way to do that, because as long as you've prepared, you can achieve a settlement on the spot instead of sending letters back and forth over weeks and months. It brings everyone's focus together on the one day to find a solution.

> Surprisingly, some of the most successful mediations are done when the parties don't even sit in the same room.

This is called a shuttle. The mediator shuttles back and forth between the two rooms (or even two phone lines) so each party and their lawyer have a chance to discuss the issues and pass messages to the other party.

What are the most significant frustrations or difficulties your clients have with regards to Family Law system?

The cost, the delay, and the complexity of the system.

Clients are pretty understanding about paying our bills, but many of them feel that their ex- is dragging things out or playing games to drive up the cost. In most cases, each party has to pay their own legal costs. It can be hard to understand why you have to pay for what you see as someone else's bad behaviour.

Clients are often shocked by the cost of independent reports, including business valuations and expert parenting reports. They really are worth the money, because the Court relies on this independent evidence to make a decision.

The system is also very complicated. Lawyers take for granted all the years they've spent studying. What seems normal and logical to us is a complete mystery to the rest of the world. I spend a lot of time preparing clients for court events, and explaining right after court what's happened.

Lawyers and Judges aren't very good at talking in plain English. I try to break it down so clients understand what's been said, and what we need to do next.

What is the one thing that you would say to someone about to go through the Family Law system?

Short-term pain; long-term gain. Think about what you want your life to look like in five years' time, and the kind of property or parenting arrangements that can get you there. Every matter takes time and compromise, but things really do get better.

Separation involves hurt and anger, but a property settlement brings closure, and parenting matters often settle down once we have formal arrangements in place.

What changes do you see in how social media and/or technology is being used in Family Law matters?

Technology has been a great help. Clients with smart phones can have a look at their banking records while we're meeting, which helps speed up property matters. They can create a screen shot of a text message exchange to use as evidence.

Social media can be tricky. My advice is to say as little as possible. Even if you have tight privacy settings on your account, things might still be visible.

However, I did have a case where we used Facebook Messenger as evidence of our efforts to notify someone of a Court date. We printed out the message with the 'seen' tick to show the Judge. The other side still didn't come to Court, so we also got permission from the Judge to send a copy of the final orders to them over Facebook Messenger. And, yes, they followed the orders.

What do you think are the Family Law implications of the recognition of same-sex marriage?

In terms of property settlements, it won't make a great deal of practical difference, because de facto property settlements are available to couples who are not married. However, it's a wonderful step for our country to have finally taken, recognising and respecting same-sex relationships. Family lawyers are usually involved at the breakup stage, so it's really nice for us to see a change to the law that celebrates relationships and brings people together.

Do you think cultural issues are sufficiently understood in Family Law proceedings?

Not always. I think there's more we can do as solicitors to understand the issues before we make our case to a Judge. Judges never want to cut off contact with a culture, but they might not understand the reasons behind particular behaviour.

For example, it's common in China for grandparents to raise children in another city. A Judge might not understand why a parent would send their children away, even if they love the children very much. If not properly explained, it might affect how a Judge sees those parents.

> It's always a good idea to ask a client about their heritage,
> and how it plays a role in their parenting.

Clients with Indigenous or Torres Strait Islander heritage might not feel comfortable raising this with a solicitor, but it is something that a Judge will want to know about, to make sure that those cultural ties can continue. The *Family Law Act* specifically asks Judges to consider this.

Are there any reforms that you believe should be implemented to the Family Law system? Please detail these and why you think this reform is necessary or desirable.

A referral system for matters from the criminal courts, where an apprehended violence order (AVO) has been granted.

For a protected person, an AVO can provide safety, but it can also be confusing. If children are involved, you should always see a family lawyer to get advice on your AVO. You might be feeling pressure from the other parent, or from extended family, to do things that the AVO says you don't have to do. For a defendant, an AVO can limit or completely stop time with children. This might be appropriate, but it might be something that can be resolved through supervised time. Creating a referral from the criminal court to a duty list before a Family Court registrar could help put some temporary arrangements in place. There are legal aid duty solicitors located in the court building to provide advice, if you aren't able to get in to see a private solicitor or obtain a grant of legal aid first. Once court has begun, it is still possible to hold mediation, and a registrar could then refer the matter to a mediator.

What are the key tips you would give readers?

Try not to compare your situation to a friend or relative's. Every family is unique, and that's why you have a lawyer who will fit their advice to suit your needs. If it were easy, we would just have computers doing the job for us.

Be patient. You are paying your lawyer quite a bit of money to write letters and prepare court documents. It takes time to get them right. It also takes time for your ex's lawyer to read them, send them to their client, ask for their instructions, and prepare a response.

Going to court involves a lot of waiting. It can feel like sitting at the airport, waiting for your flight to be called. Then you rush to board, and then you sit and wait again. You might feel more comfortable if you bring a friend or relative along.

There is no such thing as a stupid question, only a person too scared to ask. If you're not sure about something, ask your lawyer.

Stephen Page

Family lawyer with expertise in surrogacy

Be careful in the power we have

Stephen Page has a wealth of experience having worked as a lawyer since 1987. He has long specialised in Family Law and has been an accredited Family Law specialist since its inception in 1996. In particular, he is regarded as highly experienced in surrogacy matters. Stephen has spoken at local, national, and international conferences about Family Law, surrogacy, and domestic violence. He is also on the panel of private practitioners able to be appointed as an Independent Children's Lawyer.

Stephen is a member of Queensland Law Society, Family Law Section of the Law Council of Australia, Family Law Practitioners' Association of Qld Ltd, Fertility Society of Australia, American Bar Association (Associate), and the International Academy of family lawyers.

Although located in Brisbane, Stephen Page assists clients across Australia who need legal advice and representation, particularly with regards to surrogacy. He estimates he assists in about half the surrogacy matters nationally.

In his interview Stephen powerfully discusses why it is we need to change surrogacy laws in Australia, as under the current law thousands of children are having their rights and identity ignored. The message I received from Stephen's interview more broadly was that we all need to be careful in the power we have as Judges, lawyers, and other professionals in Family Law.

Where should someone start if they are separating from their partner?

The first thing I would say is there's no magic in the system. If you can keep out of the system for as long as possible, that is a good thing. It's awful.

The expectation of most people is they need to speak to a lawyer to discuss, say, their children. The reality is that most people don't go anywhere near a lawyer to discuss their children. Most people work out their own arrangements, which are good, bad, or indifferent.

I have had people go to mediation without legal advice and they have been completely done over. The process of mediation is put forward as a panacea.

> Mediation is actually a lot more stressful than you
> might anticipate. It's an exhausting process. But it's better than
> Court, most of the time.

The thinking about mediation is so pervasive. Twenty or 30 years ago, settlement occurred between lawyers, whereas today I see clients who, from the first time I see them, want to go to mediation.

So, you're saying that if there are two sensible lawyers, they should be able to able to work it out, even without mediation?

Yes, and most are sensible. Most aren't trying to recreate the Battle of Waterloo. They are trying to put out bushfires. Unfortunately, there are some lawyers who seem to be stoking the fires of discontent and making what might have been a small fire a bushfire.

I will give an illustration of a case that I found most worrying. A former husband and wife both appeared in my office, when I had only booked to see the husband. I thought, this is unusual, as you normally act for one party only and here they both were before me.

What had happened was they had split up years ago because their daughter had said to her mum, 'Dad has sexually abused me.' The mother went into shock and did all the right things to protect the daughter and kicked the husband out. She said to me, 'I couldn't get my head around the fact that my husband, who is one of the kindest, gentlest men I have ever met – and who I have been deeply in love with from the first day I met him up, until that moment – would have done this.'

As we often see in Family Law, there were no criminal charges, just an initial Police interview. There were no contact centres available at that time so the dad couldn't see the child at all. An expert interviewed the child and said that in their report, definitively, it would appear that the child had been sexually abused.

She got this report and her world got so much worse, because she had always left open the possibility it hadn't happened. She said, 'My whole world fell apart. Everything I believed about my husband was a lie.'

This whole time, the dad protested his innocence. Dad's lawyers got another expert who reviewed the video of the girl being interviewed by police and they concluded she was lying, and might have a psychiatric condition, and it would behove the first expert to review that video.

And, of course, the first expert said, 'No I don't have to. I will do it just before trial.'

Well, as often happens in our system, the matter got clogged for, say, three years, so there was a long period where the expert refused to look at the material, and said, 'I am firmly of this view'. Every time the mum got this email or letter, she firmed up.

Eventually, just before trial, some three years later, the expert looked at the police material and said, 'Oh, actually I think I got it wrong. It appears to me the child may have a psychiatric condition and I strongly recommend the child see a psychiatrist'. She [the mum] said that by this stage, her world had now been turned upside for the third time, and this was probably the worst.

So, the child goes to a psychiatrist and the psychiatrist says the child has a psychiatric condition where she has a propensity to lie.

The relationship between Mum and Dad was completely destroyed. Surprisingly, this girl ultimately went to live with her father because Mum couldn't cope anymore. They came to see me to ask if they could sue the expert.

I think that case is just an example of how we have to be so careful in the power we have as lawyers, Judges, and experts, to try and

treat people with sensitivity and recognise the real impact of what
may seem to us to be little decisions that can have a large impact in
people's lives.

So, there is a case example where you go, 'Well, how could that have
been done differently?'

Do you have any other thoughts about reform to surrogacy laws?

As you know I do a lot of surrogacy matters. We have seven different sets of
surrogacy laws across the different states, and as a result we have different
outcomes. In the Northern Territory we don't have laws, which means you
can't do surrogacy there, as you can't ever be shown to be the parent.

We have at least a thousand or two thousand children born overseas
where it's uncertain that the parents (the ones who wanted them, who love
them) are parents as a matter of law.

Whatever impact that has on the parents,
it's an obscenity that these children's rights,
status, and identity are being ignored.

Attorney George Brandis said, in 2013, there were to be changes to the law.
Well, nothing has been done. Article 8 on the International Convention on
the Rights of the Child says we are to protect the identity of children, and
yet we don't do that.

Then we had the obscene decision regarding Mr and Mrs Bernieres,
who were living in Melbourne, who went to India for surrogacy. The child
was recognised in India as their child. In the Family Court in Melbourne
they sought: 1) That the child live with them - granted straight away; 2)
That they have equal shared parental responsibility - granted straight away;
and 3) That they be declared to be the parents of the child.

And here their litigation ship hit the rocks. The trial Judge said the effect
of this section under the Family Law Act means you are noncompliant with
Victorian law and there are presumptions under Victorian law which mean
you are not the parents. They appealed to the Full Court of the Family

Court, which delivered a three-Judge judgement last year that they aren't the parents.

And why I said 'obscene' is: Who are the parents of the child? Is it the couple who intended to have the child, cared for the child, contributed at least some genetic material, and always, in a state of reality, will be the parents?

Or is it the couple under Indian law who are not recognised as the parents, have never cared for the child, never intended to have the child. So, the obvious conclusion is either the surrogate and her partner are the parents or no-one is the parent for this child. Each is a terrible outcome for that child. We need to protect this child and children like this child.

> Currently, we have couples going overseas in great numbers, because our legal settings make it too hard to undertake surrogacy here. When they bring their babies back, with only a few exceptions, it is unclear whether they are the parents of their children as a matter of law.

We had a House of Representatives Inquiry that, to its credit, said there should be national non-discriminatory laws. Then they said, well, it's got to be altruistic surrogacy, because we had everything between making it full commercial, and the Australian Christian lobby saying there should be no surrogacy whatsoever. Ok, let's strike the balance. Well, that setting will mean people will still go overseas. And then they said we should make it harder for people to go overseas, unless their standards in that country are as stringent as ours. The only country with standards as stringent as ours is New Zealand. Not the US, not the Canadians, not even in the UK.

As a result, people will have children overseas and they will pretend how they had these children. Just as how people in Europe go to the United States and Canada and pretend that they had a child via natural birth, because the legal settings there are even worse than ours.

Judges have suggested that domestic surrogacy laws should be handled by the Federal Circuit and Family Court. Of course, in Western Australia, everything is handled by the Family Court. For the rest of the country surrogacy orders are made by state courts. In Sydney, it is the Supreme Court of New South Wales.

When I thought everything was going to be handled by state courts, I was unsure as to if these Courts that did not have experience with Family Law would get it right. But what I found in practice has been surprising. The Judges in state courts have more time, flexibility, and resources than hard-pressed Federal Circuit Court Judges, for whom the constant refrain is 'We don't have enough resources; we can't get to it'. I would be absolutely opposed to transferring that jurisdiction to the Family Courts, unless the resources were also given to handle to amount of work.

Also, what surprised me is these state Judges, with little experience in Family Law, were remarkably sensitive about kids and families.

I have seen this in Victoria, New South Wales, and South Australia and Queensland, because I appear in all of these places on these matters.

One of the Victorian Judges, when Mum and Dad come in and bring the baby (also, in the Family Courts, you would never bring the baby), it is a joyous experience and photos are taken with the Judge and every child gets a teddy bear from the Court. I don't know anywhere else in the world that does that. It is such a wonderful, heart-warming experience and not what you expect to see in a Court.

Previously, you and I have talked about how shocking correspondence can be in Family Law for clients and your strategy of being very careful about when and how such correspondence is sent. Could you go over this again, please?

Sure. Clients give instructions; solicitors give advice. The usual model is that every last letter that goes in and out, the client gets a copy. That is the usual approach, so we don't have the mushroom factor, and the client can't say they didn't know.

The issue with Family Law is it is very confronting. From my own experience I know how overwhelming it can be. For me, my separation was combined with finding out my father had cancer. To put it in perspective, on the Sunday, my wife and I split up. On the Wednesday, my father was diagnosed with terminal cancer. On the Friday of that same week, I was told he had a life expectancy of between five minutes to, at most, seven days. You start to get a new appreciation of life when you are met with two huge crises at once.

I could not look at the lawyer's letters. I just found it too traumatic, because it was adding to the trauma of my dying father, topped with not seeing my kids regularly and dealing with property matters. Each one of those alone was a major source of grief that I had, all bundled together, at the same time.

Often, very to-the-point letters are sent last thing Friday afternoon. For some of them, if they are an everyday letter, it just goes through. But some of them I hold it off till Monday. Provided it is not that urgent, we can talk on Monday and I don't want to ruin their weekend.

Some clients can't even see the letters, so I will speak to them and talk them through the letter. What I don't accept is when a client says, 'You just make all the decisions'. It can't work that way. We have our respective roles. The client has to make informed decisions.

You know, it's very easy for us to send a letter getting stuck into the other side, and sometimes it's appropriate to send a pointed letter. But other times it's appropriate to tone those letters down and not make them as confronting as they are.

Do you have any other tips for someone who is reading this and is going through a separation and trying to navigate this process?

I give the following tips to my clients:

1. Firstly, you rock-up to a lawyer on day one. Don't accept this will be the definitive answer about where your matter is going. For parenting there may have to be investigations, or discussions had about what needs to be done. As far as property is concerned, what you think you own can be a bit vague at the beginning, and you need to go through this documentary trail about which way is up. The thing about property matters is that the subject is highly discretionary. There is a range of outcomes when it comes to property.

2. Always have a support network. Have friends and family who can help you. But you may not have anyone because, for example, you had a partner who is controlling and cut you off from people. So then get a support network; for example, go to the local meetup, or join a Church or community organisation.

3. Talk to someone. See a counsellor, someone independent who can tell you which way is up.

4. Have an exercise regime in place. Be fit. When you exercise, you produce endorphins and that makes you feel good. You feel better about yourself. But, above all, when you exercise, all those horrible thoughts that consume your brain are gone. Your brain is wiped clean. You have a positive view about the world. Even if you have no money, go walking. When you see the trees and the birds, it is truly beautiful, and it makes you appreciate beauty.

5. There are always people who are going to be worse off than you. You may not think it, but there are. And there are always beautiful things to see and appreciate. When I separated, I found myself doing it pretty hard. I was sleeping on a blow-up mattress, I didn't have a car. Then I suddenly had all this time, as I wasn't able to see my children much. My whole life to that point had been divided between children and work. I didn't know what to do with all this time. I started to learn a language and I went to the local market, and because I had no money, I would make all my own food. Brewed my own beer sometimes, with greater and lesser success. Life is there to be grabbed. Just because your relationship is broken down doesn't mean that all life stops. Be adaptable. Adjust your life to the circumstance that you find yourself in.

I remember my father said - the first time I separated, not when he was ill - 'Life will go on'. I exclaimed, 'I've lost the house!' Dad said, 'You'll get another one'. I was pretty hysterical and he was explaining this in a calm tone. When my dad told me this, I thought, he's right. I was looking at this all wrong and so I was able to move forward.

I'm very lucky. I feel privileged to help people whose relationship has broken down and they feel crushed by the world. I can help them get back on their own two feet and conquer the world again.

Do you have any thoughts about any other areas of reform?

> I think the greatest problem we have is a lack of Judges. We can fiddle round with the Family Law Act, but, really, delay and lack of resources is the key issue.

Having the mediation model generally, I think, is a good idea, despite what I said about if you don't have to go to mediation, then don't.

What I think is hardest is waiting. Meanwhile, the conflict is ongoing, like acid on the parents and the kids.

I have seen where the Courts have had more resources, and then when they have had less. If you can get in and out of your dispute in a year, great. That means the damage is less. If it takes three years, it's worse.

I think the idea of the docket system is good. Either way, there needs to be more Judges and there needs to be more money put in the system.

Do you have views about surrogacy and making it more viable in Australia?

Absolutely. They go to the US, Canada, and Ukraine. They are also going to Brazil, China, Laos, Kenya, Nigeria, all under the table. I have had clients look at undertaking surrogacy in Iran and Bangladesh. You ask, why are they going there? It is because they can't do it here. Either we don't have egg donors or surrogates due to our legal settings.

In Australia we say we don't want women to be victimised because of the possibility they may be paid. What instead happens is that surrogates are left out of pocket. The classic example is, in Australia, there's a one in ten thousand chance of dying when a woman gives birth, and yet, in Victoria, it is illegal for a woman who is a surrogate to have life insurance.

So why would you do it? In addition, you are going to be out of pocket for everything else. It is just a crazy way of looking at it.

Unless we have fundamental reform and allow compensation to donors and surrogates, these couples will just keep going overseas, in droves. The thing is that...

> people don't do surrogacy unless they have to. Who would want to talk to a lawyer about how to become parents when, instead, they could just have sex?

If they are going to an IVF clinic, they would rather go to one down the road than on the other side of the ocean. You just wouldn't. You'd just go to the local one.

While there has been a rise in domestic surrogacy, it will be a long time, I think, before it will match those going overseas.

Our clinics are well run and well regulated. Some aspects about how we do surrogacy are excellent. Appropriately, the counsellors are child-centred in approach. They reality-test surrogates' partners, which is wonderful. In the end, our system in Australia is decided by Judges. I can't stress how important this is, because if you are at the beginning of the process, you know you won't get through the end of the process unless a Judge is satisfied. Judges are very concerned to make sure that everyone is protected, including the surrogate, their partner, and above all they focus on the child. I think all this is a strength of how we do it.

> It's against the law to pay a donor anything other than their reasonable expenses, whatever that means. No one, as far as I know, has been charged. But it's an offence punishable by up to 15 years in prison.

We consider that our women are so pure that they have to be protected. Yet the inevitable outcome is that we can't do it here, so where can we do it? In Spain, records are kept about the donor, but it's on the basis that the donor remains anonymous.

The child will never know who the donor is. Both Chief Judge Pascoe, as he was then, and Chief Justice Bryant said, in 2014, it is a child's right to know their genetic origin, and yet that's the setting we have in Australia.

We can still have that with donors that are compensated. However, there should be a realistic cap so they aren't exploited and intended parents aren't paying too much. We don't want surrogacy to be the get-rich scheme; we want to make sure they are protected.

Those who say we have to have the current setting so they are protected, I don't think they give the Australian people or the Australian surrogates enough credit. These are Australian women. They have an expectation of equality, and systems should be there to protect them.

Surrogates are amazing because they want to give the gift of life. I have had the privilege of talking to surrogates here, in the US, and Canada. In the US, they get paid an amount of $20,000 upwards as base compensation. In Canada, the base compensation is about $20,000-22,000 Canadian.

Their prime motivation is to help others. Part of their life mission is they like being pregnant, childbirth is pretty straightforward; they've had their kids. Everyone knows someone who hasn't been able to have kids and they figure – it's not a great intellectual leap – they can have kids easily, so they will have a child for someone.

I know you also do quite a lot of work with regards to adoption. I don't know if you and I have ever talked about this but I am actually adopted too, so this is an area of interest for me. You see, I was in that first wave of international adoptions out of Taiwan in the early 80's. Where are we at with domestic and international adoption?

Oh, good on you Zoë. Well, I think the current message about adoption is 'good luck'. The numbers are bleak.

If you think back to 1971 – the era where nuns grabbed the baby from the single mums. Quite properly, since then, we have had apologies for those practices. The number of children available for adoption is miniscule by comparison. Adoptions are three times per capita in comparative countries, such as the US or UK.

Why is that?

Our settings make it hard to adopt. New South Wales has started to allow kids in care to be adopted, but they have done this from a very small base.

Everywhere else, we have tens of thousands of children in Care and very few are adopted out. These kids have, on average, six placements. They don't have any stability, like the kind of stability that would be offered by adoption. Many single women now keep their children.

Also, with the rise of India and China out of poverty, children who were once available are no longer available. In the past, there were rackets of children being exploited and sold into adoption, such as in India.

> The number of children available for adoption are a drop in the ocean. So, for most people who can't have kids, the only real option is surrogacy; adoption isn't realistic for most. It's bleak.

Tash Nolan

Family lawyer

On a level playing field

Tash has a diverse background, having gained experience in many areas of law, including Family Law, conveyancing, commercial law, wills and estate planning, probate, commercial litigation, and criminal law.

Tash has a Master's in Applied Law (Family Law). Tash chose to specialise in Family Law because she wanted to be able to help people through what is one of the most difficult times in their lives. Tash is experienced in modest property settlements to more complex property matters involving multiple assets, family companies, trust structures, and superannuation interests. Tash's commercial background complements her Family Law practice. Her commercial experience allows her to quickly identify the issues at hand and provide the most practical and cost-effective solutions for her clients. Tash strongly believes that all aspects of alternative dispute resolution should be explored to try to resolve the dispute in an efficient manner before resorting to litigation. Tash is a member of Collaborative Professionals (NSW) Inc. She is passionate about assisting her clients through their Family Law matters using the collaborative approach and engaging other professionals, including accountants, financial planners, and child psychologists, where necessary.

In Tash's interview I could see that her background in commercial law has influenced her practical outcomes-focussed approach. In comparison, she describes how other practitioners would, for example, take out an AVO simply to put their client 'on a level playing field'. Tash also is one of the practitioners who continues to prepare binding financial agreements and she discusses her perspectives on them, including her view that an area for reform could be standardised financial agreements.

⸪

So, tell me about your career history and how you came to work in Family Law.

I started working as a receptionist in a Family Law firm in Canberra when I finished Year 12. About two years later, I went to university and continued to work at the firm as a secretary to the Family Law partner.

Upon completing my degree, I took a break from Family Law and worked in criminal law for a brief six months and a commercial litigation role for about three years. During that time, I decided that I wanted to make the move back into Family Law, so I started the College of Law Masters (Family Law) course in 2012, and moved back into an exclusive Family Law role in 2014.

In April 2016, I started my own firm and I predominantly practice in Family Law; however, the firm also offers services in conveyancing, wills and estates, and commercial law.

What kind of matters do you assist parties with?

I assist parties with any property and parenting issues that arise from their separation. I also assist in preparing and negotiating financial agreements.

What would you say is your law firm's point of difference?

Having a background in commercial litigation, I take a commercial and pragmatic approach to Family Law matters. The fact that my firm also offers services in conveyancing and wills and estates means my Family Law clients have access to a full-service firm that can assist them in resolving their Family Law property settlement, refinance or assist with the sale of the matrimonial property or investment property, and then update their Will.

How do you charge for your services?

I offer a no-obligation, free initial consultation. If the client engages me, I require a $2,000 retainer to be deposited into my trust account. I charge an hourly rate and issue itemised monthly invoices with terms of seven days.

What would you suggest to a litigant with limited funds to pay for legal fees?

I recommend that litigants with limited funds approach legal aid in the first instance. I am on the Legal Aid Practitioner Panel. If they are not eligible for a grant of legal aid, in some circumstances I will agree to accept payment of my fees on completion of the matter.

And any words of wisdom to litigants going through the system?

> My view is that it's always better to try and resolve these disputes amicably and as quickly as possible,

... so that the parties, and, more importantly, their children, can move forward with their lives. Notwithstanding this, there are always matters in which agreement cannot be reached and there is no alternative but to go to Court.

Just because you are in the Court system doesn't mean that you lose the opportunity to negotiate a resolution. I always advise my clients that it is far better for them to negotiate the terms of an arrangement they can live with, as opposed to having orders imposed on them by a third party. By negotiating, they maintain control of the situation and can, hopefully, achieve an outcome that gets them out of the system and in a position where they can effectively co-parent their children, moving forward.

What are the biggest challenges as a family lawyer working within the current system?

The delays and uncertainty of the Court system. It is a cause of much frustration for clients who end up at the mercy of the Court system.

Another common complaint now is that the Courts are so unpredictable.

> You can't tell your clients with certainty what will
> happen when their matter is before the Court.

Not being able to say with certainty that your client's matter will even be heard, when they have waited three months to get the court date in the first place, is difficult.

Given the current delays in court, has this changed how you run Family Law matters?

I have always been an advocate for mediation and for parties to do all things to try and resolve their matters by negotiation rather than be subjected to the Court system. I am very honest with my clients, and I do not hold back in telling them that commencing proceedings will not necessarily be the panacea to their problems.

I encourage my clients to utilise Family Dispute Resolution Practitioners to assist with resolving their parenting disputes, and involve mediators to assist with resolving property disputes. I am a collaboratively trained lawyer and believe there is merit in involving other practitioners, such as accountants, financial planners, and child psychologists, to provide a holistic approach to resolving a Family Law matter.

I believe the system is fundamentally flawed; that is, a system whereby parties are encouraged to put on an affidavit material that disparages their former partner, put their lives on hold for two to three years while the Court progresses their competing applications, and at the end of it all, expect the parties to be able to effectively co-parent their children.

What are the common misconceptions about Family Law?

That it will cost a fortune. While fees vary depending upon the practitioner, there is a misconception about the average amount it will cost.

In my opinion, it is certainly common knowledge that the bigger firms charge significantly higher than the smaller firms, and the amounts of money that parties pay to resolve their property settlements are often significant, relative to the size of the pool available for division.

It sounds like you are very focussed on obtaining an outcome for your clients as efficiently as possible. Do you find the way some lawyers practice Family Law is unhelpful to reaching a resolution?

The most recent experience I have had is a client whose file I took over from a larger firm.

In that matter the husband had taken out an AVO against the wife. The wife was told that she now needed to go and get an AVO against the husband because the lawyer could not act for her unless they were 'on a level playing field'. This type of conduct is absurd and is, in my view, more about generating fees than getting a result for the client and acting in their best interests.

Do you believe there is any gender inequity in the system?

> I think there is a systemic bias against men in the
> Family Law system.

I have had colleagues and peers comment to the effect of 'Oh, I've never seen a dad get a good result before that Judge' all too often. I also find that, although there are no doubt serious matters involving domestic violence, unfortunately...

> some women still use AVOs as a strategy
> in the proceedings,

...and men find themselves in a position of having to defend unfounded allegations of domestic violence and get over that hurdle before the real issues, like the time they spend with their children, can be dealt with.

I know you are one of the practitioners still preparing BFAs, binding financial agreements. Can I have your views about the recent case of *Thorne v. Kennedy*?

I still prepare binding financial agreements, taking care to ensure that I am dotting the i's and crossing the t's.

I believe that the recent case of *Thorne v. Kennedy* is the exception and not the rule. The circumstances of that case are such that the hallmarks of unconscionable conduct and undue influence were obvious.

The *Family Law Act* was amended to encourage people to agree about the distribution of their matrimonial property and thus give them greater control over their own affairs in the event of marital breakdown. The amendments allow couples to make regulated financial agreements.

It is the very nature of financial agreements that their terms will generally be more favourable, and often significantly more favourable, for one party. However, despite the common financial imbalance in these types of agreements, if the agreement is signed in circumstances where the parties are aware that the terms are grossly unreasonable, then the High Court's decision confirms that the agreement may be set aside on the basis of undue influence and unconscionable conduct.

A conclusion of 'unconscionable conduct' requires a party to be subject to a special disadvantage which seriously affects their ability to make a judgement about their best interests. The other party must be aware of and take advantage of the special disadvantage. In this case, Ms Thorne's special disadvantage was known to Mr Kennedy, because he created it with the urgency in which he required the agreement to be signed, and the threat of not proceeding with the marriage if she refused to sign it.

What *Thorne v. Kennedy* has done is provide some key factors for practitioners to consider moving forward as highlighted by the High Court:

1. Whether the agreement was offered on a basis that it was not subject to negotiation;

2. The emotional circumstances in which the agreement was entered, including any threat to end a marriage or engagement;

3. Whether there was any time for careful reflection;

4. The nature of the parties' relationship;

5. The relative financial positions of the parties; and

6. The independent advice that was provided and whether there was time afforded to the parties to reflect on that advice.

Are there any reforms that you believe should be implemented to the Family Law, especially with regards to financial agreements?

I think that consideration should be given to implementing standardised financial agreements.

There is certainly a demand for them, and the legislation provides for these types of agreements to continue to be utilised. Implementing standard agreements might lead to a reduction in the amount of disputes and litigation post separation.

Lastly, what is some of the best advice you were given regarding managing the stress of practicing as a lawyer in Family Law?

The best piece of advice that I was given was that if you want to go into Family Law, you need to be able to leave work at work and not take it home with you. I think it is essential to be able to separate yourself from your clients' problems. It is easier said than done.

Sherlene Heng

Family lawyer

The bigger picture

Sherlene Heng was admitted as a solicitor in 2009 and has practised exclusively in Family Law. She completed a Master's of Law (Family Law) in 2014, and in addition to her Bachelor of Laws, also has a Bachelor of Commerce, which adds to her ability to resolve complex financial matters. Sherlene commenced the first half of her career in Western Australia and has spent the second half in New South Wales and has recently returned to Perth to work at O'Sullivan Davies Lawyers. She has dealt with varied matters in her career, and has a particular preference for financial matters, especially where there may be cultural points of difference from the 'standard' matter (although no matter is standard, in her opinion).

In this interview Sherlene talks about her hopes for the increased uptake of technology in Family Law and other areas of reform, such as a specialised list for small property pools and also interstate children's alerts. She also explains why she still believes binding financial agreements continue to provide clarity and certainty for parties entering into a de facto relationship or marriage. Sherlene explains why it is important to remember the bigger picture in Family Law matters.

What should a client look for when choosing a family lawyer?

Right now, in the Family Law Courts, matters can take three years to be heard at trial. That's three years of communications with your lawyer, sometimes on a daily basis, of your lawyer knowing the most personal details of your life, how much you spent on waxing and online dating websites, of your new relationships, of what you bought on your credit card last month.

Of course, it's important who your lawyer is, and different lawyers are bound to gel with different clients.

> Clients should feel, early in the process, that the lawyer has their best interests at heart.

This can include reviewing if the lawyer is actively seeking to resolve issues as opposed to creating them; if the lawyer is providing clear and objective advice, including whether a settlement is a preferable option to continuing litigation, even if that advice is something the client does not want to hear; if the lawyer is providing guidance through the process and is able to effectively communicate with them; and if the lawyer is able to think outside the box for alternative solutions, if necessary.

This is particularly so for parenting matters, where it can be easy to get caught up in the mechanics of the system. Is your lawyer encouraging you to litigate over those tennis lessons that happen during your time with the child, or is your lawyer conducting an effective listening exercise and troubleshooting any underlying issues? This is not to trivialise the issues, but it is important that the client, the lawyer, and Counsel work as a team, without forgetting the bigger picture (in parenting matters, the child).

What do you think are some of the biggest challenges as a family lawyer working within the current system?

I believe that the biggest challenge in the system at the moment is the delay experienced by clients after commencing proceedings. It is almost impossible to predict when a matter will be listed, and whether it will be heard at the time listed or adjourned to a date months from now. Even in the short matters list, the very short notice at which a matter is listed means that there is often significant difficulty ensuring Counsel can appear on that date, especially the same Counsel which was already briefed in the matter when the matter was put into the short matters list.

This creates difficulties in a wide range of situations; for instance, when acting for a party seeking to see their children where there are no orders allowing them to do so. While there are similarly no orders stopping them from doing so, it would be dreadful for the child to be subject to confusion and uncertainty if both parents are withholding the child from the other pending orders being made, and so sensible parents usually wait for orders to be handed down by the Court. However, the longer they wait for a hearing, the longer their relationship with the child may potentially be affected.

Another example is in relation to financial proceedings where it is often difficult for a party with no funds at the time of separation to sustain litigation pending, for instance, an interim costs order. It is also difficult for a party seeking maintenance to pay their living expenses if there is a lengthy wait for an interim hearing – it would be in the other party's interests to draw the proceedings out for as long as possible and unlikely to be in his or her interests to consent to orders for interim costs or maintenance at the early stage.

Part of the system also simply relies on there being a modicum of trust that parties will 'do the right thing'. Unfortunately, this is not always the case. There could be a refusal by a primary carer (in the case of parenting) or the party with control over assets (in financial matters) to participate in the proceedings, or, having participated, then breaching orders already in place. Although there are mechanisms in place to move such matters to an undefended hearing, or for them to be listed for a contravention hearing or enforcement hearing, the speed at which that might progress creates a number of difficulties for the other party. While, ultimately, the Court may make orders in favour of the applicant, by that time months or years may have gone by, to the detriment of that party.

What are the common misconceptions about Family Law?

The most common misconception is probably that assets will be divided equally at separation, followed by 'but women always receive 70–80%, right?'

I have also found that some people find it difficult to reconcile contributions being equal where one party worked and one party did not (for instance, if the non-working party was caring for a child/children), and, finally, a common belief that the value of the asset pool is taken as at the time of agreement, or judgement, and not at the time of separation.

Do you have any views about if there is a particularly aggressive manner in which Family Law is practised by Sydney family lawyers?

Having previously practised in a smaller capital city, I do find that Sydney has a particularly litigious culture. However, the litigious culture in Sydney does not come as a surprise to me. As the biggest city in Australia, one of the most expensive cities in the world, and a focus on being a financial hub, the willingness to litigate is likely to be an approach more readily taken by clients there than in smaller cities or in regional courts.

Certainly, depending on which party you are acting for, they may not want to settle but, instead, make things as difficult as they can for their ex-partner or spouse.

Lawyers in Sydney are not immune to this culture, and while it is the case that lawyers are a product of their instructions, it is, of course, a combination of both the client's approach and the practitioner's approach that can make it difficult to settle a matter. An aggressive client with a lawyer who, themselves, behave in a hostile, sarcastic, or unapproachable manner certainly makes the matter less likely to resolve.

Are there any reforms that you believe should be implemented to the family law system?

I would like to see a greater use of technology in the Court. I am supportive of the online Court filing system and, in addition, would be open to things such as online bookings for new or adjourned Court dates, so that one can ensure that all solicitors and Counsel are available, and increased attendances by telephone or video link, to prevent lengthy wait times in Court.

Thinking out loud, and noting that any of these would, of course, require some independent studies and recommendation, I would also be interested in whether there should be:

- greater powers for enforcement of orders by the Court, including greater utilisation of penalties for noncompliance, and increased powers for third parties to intervene if, on the face of it, an order has been breached;
- a special docket for small property pools where the asset pool is less than a certain amount, potentially with capped fees and quicker time frames; and while I note it is the intention that less complex matters are heard in the Federal Circuit Court, and that litigation should not be the first port of call for small matters, this might assist in some circumstances;
- interstate children's alerts to prevent children from being taken interstate without the other parent's consent.

I see quite a few clients wanting a prenup (binding financial agreement), but they seem very confused about binding financial agreements and often say other law firms will not prepare them anymore. What are your thoughts on binding financial agreements?

I believe binding financial agreements still provide clarity and certainty for parties entering into a de facto relationship or marriage. This is especially so for parties with relatively similar asset positions at the commencement of the relationship or marriage, who may have families with farming interests or other such inheritances to be received in due course. It is also the case with people who may receive gifts of money or real estate prior to or during the relationship, or upon the marriage taking place.

Undue influence and unconscionable conduct have long been recognised as matters which can render a contract void, and binding financial agreements should be no different. It is common practice amongst family lawyers that if a party wishes to sign a binding financial agreements mere hours or potentially even weeks before the wedding, that this should throw up red flags. Other common red flags are where there is a party with a limited command of English, or where a person puts forward a position and refuses to discuss or negotiate the terms – the 'sign this or else' position.

While the case of *Thorne v. Kennedy* in some ways broadens the circumstances in which binding financial agreements can be set aside, and to quote the judgement, 'it can be an indicium of undue influence if a pre-nuptial or post nuptial agreement is signed despite being known to be grossly unreasonable even for agreements of this nature', the specific factors in this case need to be considered. This is a matter where one party had no significant assets, basic English skills, no family in Australia, who had come to Australia at the behest of the other party, who was on a tourist visa, who signed the agreement 10 days before the wedding, and had relatives already in Australia expectantly waiting for the wedding to occur. Notwithstanding that she signed a second agreement after the wedding, removing the time pressure, the other factors continued to apply.

As with any contract entered into in any other jurisdiction, there is always going to be a possibility that the contract, in this case, a binding financial agreement, can be challenged. Our firm will still provide independent legal advice on some binding financial agreements; however, those matters are considered on a case-by-case basis. Certainly, we will not see anyone who informs us that their wedding is taking place tomorrow and they just need to someone to sign off on it.

What are the key things you would say to someone reading this book who is separating?

I really only have a few basic tips:

1. *The Family Law system is complex. Seek advice early.* Even if you think you don't intend to litigate or you are happy with a particular arrangement proposed, it is cheaper in the long run and for your peace of mind to have a comprehensive appointment with a lawyer who can tell you how the system works, and what the likely outcomes are in your matter, just so you know.

2. *Don't engage in knee-jerk reactions.* Separation is difficult at the best of times, but there is nothing worse than seeing your social media post or email to a third party annexed to an affidavit in the future. If someone says something which causes you to react, they probably know exactly what they are doing and are using it as a strategy against you. Type your first response, delete all the swear words, then maybe just go ahead and delete the response altogether. If you must respond, respond politely and briefly. There is simply no need to engage.

3. *Respond to your lawyer.* If your lawyer is asking for your instructions, provide them. This not only moves your matter along more quickly but also saves you on the fees you then have to pay for your lawyer to follow up time and time again.

4. *Sometimes this is difficult: Make sure to care of yourself.* If you need to seek therapy, get it. If you need a time out, take it. Consider if you would benefit from family therapy as well, and make those enquiries as soon as possible.

Rana Saab

Family lawyer

People who use their children as tools

Rana Saab established Saab Law Group in 2010 with a legal team of over two decades of experience. Rana, who is a principal at Saab Law Group, is on the Legal Aid Panel for Family Law and Criminal Law. She is also a registered Migration Agent and Member of the Law Society of NSW.

Saab Law Group has expertise in the areas of Criminal Law, Family Law, Traffic Offences, Immigration Matters, and Care & Protection Matters. Saab Law Group was named winner of the 2017 St George Local Business Awards for the most outstanding professional services.

In this interview Rana discusses how delay has changed her approach to matters, and reforms that could be adopted to better deal with family violence. Interestingly, Rana sees both sides in relation to matters where family violence has been alleged, and she discusses the effect of false allegations but is also is sympathetic to reforms proposed by those who advocate for victims of family violence. Rana also discusses practical payment options for clients who have limited funds for legal fees.

How did you come to work as a family lawyer and what is your background and experience?

Saab Law Group was established in 2010, and the firm is built upon solid experience in legal matters, over a wide range of legal fields, such as criminal, immigration, and Family Law matters. I wanted to differentiate myself from other law firms by creating a firm that reflected the values I hold dear, such as professional integrity, honesty, communication, and always aiming to provide a quality service consistently. In 2017 my firm won the Local Business Award within the St George area for the most outstanding professional services.

Are there any points of difference as compared with other firms?

Saab Law Group's personal and professional approach in dealing with sensitive Family Law issues distinguishes the firm from others in the industry. I do not believe there is one set recipe or way of dealing with Family Law issues. The ability to cater for and adjust to each client's situation on a case-by-case basis is necessary. Our attention to detail in all matters is another point of difference. Our success rate in finalising matters and achieving desirable outcomes for our clients reflects the level of dedication and professionalism we employ in all matters.

What kind of matters do you assist parties with?

I assist parties with a variety of Family Law issues and my services extend to cover divorce, de facto relationships, property settlements, binding financial agreements, parenting orders, children's issues, custody and care orders, mediation, and counselling referrals.

So many areas are relevant to Family Law, such as criminal, property/conveyancing, bankruptcy, taxation, and international law, so I think it helps that I have experience in and still practice in other areas.

What should a client look for when choosing a family lawyer?

A client should always look for a lawyer who is a confident and competent professional with whom they are able to communicate with effectively about their matter.

How do you charge for your services?

We charge in a number of ways: we can estimate our fees at the completion of the matter, charge an hourly rate for private clients, or payment is made through Legal Aid funding.

What would you suggest to a litigant with limited funds to pay for legal fees?

Some suggestions could be, say, paying in instalments, applying for legal aid, or providing other methods of security for payment. Saab Law Group do legal aid work so you can apply for legal aid and then nominate Saab Law Group as legal representative.

Given the current delays in Court, has this changed how you run Family Law matters?

The delays in having matters heard, highlight the benefit of utilising alternative dispute resolution. In that sense, the delays have increased the number of mediations that I have resorted to, especially in property settlement matters.

> In a congested court system, mediations are cost efficient, time efficient, and are more likely to yield a positive outcome for both parties involved in a family dispute.

It not only offers a chance for the parties to resolve their issues without litigation, it also maintains a certain level of communication between them overall.

What are the most significant frustrations or difficulties your clients have with regards to the Family Law system?

Long delays in the court system are a huge setback for many clients who have very limited options or avenues to pursue a resolution outside court orders. Another difficulty for clients are the legal costs associated with delays. Often fathers feel they are not supported in the Court process.

What are the common misconceptions about Family Law?

Perhaps that it is a very convoluted or confusing system. Despite the need for a specialist family lawyer in most cases, a good family lawyer is one who can communicate the legal issues to their clients and the ways to resolve them in a clear and effective way. Numerous clients tell me they did not anticipate how long their matter was going to be and how exhausting the process is, as it can be very cumbersome at times.

Other common misconceptions about Family Law are that the mother *always* obtains orders that the child primarily live with her, and, in property disputes, everything is always split 50/50.

Do you have tips for those going through a separation?

Seek advice from a family lawyer early who understands the full scope of your situation. Too often, clients are unsatisfied with legal outcomes simply because of a miscommunication of facts or events. Family Law is a lengthy process, and is unfortunately a very costly road to go down, so it is impor tant to ensure that your legal representative is fully aware of your situation, so they can make the best recommendation for your situation to save you money and time.

The way you communicate is important. Transparency with your legal representative is crucial.

Do not hide information from your lawyer, as this can and likely will come back to damage your case and make a bad situation even worse.

It is also good to note that a court is not always your first option, as mediation can assist you and may even solve your situation without you having to waste a lot of time and money. There are various avenues which can be explored, other than Court.

> Alternative dispute resolution can create good outcomes for families that cannot afford lengthy litigation.

I have also witnessed people who use their children as tools to gain a better advantage over the other side.

Sometimes one party will begin to make false allegations about the way the other has treated their children, in terms of physical safety and security. This then leads to an AVO being created based on false allegations, which then acts as a spark to fast-track the side that has made the false allegations to gain housing from the government, and also can prevent the other party from seeing their children.

In cases such as these, parties use their children as tools, saying things about the care of the children that is misconstrued or altogether false to hurt the other side. The role of the Independent Children's Lawyer is so important to ensure the best interests of the child are met.

> It is important to not be driven by revenge, and always be mindful of the best interests of the children involved.

It is ugly when parents fight and the children must sit on the sidelines, feeling powerless and hopeless as to why the parents cannot get along. It is necessary to prioritise the children and to make sure that all decisions made are for the best interests of the child.

You mentioned the use of AVOs being used – or misused – as a strategy in Family Law. Do you think there is a gender bias in the way these are used?

Fathers who have been extremely loving and compassionate towards their children and who pose no risk to their children sometimes become neglected within the Family Law system. One bad reaction by the father during a separation matter which is taken out of context or exaggerated by the wife may lead to an unfair AVO being imposed, causing the father to be separated from his children.

However, on the flip side to what I said about AVOs sometimes being unfairly imposed, I do think family violence, when it has genuinely occurred, is a serious issue.

Do you have any thoughts about family violence in Family Law; for example, ideas about reform?

Rosemary Batty presented and discussed her views on the issue of violence and Family Law with the major political parties prior to the last federal election. In conjunction with Women's Legal Services Australia, she presented a petition calling for reform and urging political leaders to adopt the following five-step plan to prioritise safety in the Family Law system:

- develop a specialist pathway for cases involving family violence
- reduce trauma and to support victims, including legislative protections that prevent victims from being directly cross-examined by their abuser
- intervene early and provide legal help for the most disadvantaged
- support victims to recover financially
- strengthen the understanding of all Family Law professionals on family violence

I am personally of the view that the above plan has the potential to reshape the current legislation over years to come. The culture of family law and the way it is practised is changing.

Tina Lohitharajah

Family lawyer

The most important decisions of your life

Tina is an Accredited Family Law Specialist and Senior Associate at Matthews Folbigg Lawyers. In addition to her Law degree, she has undertaken a Bachelor of Arts, majoring in Psychology. This has placed her in the unique position to cater for the legal needs of clients whilst understanding the emotional impact that separation has on families.

Her passion and empathy for individuals going through a separation was initially nurtured whilst working for the Federal Magistrates Court (now known as the Federal Circuit Court).

As an experienced family lawyer, Tina understands the difficulties people face with the Family Court system. Consequently, she takes a holistic approach to achieve a balanced, fair, and time and cost-effective outcome for clients.

Tina is also a nationally accredited mediator and believes alternative dispute resolution services such as mediation are crucial in the Family Law process and allow individuals to have some control over the outcome.

In this interview, Tina gives practical tips about how to best support children through a separation, why mediation is such an important part of the Family Law system and the importance of proper resourcing for the entire family law system, not just in relation to the appointment of more Judges, but also that there be more family consultants and more supervising contact centres.

What are the key tips or pieces of wisdom you would give readers who have children regarding how best to proceed after separation?

The best advice I can give to any person who is going through a separation is to minimise the impact that the separation has on your children. There are things you can do to make this process easier for you and your children.

Help your children transition by minimising conflict, introducing changes gradually (including new partners), maintaining routines and seeking support.

There are some instances however, that may require more urgent action. For example, if there is a risk that a child may be removed from Australia, then it is appropriate for you to act quickly and obtain legal advice as soon as possible.

Lastly, surround yourself with support. At the difficult time of separation, it is important to seek all the support and assistance that you need to sort out your Family Law matter. Seeking legal advice is always a good place to start, so you know what to expect and where you stand. However, it is equally important to consider other support services that can help your family through the transition. These include post separation parenting programs and family dispute resolution services that can help you work out the best way to co-parent with the other party.

I know you frequently use mediation to resolve matters. In your view, why is mediation a good idea in Family Law disputes?

Yes, mediation has a vital role to play in the vast majority of Family Law disputes, whether it is children's matters or division of financial assets. Agreeing to participate in the mediation process can have many advantages that may not be apparent when you are first considering this process.

Mediation is run by the mediator who facilitates open discussions and assists you in sorting through the issues in dispute and generating options for resolution. Final resolution can only be reached with the consent of all parties, and therefore you control what agreement will be put in place for your family and your future. Although litigating through the Court system is necessary in some instances, having a Judge determine your matter means that some of the most important decisions of your life are left to someone else to make.

Reaching an agreement through mediation allows specifically crafted arrangements to be explored that suit your family best.

> Mediation also offers you the opportunity to
> resolve your matter immediately.

Particularly if your lawyers are present, legal terms can be drafted and signed by the parties and shortly thereafter made into Court orders without the parties having to go through the tedious and costly Court process.

It is not uncommon for parties to be waiting three to four years in the court system for a final determination, and another six months for judgement to be delivered.

The benefits of mediation are huge when you consider the alternatives. Even if the mediation process ultimately does not yield a final resolution for you, often other smaller disputes become resolved and, if nothing else, at least you better understand where the other party is coming from.

In my experience as a family lawyer, my clients are increasingly embracing the process of mediation. Even those who insist that an agreement with their partner is not possible are often pleasantly surprised that an agreement was reached after options were explored. As a nationally accredited mediator, I also offer mediation services through Matthews Folbigg Lawyers as an alternative for those clients who wish to have more control over their outcome.

> It is my experience that clients who resolved their matter through
> mediation had a greater level of satisfaction
> with the outcome because of the control they had
> over the process.

Are there any reforms that you believe should be implemented to the Family Law system?

The appointment of more Judges is necessary in order to timely address the overwhelming caseload that the Courts face. However, there are other things that can be done to provide assistance to this process. For example, an initiative that focuses on appointing more registrars and broadening their powers would enable them to address less complex matters. This would then ease the load on Judges by freeing them up to hear those matters of a more urgent and complicated nature.

More appointments of family consultants who prepare reports to assist the Court in parenting matters could also reduce wait times for a final hearing.

Another issue that needs to be addressed immediately is enabling greater access to Supervising Contact Centres. These Centres provide alternatives for parents to see their children in circumstances where allegations of risk or family violence have been made.

This option is particularly important where there are no suitable persons available to supervise the time. These Contact Centres provide a means for parents to maintain a relationship with their child until such time as the allegations can be properly addressed by the Court. However, due to the lack of resources available at these Centres, it is not uncommon for parents to be on waiting lists for months before an initial intake session can occur.

In the current circumstances of extraordinary Court delays, additional funding for Supervised Contact Centres is a necessity to provide accessible alternatives for parents to see their children.

Beth Jarman

Family lawyer

A clear pathway forward

Beth Jarman was admitted in December 1986 and worked in private practice for seven years in a wide area of law, from insurance, general civil, family, and commercial and criminal litigation to property law, wills and probate, and other related fields. She has appeared in many courts, including The Supreme Court of NSW, District and Local Courts, Family Court, Workers Compensation, and Land and Environment Court.

In 1994, she commenced work in the NSW Public Service with the Legal Aid Commission of NSW. Soon after, she was asked to begin a new Family Law practice in one of the Commission's suburban offices and went on to be in charge of that Family Law Practice, and occupied other positions within the commission. Since 1994 Beth has worked exclusively in Family Law. In 1996 Beth began work as an Independent Children's Lawyer, and in 2001 she obtained specialist accreditation in Family Law. In 2004 she spent approximately 10 months as Deputy Registrar of the Family Court at Parramatta on a temporary basis.

Beth returned to private practice at Coleman Greig, Parramatta, in 2013, and then moved to Mills Oakley. In 2017 she was appointed Special Counsel with Mills Oakley.

In this interview, Beth discusses in detail how to manage legal fees and what free legal resources are available in Family Law. She also talks about the ways in which she believes Family Law needs to change and the importance of finding a lawyer with a clear pathway forward through the complexity of the current Family Law system.

What kind of matters do you assist parties with?

At Mills Oakley we assist clients in all areas of Family Law. Our clients' situations can vary greatly. Our assistance includes providing initial legal advice, drafting letters to assisting parties with mediation, drafting consent orders, drafting binding financial agreements through to commencing proceedings and acting on behalf of our clients in bringing or responding to matters before the Court. We also undertake work in the collaborative field of Family Law.

There is a wide range of problems that people can experience resulting from a breakdown in family relationships. We are there to assist clients with whatever problems they face.

Describe what it is you do.

As a family lawyer I assist people to separate their lives following a breakdown in their relationship or their marriage. This can also include resolving the parties' financial relationship with each other and also assisting to make appropriate arrangements for their children. This can involve also making an Application for Divorce on behalf of a client. There are many ways that parties can resolve disputes quickly and in a cost-effective manner without resulting in litigation.

Do you have any special areas of interest or expertise within Family Law?

To attain Family Law specialisation, you have to demonstrate specialist knowledge in all areas of Family Law practice and procedure. However, as I have been an Independent Children's Lawyer (ICL) since 1996, I have had approximately 20 years of experience in acting on behalf of children in the

Family Court and Federal Circuit Court of Australia in many complex and difficult children's matters.

By definition, matters in which an ICL is appointed are generally complex matters. The challenge is to represent the children and act in their best interests, achieving the best outcome in as quick a timeframe as possible. It is well known that protracted litigation between parties has a deleterious effect on children.

I think children suffering ongoing stress as a consequence of protracted Family Law litigation is currently a very topical problem.

What is your law firm's point of difference as compared with other firms?

Mills Oakley commenced in 1864, in Melbourne, and has grown to be a large national commercial firm. In 2017, the firm was voted Law Firm of the Year in the competitive Australasian Law Awards.

As a point of difference from other large commercial firms, Mills Oakley seeks to service our clients by ensuring that all areas of law are practiced. Mills Oakley has one of the largest Family Law practices in Australia.

The firm prides itself on solicitor-client relationships and always strives to improve our solicitor-client service.

What should a client look for when choosing a family lawyer?

Most importantly, in Family Law proceedings I believe it is imperative that you have a good relationship with your lawyer. It is important that you are able to trust your lawyer and trust their advice. You need to feel that your lawyer is empathetic and stands beside and with you in your matter.

However, you should also trust your lawyer for clear and objective legal advice. If possible, your lawyer needs to provide you with a clear pathway forward to assist you to resolve your matter in the fastest and most cost-effective way.

At your first consultation with your family lawyer, I believe it is important that you have a good rapport with that person so that you feel confident they will act in your best interests and support you in finding a solution as soon as possible.

Your family lawyer should also preferably have expertise in Family Law and solid experience working in the field.

How do you charge for your services?

At Mills Oakley we charge for our legal services on an hourly basis.

All our clients enter into a costs agreement with us. The costs charged are clearly set out in that agreement, as well as an estimate of costs provided.

What would you suggest to a litigant with limited funds to pay for legal fees?

This is a difficult question, as many people cannot control the resolution to their problem. There are always two sides to every problem and, conversely, two parties to every solution.

To start, it helps if all relevant facts and dates are collated before coming to your lawyer; for instance, in property matters, the Court considers financial and non-financial contributions. Compiling a history of who contributed and paid for various assets and expenses can reduce the time your lawyer needs to spend on collating this information, and hence reduce costs.

Ensuring that you also have all relevant financial disclosure documents in an ordered fashion can also cut down costs significantly.

> The most cost-effective way to resolve any Family Law breakdown is to reach an agreement with your opposing party.

If an agreement is quickly reached, consent orders can be prepared and filed with the Court. Alternatively, a binding financial agreement can also be prepared. This is the least costly way forward and enables parties to maintain control of both their problem and solution to their problem, as well as minimise costs.

If you have a close working relationship with your ex-partner and the dispute centres on children, with the assistance of mediators it is possible to enter into a parenting plan and work to arrangements that are contained in that document.

There are also numerous free legal advice services, such as the Legal Aid Commission of New South Wales and various legal community centres scattered around both the Sydney metropolitan area and suburban and country areas of New South Wales. In New South Wales, Law Access is also available for advice.

In certain cases, if you have very limited funds, you may be eligible for a grant of legal aid. Each State and Territory has its own Legal Aid Commission with similar policies and guidelines operating for clients who require Family Law assistance.

As Local Courts also have jurisdiction in Family Law matters in country areas...

> sometimes a quick and effective method to resolution would be to enter consent orders at your local court by your local court magistrate.

The Family and Federal Magistrates Court also have many excellent information and fact sheets available online to assist parties. Legal information is also available through local libraries and the Mitchell Library.

Are there any Family Law matters you would not assist in?

No, there are no Family Law matters we do not assist in. Our firm will prepare binding financial agreements; however, our preference is, for parties who have separated, to have their agreement converted to consent orders, which are then approved and made by the Court.

What are the biggest challenges as a family lawyer working within the current system?

In matters which are required to be determined by the Court, I think...

> the current biggest challenge facing the Family Law jurisdiction are the current delays experienced in having

*a client's application resolved both on an interim
and final basis.*

Given the current delays in Court, has this changed how you run Family Law matters?

I think delays have increased the emphasis on alternate methods for dispute resolution. Alternatives to court action, such as arbitration and collaborative law, are gaining more traction. Family Law practitioners are required by the *Family Law Act* and Rules to advise their clients of family counselling and mediation assistance available to them. However, the emphasis on family counselling has always been enshrined in the *Family Law Act* since its inception, in 1975. I have found, particularly in my experience as a registrar, that solicitors genuinely want the best for their clients and want to assist their clients to resolve their matters at the earliest opportunity.

Unfortunately, as Family Law practitioners, we have to work within the constraints which are presented to us by the current structures and practices of the Family Court and Federal Circuit Court of Australia.

What are the most significant frustrations or difficulties your clients have with regards to the Family Law system?

I think the predominant frustration that our clients have is that matters are not determined fast enough, and the delays that are being experienced. This can often have the result that disputes broaden and become more complex as time proceeds, and can be more difficult and costly to resolve.

What are the common misconceptions about Family Law?

I believe there are many misconceptions about Family Law.

Clients can be surprised at the complexity of process and procedure involved in bringing or defending an application in court. The Family Court or Federal Circuit Court of Australia, like other courts, are courts of law, and matters are determined by judicial officers on the evidence before them. Collating that evidence can be time consuming and complex.

From my experience, people often think that in the Family Court it is 'first in, best dressed', that is, the first person to apply has the advantage. This is not the case.

The other misconception is often that the Family Court favours women. I don't believe this is the case. However, in property matters The *Family Law Act* does attempt to give value to work undertaken as homemaker and parent, and does give consideration to those persons who have primary care of a child into the future.

What is the one thing you would say to someone who is about to go through the Family Law system?

Try, if possible, to be willing to discuss a solution moving forward, even if that is with the assistance of a third party, such as a mediator or counsellor, so that an agreement can be reached at the earliest opportunity. This, of course, is not always possible.

How has Family Law changed from your perspective over the years in terms of the kind of matters that are being run and the way they are being run? What changes do you see around the corner?

I do believe that matters coming before the Court appear to be becoming more complex. There seems to be more matters before the Court with multifactorial problems involved, such as mental health issues, abuse issues, clients with drug or alcohol problems, or a combination of all of these.

There are also more self-represented litigants coming before the courts.

Do you have any views about the intersection of child protection and Family Law Courts?

Pursuant to sections of the *Family Law Act*, there are many necessary closely enshrined obligations designed to prevent and protect children from abuse in its many forms. I believe these are absolutely necessary.

Pursuant to Section 91B of the *Family Law Act*, a court can make an order requesting a child welfare authority to intervene in court proceedings.

In most matters the authorities will decline to intervene. My view is that in matters where the court makes these orders, intervention by child welfare authorities is required. I would like to see an increase in participation by child welfare authorities in Section 91B matters.

What are your views with regards to the way family violence is understood in Family Law matters?

Historically, I think that the interplay of family violence in Family Law matters has not been properly understood by some judicial officers and has not, in all circumstances, been given due consideration.

With the implementation of the *Family Law Legislation Amendment (Family Violence and Other Measures) Act* 2011, this has changed and there has been an improvement in the serious consideration of family violence and protecting families from family violence in matters that come before the Court.

In relation to the presumption of equal shared parental responsibility, it is my experience that in matters involving family violence, the courts have consistently applied the law correctly. I have not seen a matter where the presumption of equal shared responsibility has been applied inappropriately in a family violence matter.

Are there any reforms that you believe should be implemented to the Family Law system?

I believe that the establishment of what is, in effect, a three-tiered system of the Local Court, Federal Circuit Court, and Family Court was not a great advance.

In my view, the Federal Circuit Court and Family Court should be rolled back into one institution to avoid ongoing duplication of costs, which has to have occurred.[3]

---

3   This interview occurred just prior to the announcement that the Family Court would merge with the Federal Circuit Court.

The appointment of more Local Court magistrates with experience in Family Law, or the re-establishment of the previous 'Local Court Family Matters', which had jurisdiction in child welfare proceedings and Family Law matters, might be helpful.

I would also like to see a recall of more court counsellors involved in proceedings, such as case assessment conferences, information sessions, and conciliation conferences in children's matters. In my past experience, these counsellors had great effect under the court's umbrella to effect resolution between the parties.

A stricter regime for financial disclosure needs to be introduced. Delays and failure to comply with directions in relation to disclosure can add significantly to time delays and clients' costs.

Contravention proceedings need to be quickly dealt with and orders should be more strictly enforced.

Finally, and obviously, more funding is required.

Alison Brown

Family lawyer

Speak up

Alison Brown is an experienced family lawyer, having practiced exclusively in the field since 2007. She holds a Bachelor of Laws, is a registered Family Dispute Practitioner (mediator), and prior to becoming a lawyer, Alison completed her Diploma in Youth Work. She has experience in complex parenting matters and also property matters involving high-net-worth clients in one case in particular, the asset pool was valued at over $1 billion.

Alison is passionate about helping people, and has worked as a lawyer at the Attorney-General's Department, providing legal advice to clients in crisis situations, and volunteers at a legal centre assisting disadvantaged members of the community.

In this interview Alison discusses the importance of seeking the assistance of a counsellor during separation, and the need to be honest with your lawyer and not be 'creative with the truth' and how mediation has helped change mindsets and approaches to Family Law. She ends her discussion with an important message for those who have experienced family violence to feel free to 'speak up' about what has happened.

How did you become a family lawyer, and what is your background and experience?

I've always had a keen interest in assisting people, and after leaving school I completed my Diploma in Youth Work with a view of working in the Community Services Field. However, after completing several work placements, such as a youth refuge and adolescent psychiatric unit, it was my placement at Juvenile Justice that inspired my interest in law.

It was a natural progression for me to start working in Family Law, as I saw it as an extension of my background in Community Services. I have worked in private practice, Community Legal Centres, and the Attorney-General's Department during my career. I enjoy working in this area of law, although it is very challenging. I enjoy working with people to try and achieve the best outcome for them but also for their family as a whole. I am of the view that having a professional yet empathetic relationship with my clients assists with achieving the best outcome. I am also a Family Dispute Resolution Practitioner.

What would be some key tips for someone navigating the Family Law system?

My first tip to anyone embarking on a separation is that it is not a quick process and can be dragged out by parties not complying with the process or by lengthy Court lists. One of the main complaints from people is that they want the process to be over as soon as possible, which is understandable; however, generally it is not a quick process, even if parties are reasonably agreeable. I often say to my clients to just sit tight and understand that one day the process will be over and you can move on, to please be patient.

My observations about parties that are involved in the Family Law process is that they often try and use the system as a mechanism to hurt the other party. Often, parties are at different stages of grieving after the end of the relationship and want to punish the other person. I am a huge advocate of people seeking professional help from counsellors and the like to manage this process better. It's also much more cost effective.

On the flip side, people are often very frustrated by the Family Law system. I would say that to propel the process, make sure you...

tell your lawyer all the relevant information they need to manage
your case effectively and ensure that all the information the Court
needs to make the right decision is presented.

Then there are those who like to get creative with the truth. To those
people I say beware! Firstly, integrity is everything in a Family Law matter.
If you lose your integrity, then your case is going to take a nosedive – fast.

Secondly, being cross-examined in a witness box is one of the most intimidating experiences you may ever have in your life, and no matter how good of
a liar you think you are, that will likely be the moment when you come unstuck.

Do you think there are any misconceptions about Family Law?

A misconception that people have in relation to spending time with their children is that they have a right to have time with their children. This is not correct.

Your child has a right to have a relationship with you,
but their needs must be met first.

Social science supports that young children should not be away from
their primary carer for long periods of time; if they are, this can cause anxiety. I often have to explain to parents that this is to protect the development
of the child so that they can grow to be well-rounded healthy children and,
by extension, adults. An equal-time arrangement is achievable; just wait
until they have grown up and can cope with an already challenging routine.

One of the biggest misconceptions about lawyers is that our job is to
make decisions for you. Our role is to advise you of the law, the available
options of dealing with your matter, and the potential outcomes regarding
the decisions you make. You are the driver.

Any tips for choosing a family lawyer?

When somebody is looking for a family lawyer, they should meet with a
couple of different lawyers and see who they like as a person or whom they
feel they can work well with long term. I think they should look for some-

body knowledgeable, who has some personal skills, because this person is going to know intimate aspects of their life and they could be working with them for some time. Also, I think it is important that you trust your lawyer and that they are going to provide you with proper, well-rounded advice.

Are there any reforms you believe should be implemented?

In my view, reform is challenging. The system is not perfect, but in a bid to try and protect the interests of all parties and children, it's a delicate balance. Unfortunately, people who separate sometimes cannot reach an agreement about arrangements for children or division of property, and there can be a multitude of reasons why this cannot be achieved.

I am of the view that mandatory mediation (in parenting matters) has assisted in changing people's mindsets, from 'See you in court!', to 'Let's try and work this out'. I also think people are savvier about the economics of separation and are trying to resolve matters without a lawyer. The flip side of that is that self-represented litigants add to the strain of the Court being able to deal with matters in a timely manner.

I also think practitioners need to be a little more collaborative in their approach in dealing with other practitioners.

> Often, family lawyers take on their clients' personal feelings and emotions which, in my view, is not helpful to the process.

There are three sides to every story. I agree with the comments of Justice Benjamin in relation to Sydney Law firms to become more focussed on results for the client rather than results for the firm.

One of the fundamental flaws with the system is the lack of acknowledgement of family violence within our society, and that a lot of family violence occurs unacknowledged. The fundamental issue with family violence is that usually the victims of any form of family violence find it very difficult to speak out. In my view, it is not just the Family Law system that needs to work to protect people but society as a whole.

> I would say to people that if you have experienced violence in your relationship, please speak up.

Claire Neilsen

Family lawyer

A long view

Claire Neilsen is an accredited specialist in Family Law working in Manly, on Sydney's Northern Beaches. She started her career in law as a legal secretary in the Family Law area in 1999 and continued working in this role whilst studying at night. Claire won the Thompson Legal Prize for Family Law when she graduated, was admitted as a solicitor in 2008 and became an accredited specialist in 2015. In 2017, Claire became the principal of the firm Shipton & Associates.

Claire has run many types of Family Law matters during this time and has a wide range of experience, including matters that are somewhat outside the norm. Claire has acted in matters where more complex issues have arisen, such as whether property is held on constructive trust for one or other party to the marriage, third-party companies seeking to enforce a debt against one or the other party to the marriage, and enforcement proceedings where a party has multiple enforcement applications by other parties over the subject property.

In parenting cases, Claire has acted in many matters which are commonly referred to as relocation cases, as well as the difficult and sensitive matters involving allegations of serious abuse and family violence. Claire assists clients to navigate these matters, which tend to be highly emotional and have the potential for serious consequences for both sides, with sensitivity and practical advice.

Claire has a very strong focus on negotiating settlements for clients in an efficient, time and cost-effective manner. She is very firmly of the view that parties who can manage to agree on an outcome in both parenting and property matters recover far better from the process of separation, both financially and emotionally.

Outside of Family Law, Claire also has experience in conveyancing, commercial transactions, and succession law, which gives her a broader understanding of the issues which arise for Family Law clients.

In this interview Claire discusses her special interesting in binding financial agreements and her ideas for reform, including a more inquisitorial system, harsher penalties for breach of orders, and how interim hearings could be streamlined. Claire provides common-sense tips for those separating and reminds us that often after a matter resolves, parties move forward and there are 'happier times ahead'.

How did you come to work as a family lawyer?

I fell into the law more by chance than by design. In about 1998 I moved back to Sydney from Queensland and was offered a temporary position in the mail room of a large firm. I took it and was then offered a junior secretary role supporting their Family Law team. After a few years as a secretary, interspersed with overseas travel, I decided to study at night, taking the Legal Profession Admission Board exams to obtain my diploma in law. I was admitted in 2008 and attained my Specialist Accreditation in Family Law in 2015. I have worked for the same firm, Shipton & Associates, since 1999 and took over as principal of that firm in September 2017.

Tell me a bit about your firm.

We are a general practice located close to Manly Beach. Our primary areas of law are family law, wills and estates, and conveyancing. We also do some criminal and commercial work. We take on all types of Family Law work, from helping people to finalise and document an agreement they have reached to dealing with complex property and/or parenting matters and drafting binding financial agreements.

At our firm we pride ourselves on being customer-focused. Over the course of a matter we generally get to know our clients well and we work hard to achieve the best outcome for them. We do this by exploring all avenues for resolution of matters by negotiation as the first priority, and if there is no prospect of such an outcome, then we prepare our client's matters for court with careful strategising and attention to detail.

What types of matters do you do?

I carry out work in all types of Family Law matters, including complex children's and financial matters.

I have also developed a particular interest in preparing and advising clients in relation to binding financial agreements. I have watched the law in this area fluctuate and change over the years and I believe it still has quite some years to go before we could consider the law with regards to binding financial agreements to be settled.

Well, speaking of this, do you have any thoughts on where we are at with binding financial agreements?

Leading up to the decision in *Thorne v. Kennedy*, I had started to see decisions being handed down which upheld pre-relationship agreements, even in circumstances where there was not full disclosure of the parties' financial circumstances, where the parties had had children after the signing of the agreement, and/or where the agreement had been signed shortly before the wedding in somewhat pressurised circumstances.

However, the decision handed down by the High Court in *Thorne v. Kennedy* received a lot of media coverage, as well as a lot of discussion within the Family Law legal community. The media did report with some gusto the decision in *Thorne v. Kennedy* as being the 'death knell' for agreements entered into, pre-relationship, and many legal commentators agree that it signals a shift away from the growing trend in the Family Court towards upholding these types of agreements, even when a person has entered into a 'bad bargain'.

In my view, a lot will depend on how the lower courts apply the High Court's judgement. The case of *Thorne v. Kennedy* had something of a perfect storm of circumstances which, when taken together, resulted in the wife having vastly unequal bargaining power with the husband.

Whilst these circumstances (or at least some of them) will no doubt occur in other cases, it is a question of fact and degree in each matter as to whether it reaches the standard of duress, undue influence, or unconscionable conduct sufficient to void an agreement.

If you are considering entering into a binding financial agreement, there are particular pitfalls with each category of agreement (pre-relationship, during relationship, and post-relationship), so they need to be very carefully drafted, but the pre-relationship agreements particularly. Often, people want to have an agreement drafted to protect their assets but would like to just fill in a form and be done, without careful consideration or negotiation with the other party. These are very complex and, at present, high-risk documents, so...

> for people who have significant assets which they want to protect, we suggest taking the time and spending the money to have the preparation of binding financial agreements done properly.

How do you charge for your work?

In our firm, we charge on an hourly rate basis for most Family Law work. Conveyancing and wills (aside from complex wills) are generally done for a fixed fee, and we are now also looking at introducing fixed-fee components to our Family Law work over the course of 2018. We understand that accessing Family Law services is daunting for everyone, and having clarity as to how much the matter is going to cost is a key issue for our clients.

What are some of the biggest challenges for your clients?

One of the biggest challenges which has arisen in the last few years in Family Law has been the extended delays in the Court system. Although we try at every opportunity to resolve matters for clients by negotiation, there are some matters (or even sometimes just discrete issues within matters) which just can't be settled and require a judicial determination. It was hard enough on clients when they had to wait a year to 18 months before their matters were resolved, but now the delay can be three to four years.

This delay has terrible flow-on effects, as parties' lives remain in limbo for that time. We have found that the bitterness between parents, for example, is very often increased by the delay as the parties seek to manage their children's arrangements without any certainty as to what will happen long term. Often, the parties are very entrenched on a particular issue and will only communicate via solicitors.

> Surprisingly, in the vast majority of cases, we find that once the matter is finalised, the orders are made, and the lawyers are not engaged anymore, parents tend to just get on with it and manage their co-parenting of the children in a reasonably cooperative way.

The delay also often leads to situations arising where one or other of the parties needs to have a decision made on a particular issue without a final hearing. If that issue can't be resolved by negotiation, then the only alternative is an interim hearing. These interim hearings invariably increase the cost to each party enormously, with the preparation of affidavit evidence and attendances at Court (often more than one if the matter is not reached the first time it is listed), and also increases delay, because whilst the matter is listed for an interim hearing, the Court does not progress it forward in the pathway to the final hearing.

> The number of interim hearings being filed also increases delay in the system generally

... as Judges are so busy hearing the interims, they don't have time to do the final hearings!

In property matters, the delay is very often unequal in the effect it has on each party. Particularly in situations where perhaps a party who is not in employment is applying to the Court for orders to relocate with children to an area of Australia where they can afford to live comfortably and raise the children, but pending the Court's hearing, they are trapped in an expensive area of Sydney with the capital from the sale of their home being eaten away in rent.

The ongoing delays and the feeling for parties that they are stuck in a 'never-ending' conflict with the other party can place people at risk of depression and anxiety, and can also lead to a party wanting to accept an offer from the other side which is inequitable, or not in their best interests, just to end the proceedings.

Given such issues, do you make use of mediation or other alternative dispute resolution?

Mediations with effective mediators (usually Family Law lawyers, barristers, or former judges) can be very useful in resolving matters, particularly if proceedings have not been commenced but the parties are not making significant progress by exchange of correspondence. We find that if each party is well-prepared for the mediation and exchanges position papers beforehand, it can be a very effective means of either settling the entire matter or in significantly narrowing the issues in dispute. Sometimes a first mediation can identify pathways for the parties to obtain further reports on issues that remain in dispute, and then a second mediation can be held to try to resolve those issues after the reports have issued.

You mentioned relocation earlier. Are you finding that there are an increasing number of international issues in Family Law?

Yes, another area of interest in our practice is the increasing need to consider international issues in Family Law matters. We are seeing many cases where people have assets in foreign countries as well as Australia, who work overseas regularly, or couples who split their time between two or more countries each year. We have had more than one case in the last year where a partner has engaged in a deliberate course of conduct in transferring the marital assets offshore over some years prior to the breakdown of the relationship. This can present particular problems in finding out what assets exist and even more difficulties in compelling the return of assets to Australia in order to effect a division of property.

Having raised all the current problems with Family Law as it currently is, do you have any thoughts about possible reform to Family Law?

Change is very likely coming to the Family Law area with the first wholesale review of the *Family Law Act* by the Australian Law Reform Commission in over 40 years. Some of the key issues which the Commission will examine will be the Family Law system's approach to family violence and the need to protect children and give them a voice, as well as the funding of the Court system and minimising the financial burden on people who need to resolve Family Law disputes.

One change which is already underway is the introduction of Parenting Management Hearings which are intended to commence in the Parramatta Registry in mid 2018. These hearings are aimed at self-represented parties dealing with parenting disputes, and rather than being adversarial in nature (where each side gathers their evidence and presents it to the Judge), they will be informal and inquisitorial (where the Judge or other decision maker will gather evidence to inform their decision).

The hearings will be free to the parties and the decisions binding. I am cautiously optimistic that these hearings may go some way to providing quick and cost-effective resolutions to disputes for the category of people who are eligible to participate. My main concern, however, is the power imbalance which is often present between parents as a result of past family violence, current family violence, or just one parent having a significantly stronger personality and verbal skills than the other. Also of concern are the number of people who pass through the Family Court system with personality disorders or mental health issues.

It is unclear to me from the announcements currently available in relation to these hearings whether matters which involve an element of family violence or mental health issues will be accepted into that program. If they are, then the decision maker has the very difficult task of gathering the evidence, making enquiries, and, to some extent, no doubt mediating disputes which arise in the course of hearings, all whilst trying to analyse and identify any power imbalance and ensure that the 'weaker' party has a proper opportunity to be heard.

I also have some concerns regarding the direct contact between the parties and the decision maker. Often when representing a client in high-emotion matters, I see the other side develop a view that the opposing lawyer is the enemy. We can be the target of vitriolic statements, angry correspondence, and sometimes threats made by the other side. Whilst it is uncomfortable and difficult for us, it does deflect that behaviour away from the client, who may have to go on and have a continued parenting cooperation with the other party.

Presenting evidence which is likely to anger or inflame the other side can be difficult for parties, even with the buffer of it being the lawyers who prepare the documents and speak to the Judge about it. Having to present that evidence in person may be even more confronting for a party, and I have some concerns about whether evidence which might otherwise be very relevant in parenting matters might go unsaid or, if said, increase the risk of family violence.

Having said that, there is little detail available regarding the precise structure of these hearings, and it may be that systems will put in place which give a voice to parents and children in Family Law disputes without compromising their emotional and physical wellbeing.

It is my view that the Family Law area is one which lends itself to a more inquisitorial system. I would like to see change introduced which, first and foremost, provides adequate funding to the Courts so that matters commenced are finished within 12 to 18 months. I think the docket system of allocating a matter to a particular Judge is very effective and should be adopted across both Courts (or make the Family Court solely a court of appeal and fund the Federal Circuit Court to handle all matters).

I believe that the docket system should be expanded so that every matter has a substantive first return date where the Judge is actively involved in narrowing the issues, including making enquiries and having input into what evidence they want to see in relation to parenting issues, and making necessary orders for the protection of children, and/or to provide clarity and certainty as to the most basic children's arrangements pending the hearing.

On that first return date, the Court should also consider making short interim orders to protect assets and provide stability in the financial matter, and then the matter should be referred to a conciliation conference.

Tougher penalties, including costs penalties and orders made in the absence of parties on an undefended basis, should be imposed on parties for non-disclosure, failure to engage in pre-action procedures, failure to comply with the Court's directions, failure to appear, or failure to be adequately prepared for hearing.

If the matter progresses and either party requires interim issues to be dealt with before the final hearing, then there should be one hearing date where two hours is allocated to deal with any interim issues, and if an interim hearing is held, then costs should follow the event in most cases (as opposed to the usual starting point, that each party pay their own costs). I think this would go a long way to ensuring that only truly urgent issues are sent to interim hearing. Following the interim hearing, the matter should be immediately listed for final hearing with the same Judge at the earliest opportunity.

Clearly, the biggest issue facing the Court right now is underfunding and extensive delay. Whilst there are many criticisms of the system as a whole, and the current review may lead to positive changes, it is my view that the system will operate at its best when appropriately resourced and will provide immeasurably better outcomes to parties if they can finalise their matters quickly, with the attendant cost savings.

Any tips for litigants?

Some of the tips I tell my clients to keep their matters on track and have them resolved as quickly and cost-effectively as possible include:

1. Make sure that you have good supports around you in the form of friends, family, and professional counsellors, if necessary. Separation is an extremely stressful time and you will need to talk and cry and sometimes rant about how unfair life can be. As much as we care about our clients and want to help you resolve your legal problems, you will find that your costs are much lower if you mostly keep your communications with your lawyer limited to the work they need to do for you.

2. Don't bite back! Even when your ex-partner says something horrible in person, by SMS, by email, or on Facebook, don't retaliate. It

achieves nothing – you will generally not convince them of your point of view in that way – except to inflame the dispute and reduce your chances of settlement. Anything in writing (including emails and posts on Facebook) will often end up as evidence in any proceedings.

3. Speaking of evidence, do not discuss your case or your former partner on social media, including in closed-group forums. This is one of the first places the other side's solicitor looks to get information about your attitude to your former partner. This can be especially damaging in parenting cases.

4. If the other side requests that you do something, such as change a child's arrangements for one week, make an interim property distribution, etc., put aside the anger and the hurt and ask yourself 'Is it reasonable?' 'Is it in my child's best interests?' 'Does it harm me to agree?' If it is reasonable and does not harm you or a child to agree, then do so and quickly. Being reasonable and conciliatory (without being a pushover) increases your prospects of getting a settlement. If you do end up in court proceedings, narrow the issues that are in dispute and avoid interim hearings if at all possible! All of those things will save you money and time during your matter, and, most importantly, will help to preserve a civil relationship with your ex-partner, which is crucial if you have children together.

5. Hang in there!! It will end, you will move forward, and life for you and your children will improve. Navigating almost any separation is difficult, stressful, and financially straining, but try to keep a long view, think about where you will be one year after it is finished, five years after, 10 years after.

There will be happier times ahead.

List of Key Topics

covered by each interviewee

Review of family law
Presumption of equal shared parental responsibility
Developmental needs of children
Gender issues in family law
Feminisation of poverty
Spouse maintenance
Attachment theory and children
Family violence
Supervised time
Preliminary hearing on issue of family violence

The Honourable Justice Peter Rose AM QC   40

Changes to family law
Parenting matters and parental responsibility
Reform to *Family Law Act*, parenting
Independent Children's Lawyer
Children's participation in family law proceedings
Family violence
Education regarding family violence
Ministerial portfolio regarding family violence
Children's Court
Judicial appointments to family law Courts
Court delays
Pre nuptial agreements
Arbitration
Cross cultural issues
Gender bias in family law
Tips for family lawyers (real issues, advice with integrity)
Tips for litigants (range of results, costs, settlement options)
Social media
SMS messages
Legal fees
Self-represented litigants
Child support

Judge Joe Harman 53

Parenting Matters: Court experts and other professionals   77

Dr Antony Milch, Expert psychiatrist   78

Court ordered family therapy
Psychological abuse of children
Tips for family lawyers
Suspension of time between parent and child

Purpose of expert psychologist report
Process for preparing expert report
Challenging an expert report
Matters that require a report
Mental health issues of parents
Supporting children through separation
Tips for parents (routine, child's best interested, school, settle matters)
Possible reform to the family law system (training, consis-
    tency for experts, earlier consultation with experts)

Family expert reports
Single expert reports
Issue of bias in reports
Supporting children in a separation
Potential reform to family law system (collaborative, child centred approach)

When therapy can assist
Emotional stages of separation
Supporting children through separation
Mental health issues of parents
Children exposed to conflict
Telling children of the separation
Effects of conflict on children

Mark Lipson, Specialist forensic accountant, expert business valuer 152

Adversarial experts

Forensic accountants

Problems with inexperienced accountants in family law

Valuation methodologies

Investigative work and money trail

Hidden assets and monies

Tax fraud

Cross referral of matters to ATO

Cost of expert valuation of business

Changes in role of forensic accountants

Delays in Court

Updating reports

Cross examination of forensic accountants

Face to face interviews in preparing reports

Individuals who have navigated the family law system   165

Simone: I never had that   166
On being a child with parents
going through bitter litigation about parenting

Exposure to conflict

Parenting arrangements

Changeover

Exposure to family law process

Father's alcohol abuse

Estrangement from father

Affects into adulthood of bitter separation

Tips for parents separating

*On how the court process facilitated
ongoing abuse from an ex-husband*

Financial issues
Separation
School enrolment issues
Self-managed superannuation
Parental responsibility
Psychological abuse
Interim hearing and parenting arrangements
Child support – objections, Administrative Appeals Tribunal hearing
Delays
Financial abuse
Past mental health issues
Subpoena of psychologist notes
Cross examination
Lawyer
Legal fees
Mediator
Child Dispute Conference
Family report writer
Independent Children's Lawyer

On being a father and survivor of domestic violence and misuse of child support

Child support overpayment
Suspension of time with children due to change in child support payments
Property and superannuation
Legal fees
Gender bias
AVO's
Psychological abuse by former wife
Tips for men separating
Male victims of domestic violence

Delay – advantageous to one party
Attachment theory
Chinese families
Grandparents
Cultural paradigm

Barristers' role
Choosing a barrister
Aggressive culture in family law litigation
International matters
Conflict of laws
International parental child abduction
Orders of an overseas Court
Overseas binding financial agreements (includ-
    ing pre nuptial agreements)
Weight given by Court to foreign decisions
Weight given by Court to foreign Binding Financial Agreement
Additional cost and delay in international matters
Expert evidence in international matters
Delay
Forum shopping

Barristers preparation process
Choosing a barrister
Charges and barristers' fees
Limited funds for legal fees
Binding Financial Agreement
Thorne v Kennedy [2017] HCA 49
Delays

Alternative dispute resolution

Hague convention

Judgments of foreign countries

Aggressive approach in family law

Gender bias

Family violence, false accusations of

Potential reform (Judges, phone conference)

Tips for lawyers

Wishes of children

Rules of evidence

Matters in the Family Violence Court

Lack of understanding of family violence

Ideas for change in the Family Violence Court (appointment of more female magistrates)

Lack of resources in Family Violence Court

Drug use, in particular use of ice

Tips for someone being subjected to family violence (gathering evidence, police involvement, family violence desk
   at court, women's legal service, duty solicitor)

Choosing a barrister

Representing children in Court

Cultural issues

Family violence

Potential reform (short form summary decisions)

Tips for lawyers (affidavits)

Tips for clients

Cost of expert reports

Complexity of the system

Technology

Social media

Same sex marriage

Cultural issues

Chinese families

Potential reforms to family law (referral system, criminal court)

AVO's and family law

Key tips for those going through a separation (every situation is unique, get support, ask questions)

Stephen Page   332

Be careful in the power we have

Mediation

Child sexual abuse allegations

Police interview evidence

Psychiatrist expert

Delay

Surrogacy laws

International convention on the Rights of the Child

Case of *Bernieres and Anor v Dhopal and Anor* (2017) FLC 93-793

House of Representatives Inquiry into Surrogacy

Supreme Court of NSW

Correspondence in family law matters

Difficulty in reading confronting letters from other side lawyer

Tips for those going through a separation (discretion in property, counsellor, exercise)

Reform (more Judges)

Surrogacy overseas

Surrogacy domestically

Payment to surrogates

Criminal offence re payment beyond reasonable expenses

Adoption

Children in Care and Protection

Delays in court

Key tips for those separating (seek advice, communication and
transparency with solicitor, mediation, be child focused)

AVO's

Gender bias

Family violence and reform

The most important decisions of your life

Fixed fees

Tips for those separating (minimise conflict, introduce change slowly)

Mediation

Potential reform (resources, Registrars, family consultants, contact centres)

A clear pathway forward

Independent Children's Lawyer

Choosing a lawyer

Legal fees, tips for those with limited funds (compile relevant
facts, settle the matter, advice services, legal information)

Delay

Mediation

Complex parenting matters

Child protection

Family violence

Potential Reform (Merge Family and Federal Circuit Court,
recall of Court counsellors, financial disclosure)

Speak up

Delay

Tips for those navigating the family law system

Counselling and supports
Attachment theory and anxiety
Choosing a family lawyer
Mediation
Family violence

Binding Financial Agreements
Thorne v Kennedy [2017] HCA 49
Delays
Mediation
International family law issues
Parent Management hearings in Parramatta (benefits and concerns)
Potential ideas for reform (Inquisitorial system,
     docket system, penalties, interim hearings
Delay
Tips for those separating (counselling and support,
     social media, narrow the issues in dispute)

More about Zoë Durand

ZOË DURAND has a wealth of experience, having worked as a lawyer since 2007, primarily in family law private practice at the coalface of the family law system.

Prior to changing the direction of her career to focus on family law, Zoë worked at leading national and international commercial law firms HWL Ebsworth and K&L Gates, giving her a financial acumen that is highly desirable in family law property matters. Additionally she has worked as a Court Appointed Independent Children's Lawyer, giving her an insight into the needs and perspectives of children, which is sought after in parenting matters.

Zoë is a principal at Mediation Answers and is currently focusing on her work as a mediator. She is both a Nationally Accredited Mediator and Family Dispute Resolution Practitioner (FDRP). Zoë is also a trained Collaborative lawyer, holds a Masters of Applied Family Law and also a Bachelor of Law Degree and Bachelor of Arts Degree (first class honours in Sociology) from UNSW.

Zoë has authored the family law case notes for the *NSW Law Society Journal* and opinion pieces for *Lawyers Weekly* and other media. She is often featured in the press for her insights on topical family law issues, including ABC and *Sydney Morning Herald*.

Zoë is the co-founder of a professional and business networking organisation which has hosted talks from Judges, Court experts and leading lawyers in family law. She is a member of the Family Law Section of the Law Council of Australia, the Women Lawyers Association of NSW, the Asian Australian Lawyers Association and the French Australian Lawyers Society. She holds dual Australian and Taiwanese Citizenship and French permanent residency.

Prior to her admission as a solicitor Zoë worked at Kingsford Legal Centre and Youth Law Australia, which empowers children and young people with legal advice and information and works to promote their human rights. She continues to be passionate about this purpose.

For more on *Inside Family Law* see: www.mediationanswers.com.au